THE LANGUAGE OF
DREAMS

BY

PATRICIA TELESCO

THE CROSSING PRESS
FREEDOM, CALIFORNIA

Table of Contents

Foreword

When I first started writing this book, I counted myself among those people who rarely remember their dreams. However, as I began to form the wealth of dream materials I'd collected into my own words, this writing process manifested itself in my daily life in two ways. First, I began having and remembering symbolic dreams more regularly, and some were startling in detail. As each occurred, I worked on the alphabetical section of this book that directly relates to the images in the dream, and found myself amazed by the insight the symbols offered. After years without having this spiritual key in my life, it was a blessing to have these friendly night-visitors that teach, inspire, and provide alternative perspectives. Second, I began meeting more people who would ask my opinions about their "odd" dreams. This gave me a unique chance to test many of the entries in this book with strangers and friends alike. The results were astounding, and I learned a great deal from the experience.

For one thing, I discovered that despite our differences, humankind has a core of instincts and learning around which dream symbols seem to revolve. Our common primitive and tribal roots bind us together in an invisible weave that goes far beyond conscious awareness. The subconscious, however, appears intimately aware of our ties. Thus, dreaming of a modern condominium can equate equally well to the symbolism of a castle, a hide tent, or a primitive cave, no matter the dreamer. The only thing that alters or colors this symbolism is an individual's life experiences.

I also discovered that people have dreams that are far more intricate than I ever imagined. This speaks of the potential of the imagination, the creative human spirit, and the wonders of the mind. Anything is possible on the dream plane. If we dream of flying, we do not question that ability, it simply *is*. If we could apply such confidence to our daily lives, what wonders would we be capable of?

So, my friends, dare to dream! In that moment of sleep, in the moonlight and the shadow of a star, may some of those dreams begin to come true.

Introduction

"All that we see or seem is but a dream within a dream."

—Edgar Allan Poe, 1809–1849

Dreams: mysterious visions that visit the sleeping mind. Upon waking, residual feelings and fleeting images remain behind like ghosts, with their stories wholly or partially undisclosed. Where do these elusive portraits originate, and why? Is there some important purpose for this experience?

Down through the ages, commoners and kings alike have voiced these questions. The answers they received, influenced by their era, culture, and individual perspectives, have ranged from the metaphysical interpretations of the ancient Greeks to the analytical views of Freud and Jung to today's rather dry psychological explanations.

Stoic philosophers in ancient Greece viewed dreams as a kind of clear sight from the soul, other spirits, or the gods themselves. People following this tradition sometimes secluded themselves in a sacred temple (like that of Asclepius) to receive healing or visionary dreams.

Other civilizations exhibited similar beliefs and practices. In pre-Christian Iceland the art of Dreaming True (a prophetic ability) was respected as inspired by the gods, and the Arabic prophet Mohammed received the Koran, the Holy Book of Islam, through a dream. In each of these instances, our ancestors believed the dream to be far more than happenstance or flight of fancy.

In the 19th century and early 20th century, psychoanalysts like Sigmund Freud and psychologists like Carl Jung began questioning the popular dream theories. These investigations weaned dream analysis away from metaphysical explanations toward more psychological views. For the first time, dreams were regarded as an inner conversation between a person and her/his subconscious.

Oddly, these reforms did not significantly alter the symbolic meanings previously prescribed by dream experts. The guides written in ancient Egypt, Macedonia, and Babylonia read with striking similarity to Victorian texts. In both settings, humankind's dream experiences could be reduced to archetypal, universal imagery, with minor philosophical disparities. These symbols and their interpretations have remained basically unchanged to this day.

Today, most psychologists still concur with Freud and Jung, saying that dreams reveal our temperament, hopes, and fears, and other subconscious issues. *Webster's New World Dictionary* defines dreams as mental images, ideas, and emotions that appear during sleep. Is this skeletal explanation really adequate for unlocking the riddle of what dreams are, and what they should mean? I don't believe so. The appropriate keys for this task are much more intricate and multifaceted, having foundations in the past, present, and future.

This book approaches the keys to our dreams in a whole new way. Part One, A Time to Dream, opens the historical treasure chest of dream interpretation, revealing a legacy of oracular messages, religious insight, and political decision-making. Part One then discloses step-by-step instructions for deciphering or clarifying your dreams, with hints for recognizing which bear the most significance for interpretation.

Part Two, The Dream Symbol Key, examines dream symbols as phenomena strongly influenced by contrasting human experiences and perspectives. Honoring this diversity required the careful balancing of traditional archetypal imagery against changing times.

The way a symbol was interpreted in the past is frequently quite different from the way we view it and react to it today. For example, during the Middle Ages gloves were given to people as a sign of honor and approval. In the Victorian era, gloves represented propriety, convention, and refinement. Today, white gloves project an image of a finicky person who is overly concerned with details (e.g., "the white glove test"). Each of these meanings is perfectly valid in its appropriate setting.

Further, since society and science have advanced rapidly over the last century, there are hundreds of new technological items and social circumstances that can find their way into our dreams. Since dream specialists of the past had no idea that such contrivances or conditions would ever exist, there are few frames of reference to build our conclusions on. So, besides traditional imagery, the Dream Symbol Key introduces contemporary objects and situations with suggested interpretations.

This expanded listing draws from several sources, including correlations with established symbols, modern myths and aphorisms, common reactions or associations, and a little instinct. Wherever possible, the Dream Symbol Key also incorporates alternative cultural, folkloric, spiritual, situational, and psychological interpretations. Please bear this in mind while you read, remembering that personal insight is nearly always the best, most dependable guide.

Ultimately, dream interpretation is a tool that helps us discern who we are, what we desire, where we are going, and how to get there successfully. It allows us to peek through a keyhole in the door of self into another world—a world that reveals the subconscious, provides insight from the Collective Unconscious, and potentially relays messages from the Divine. Thus, the study of our dreams can aid creativity, expand universal awareness, develop focus for one's spiritual path, encourage personal growth, and improve self-understanding.

Sweet dreams!

PART ONE

A Time to Dream

CHAPTER ONE

Of Dreaming and Believing:
Historical Overview of Dream Interpretation

"We are the music makers; we are the dreamers of dreams."

—Arthur W. E. O'Shaughnessy

Dream Symbol Keys have a long, multicultural past. The oldest surviving written record of dream interpretation is the Chester Beatty Papyrus from Egypt, dating from 1350 B.C.E. The Babylonians sought clues to their future in dreams by reviewing the images as one complete message. Conversely, in the 7th century B.C.E., an Assyrian king named Assubanipal wrote about each element in a dream as a separate cipher with distinct meaning. In 350 B.C.E., the Taoist philosopher Chuang Tzu pondered if all life was but a dream.

By 400 B.C.E. onward, many dream guides appeared in Greece. Notably, Socrates (470–399 B.C.E.) spent the latter days of his life rewriting a version of *Aesop's Fables* because he received instructions to do so in a dream. Around the same time, the Father of Medicine, Hippocrates, wrote and spoke about dreams as indicators of unmanifested physical ailments.

From the cultural hub of Athens, dream dictionaries spread around the world, carried by merchants and travelers and adapted by clever scribes. Of these, the *Oneirocritica* by Artemidorus (140 C.E.) was the most influential of all, basing its observations on collected previous sources. This book was so popular that it survived well beyond its originator, with 20 editions published by the 1700s!

It becomes apparent that this art has been an important element in human experience. While sophisticated minds might scoff at pursuing hidden meanings in their dreams, seekers can count themselves in good company. Some of the greatest thinkers and theologians of all ages believed in dream symbolism as a way to understand themselves and the world they lived in.

This group included such leaders as the Persian king Xerxes (400 B.C.E.) and the Roman general Julius Caesar (100–44 B.C.E.); religious figures like the Magi (7–6 B.C.E.) and St. John; writers like Shakespeare (1564–1616) and Robert Louis Stevenson (1850–1894); musicians like Mozart (1756–1791) and Handel (1685–1756); inventors like Benjamin Franklin (1706–1790); and such visionaries as Edgar Cayce (1877–1945), also known as the Sleeping Prophet. With such people using dreams to foresee the future, determine matters of state, create magnificent art, and cure ills, it is no wonder that dream interpretation survived into modern times.

The popularity of dream interpretation has vacillated as has the interest in the occult, palmistry, and other divination methods. During times of religious persecution, for example, the number of dream books dwindled. At the turn of the century, a veritable sea of dream books reappeared. Likewise, when the Swiss psychologist Carl Jung wrote in the early 1900s about dreams as a storehouse for universal human perceptions, dream interpretation experienced another revival, even as it is enjoying today with the New Age movement.

Dreams and Sleep

Psychologists now recognize that messages from the subconscious are much easier to receive during sleep. So our forbears were essentially correct. While we sleep, the veil of consciousness that conceals a great many things gets set aside. Dreams filter through, containing symbolic or direct representations from the hidden realms of self, or the universe.

Dream Oracles

Many sacred sites around the world were once places where seekers could go to understand their dreams, where they would receive visions from the Divine either personally or through the aid of a professional dreamer. Historians believe that the Delphi was originally a dream oracle where prophetesses and priestesses known as the sibyls presided over divinatory matters. Epidaurus, another Grecian oracle, was one of the best known incubation centers in the world. People traveled there to sleep in the sanctuary, hoping to receive inspired dreams.

Using dream interpretation as a divinatory tool stems from the Grecian belief that the soul is free during sleep, and therefore able to recover truths normally hidden in a waking state. Experts in this art were called *oneiropoli*. Besides providing meanings, the *oneiropoli* also instructed people in the proper groundwork for experiencing inspired dreams. The seeker would have to bathe, eat a special diet, and sometimes even take a drug to help induce a trance state. This was a ritual of cleansing, purification, and preparation.

The Japanese Buddhists had similar rituals beginning in the 4th and 5th centuries. These rituals were popularized around the 1400s, and still show signs of use in the 20th century. Pilgrims traveled to a known holy site such as the temple in Sakata, hoping for a dream to resolve their difficulties or reveal their future. During the journey, they would abstain from eating meat and strong vegetables. At the temple, it was customary to leave an offering and make a vow to the gods. The traveler then remained a specific number of days, the most favorable being 7, 21, and 100.

The Japanese dream oracles regularly produced visions of a beautiful woman, a shining boy, or an old monk wearing dark robes, bearing the seeker's answer. Each of these was significant in the Eastern psyche: the great goddess, the wise child who also represents the hope of the future, and the elderly religious man who has dedicated his life to one path. No matter who appeared, however, it seems that the gods either had a sense of humor, or enjoyed teaching seekers forbearance. The much sought-after dream usually arrived on the last night of the vigil!

In this culture, dream divination was so respected that the emperor acted as the official dreamer for the entire country. There was even a special sleeping chamber and bed constructed during the 7th century C.E. for this purpose. Once a dream arrived (often "coincidentally" supporting his political position), it was announced to the populace or the palace staff, so that divine wishes could be met without delay.

Dreams in Religion

The Egyptians, Mesopotamians, Hittites, ancient Hebrews and Druids alike practiced some form of sleep incubation. The Egyptians so adored their dream oracles that they kept using them even when Constantine (280–337 C.E.) tried to suppress such practices. In Mesopotamia, there was the *baru* who was an expert in all forms of omen interpretation, including those coming from dreams.

The Hittites (1700–700 B.C.E.) specifically asked in their prayers to the gods to reveal themselves in dreams. This civilization also had professional dreamers in their ranks called *apilu*. This literally translates as "answerer." Their god of dreams was *Ziqiqu*—a book of omen interpretation was given his name later in Hittite history.

Hebrew peoples considered dreams as acceptable indicators of divine will. The Old Testament recounts many instances of God speaking to his people through dreams, including communications to Jacob, Joseph, and Solomon. During the Talmudic period, rabbis used dream interpretation to teach believers religious or social lessons. The root word for dream or vision in Hebrew means "to see." This explains why the term "seer" is readily applied to biblical prophets as well.

In Chinese Taoist folklore of the Yuan Dynasty (13th–14th century), the last of the eight immortals, Lu Tung-pin, found his calling and credited his conversion to dreams.

The eight immortals were people who so strictly walked the Taoist path of simplicity and selflessness that they were granted immortality. Lu Tung-pin decided to renounce the world after waking from a dream in which his life took a frightening turn. This made him realize the folly of worldly concerns.

St. Augustine (354–430 C.E.) regarded dreams as a tool for understanding his mind and relationship with God. Martin Luther, toward the end of the Middle Ages, felt that dreams improved self-awareness, especially with regard to recognizing sin.

There are many people who believe that the Divine can, and does, use dreams as a vehicle. Native Americans look to dreams, visions, and trance states to guide and direct them, as do Australian Aborigines and Tibetan monks. Considering the hectic pace of our world, this may be the Great Spirit's best avenue of direct communication. About the only time we slow down enough for the Divine to get our attention is when we sleep!

CHAPTER TWO

The Dreamer Awakens:
Modern Guide for Applied Dream Interpretation

*"Nothing so much convinces me of the boundlessness
of the human mind as its operations in dreaming."*
—William B. Clulow

Dreams help us cope with the complexity of existence in a simplified or symbolic structure. They speak of our emotions, beliefs, careers, attitudes, and habits, who we were yesterday, who we are today. In other words, the subconscious houses the entire range of information that is the sum of our life, the totality of our "Be-ing," and releases that information to the conscious mind during dream time.

Dreams provide clues to something that has occurred or is occurring inwardly. Dream interpretation is one way, therefore, to reconnect with our *true* nature, restoring self-awareness, empowerment, and wholeness to our daily lives. Carl Jung felt that the unconscious mind contained a blueprint for human actualization and psychic balance. He taught that dreams both express something and impress the importance of that "something" on the dreamer. The dreamer then can use that revelation to solve problems and to shed light on daily concerns.

Freudians theorize that dreams embody information we are not consciously aware of, or something we are reluctant to tackle directly. Dreams become tattletales of innermost feelings, wishes, tensions, and perspectives. The Gestaltists approach dreams as compositions, or portraits of all the meaningful patterns of our lives with the whole picture being greater than each part, with each part significant.

No matter which approach to dreams is chosen, in all cases a dream may cover several levels of meaning ranging from the straightforward to the subliminal. Exactly which interpretation is "right" is best determined by the dreamer. Such intimate visions cannot be wholly explained by any book or advisor. At best, this book will provide several overviews and options in the hope that one interpretation will touch the uniqueness of the reader's experience. A good counselor will likewise offer alternatives for the dreamer's consideration. In either case, it is important that dreamers be totally honest about the most significant or troublesome areas of their lives. Without such honesty, it is easy to overlook the obvious cues from night visions.

As we become more attentive to impressions received from the subconscious, many areas of our lives will improve that have nothing to do with dreaming. Our awareness creates a balance between thought and intuition, between logic and instinct, that is tremendously beneficial on both mundane and spiritual levels. For example, we may react negatively to a particular stimulus without any consciously known cause. Then, we begin having dreams that reveal the cause. Knowing the root of a problem wins half the battle. By understanding the "whys," we begin to release our anxiety, and slowly learn to regulate and transform those negative reactions.

The Physiology of Dreaming

Everyone dreams, even though some people claim they don't. In fact, dreaming is an important part of maintaining mental stability. An inability to remember dreams is often due to how we awaken. Once a dream cycle completes itself, retention decreases gradually. Memories continue to wane upon waking. So, the window of opportunity for integrating and mobilizing a dream's message is relatively small.

Mental activity levels change at various stages of the sleep cycle. According to research, approximately 80 percent of all dreams take place during REM (Rapid Eye Movement) sleep. Exactly why this occurs is uncertain. We do know that people are very difficult to wake during REM, often ignoring loud sounds and other externals. During this time the body is limp, but may move periodically to act out particularly vivid dreams.

Our normal sense of time has little meaning within the dream world. While time outside the dream story goes by without change, a very complicated dream can take place in minutes, and several short dreams can occur in seconds. This is why we sometimes feel disoriented upon waking; our clocks say one thing while our mind has experienced something else. Here is the power of dreaming. It can symbolically reach beyond the normal barriers of time and space, of the "real" world into the realms of the miraculous.

The Third Dimension: Spirit

The first chapter in this book presented a brief overview of dreams in a religious setting. We often hear the saying that humans are three-dimensional beings, composed of mind, body, and spirit. We have already covered the mind and body. Now let's turn to the spirit.

An overwhelming majority of people believe in some type of spirit or soul—the energy that makes us each unique. We'll take the idea one step further. The mind still affects the body while we sleep, so it may also affect, or interact with, our spirit. Using this reasoning, the spirit can be compared to a telephone line between this world (our mind) and the next, potentially conveying messages from deceased friends and family members through a dream.

To provide a personal illustration, my son Karl had a dream of my father right after he died. In the dream, Dad told Karl not to be sad, that he "felt much better now." This three-year-old boy then recounted his tale to everyone in the family who would listen. This dream provided us with a sense of peace and closure, from the mouth of one who didn't even know that Dad had passed over!

Likewise, the spirit may be able to access the Higher Self, or what Jung called the Collective Unconscious, for spiritual information and insights. This is like a giant fountain of knowledge and experience. Because we all have the same origin, anyone can drink from and be nourished by this source, if we know how to find it. Dreams allow this fountain to spill over into consciousness. So, if you have struggled to find your spiritual path, or wish to reconnect with sacred powers, consider your dreams as potential allies in this quest, and review the symbolic meanings accordingly.

Programmed and Lucid Dreaming

The ideas of programmed and lucid dreaming are relatively new, and still somewhat unexplored. In programmed dreaming, a person attempts to elicit a specific vision through the use of emblems or suggestions. In lucid dreaming, the individual interacts with the dream once becoming aware of it.

For example, I have repeatedly told my son that if he dreams of monsters, he can make up a weapon to frighten them off, or he can call for aid. This instruction serves two purposes. It gives Karl the knowledge that he can control his own fears and regulate the nightmare so that it turns in his favor. Additionally, the subtle repetitive suggestion to his subconscious will eventually manifest on the dream plane. In this situation, the result has been positive. On several occasions, Karl has told me of a victory in his dreams because, in his words, "I remembered what you told me."

Besides overcoming nightmares, programmed and lucid dreaming may be useful for personal growth, improving spiritual insight and leading a more fulfilled life. Even so, I strongly suggest consulting an expert on this technique before trying it yourself. In programmed dreaming, you will initiate a dream sequence on a conscious level, and have an awareness of the symbols used. Therefore, you probably won't need to refer to a dream guide unless unexpected symbols and images crop up. Similarly, lucid dreaming changes the outcome from what the subconscious prescribed. This change can obscure or confuse the originally intended message.

Telepathic Dreams

Another type of dream is one stimulated by telepathy, a form of extrasensory perception that allows us to communicate between our mind and that of another person without words. As previously illustrated, the human mind seems much more open to impressions from "unseen" realms while we sleep, whether generated from our own subconscious or from the energy fields of others.

For example, the next time you dream of a close friend being in trouble, you might call that friend the next day to see if all is well. Tell the person about the dream and see if it makes any sense to her/him. Inevitably, when I have a dream like this, the friend, family member, or acquaintance in question really did need a good ear.

Another example of a telepathic dream is one that occurs when someone we know is close to death or seriously injured. Numerous people report waking for no apparent reason at the exact moment of an accident, or dreaming that the person involved came to them with a message. In both cases, the dreamers received specific energies from the individual who, for whatever reason, was thinking of them in their hour of need.

Generally speaking, telepathic dreams involve people we know more intimately, but in rare instances may include someone you've never met, those from different eras, or even people in different dimensions. To relate a personal experience: one night I dreamed I heard the sound of weeping, but it was far away from me. I listened closely and tried to follow the sound to its source, only to find a young girl weeping in her bedroom. Her clothing was that of someone living in the Old West, as was the furniture in the room. She was distraught because her ideas were laughed at by people, as she was too mature and insightful for her years.

I stood there, knowing she could not see me, but tried to reach out my hand to her. When it touched her shoulder, she shivered and looked around as if expecting someone. So, I tried to communicate simple thoughts of acceptance, assuring her she wasn't silly or crazy. As I did, her face grew calmer as if she suddenly understood something that had eluded her before. Then I awoke.

To this day I do not know who that girl was, or where (or when) she lived, but I know beyond any doubt that the experience was real to me. For a moment outside of time I held close another soul in need, and we both benefited from the experience. There is a chance this may have been both an OBE (Out-of-Body Experience) and a telepathic dream, but in either case the effect on me was profound.

When telepathic dreams take place, the dreamer becomes like an inter-dimensional telephone line communicating messages that otherwise would be impossible to impart. So instead of merely interpreting a telepathic dream, act upon it. Find out the reason it occurred and respond in any way you can.

Pizza or Prophesy?

People comment regularly about an odd dream, postscripting the conversation with a physical explanation for the event. The idea of unusual dreams being caused by food or other influences is quite plausible.

Ponder all of the experiences that surround you daily—from noises caused by radios and traffic, to variations in lighting and your eating habits. The mind catalogs each moment, at least part of which may be released through dreaming (see also step 4 to follow). So, if you dream about a loud radio, this symbol may not need extensive analysis, other than recognizing that you were annoyed by someone's musical tastes earlier that day!

It's not always that easy to discern the difference between visions evoked by simple happenings, and dreams that deserve intense examination. Here are some guidelines that may help:

- The dream seems profoundly realistic, so much so that you wake up feeling displaced. This feeling lingers for some time.
- The dream leaves you with a sense of déjà vu that isn't easily shaken (see also step 7 to follow).
- The dream nags at you all day.
- Certain images or scenarios from the dream continue to flash in your mind long after you wake. If this occurs, these portions of the dream should be closely scrutinized before seeking hidden meanings. I call this discovering the central issue or emblem that unlocks the entire interpretation.
- Rereading your dream entry elicits an unexpected physical or emotional response such as feeling chilled or crying. Our bodies remember things that we consciously do not, so these responses strongly indicate important lessons or revelations.
- The dream centers around someone or something from the distant past. This shows that something *now* inspired a memory that's important to your current situation.
- The dream includes historical knowledge that you should have no awareness of. In esoteric traditions, people believe this type of dream recounts a past life experience, or reflects an ancestral memory. In either case, the information has some bearing on your present needs or circumstances.

In any instance when you're uncertain, I always recommend making notes of the dream in a journal (see step 1 to follow). Write down your initial impressions, and scan the Dream Symbol Key section of this book. If you still find yourself doubtful of any conclusions, put the matter aside and wait.

Over time, of two things will happen. The dream will never recur, and even upon reading it months or years later it holds no import, or you will suddenly experience a revelation. This is where the proverbial light bulb goes on, and you recognize the meaning of a dream that previously eluded you. This is but one reason why maintaining a log of your dreams is so valuable.

Nightmares

While one may not want to think too long or too hard about a horrifying dream, nightmares are a loudly voiced cry from the human psyche. They reflect our fears, guilt, traumas, and unresolved issues, especially those we continually try to deny or avoid. Consequently, analyzing your nightmares may be far more important and revealing than pastoral, lovely dreams. In effect, your subconscious is kicking you, trying to get your attention.

In reviewing your nightmares, it is important to step back and compose yourself first. Consider any obvious circumstances that may have inspired the vision. For example, if you spent a lonely night watching horror movies, the chances of having a nightmare increase. The last violent or scary images your mind experiences before going to sleep are often the first to reveal themselves in a nightmare.

If it appears that nothing you recently saw or experienced prompted the fearful imagery, then it's time to ponder the worries or thoughts that have lain heavy on your heart. Break down the images in the nightmare as you might any dream, but realize these will likely have intensely personal meaning. For example, seeing a lover drive away from you and end up in an accident might reveal your fear of losing that individual on an emotional level. Monsters, on the other hand, are usually facets of our personality that we don't always show to the world, like rage and bitterness.

Should the same nightmare repeat itself, the core issue of that dream has not been resolved and you need to dig deeper. No matter the scenario, don't let the lingering emotions from the dream hinder your capacity to face nightmares for what they are—a part of you that needs expression, understanding, and integration.

Ten Steps to Effective Dream Interpretation

1. Create a dream diary.

Find a sturdy notebook that opens easily and attach a pen or pencil to it with a long string. As soon as you wake up, write the dream down in detail. Include everything you can remember sequentially from beginning to end, including seemingly trivial things like colors in clothing, directions of movement, placements, numbers, geometrical shapes, creatures, jewelry, seasons, buildings, flowers, and anything that's exaggerated (vocally, physically, etc.).

Not every dream will contain specific details (or perhaps you won't recall the them), but those that do should be so noted. Sometimes the peripherals of a dream tell us more than the direct impression. People don't always like to face their problems or fears head-on, so through dream imagery the subconscious presents these issues in a less candid but more palatable manner.

Make sure to date each entry. For individuals who have visions of the future, dating an entry can confirm an honest talent for prophetic dreams. In the days, months, and years ahead, you can return to this journal to see how much your dreams have taught you about yourself (see also The Human Factor, later in this chapter). In both respects, a dream diary becomes an excellent reflection of personal growth.

2. Note immediate impressions.

Often, our first intuitive response to a dream is far more accurate than later research on the matter. Sometimes it's tempting to overintellectualize dreams, thereby diminishing the emotional, spiritual, situational, or experiential value. For example, say you dream of a movie star whom you admire. This is probably just a creative reenactment of a well-loved movie, where you get to appreciate that person's talents again. It really can be that simple!

To balance this statement, exactly what that person is doing in the dream may hold import. For example, if the actor is confronting an ill-mannered individual in the dream, you may likewise wish you'd confronted someone similarly during the day. In this instance, swallowing your words produced a dream that expressed your unvoiced feelings through a safe medium and a familiar, respected face.

3. Analyze the obvious.

If a dream repeats occurrences from your daily routine, then that's probably all there is to it. If you dreamt of eating, perhaps you went to bed hungry. Similarly, people often dream about topics recently viewed on TV or read somewhere. You can recognize each of these causes fairly easily, and such dreams require little (if any) analyzing. In fact, these examples illustrate the most predominant types of dreams—those that repeat or reflect mundane life.

On the other hand, if the day's overview was different from what actually occurred, or the story line replayed from the media took a different turn, this may be quite significant. It can illustrate personal concerns, fears, hopes, and desires, and provide other insights upon closer examination.

If the obvious, central themes of a dream don't make sense, look at the peripherals for meaning or try a little word association. If you had to describe the dream with one word, or a short phrase, what would it be? What is the first word or phrase that comes to mind next? Allow this sequence to continue unhindered like free-flow writing until you feel finished. Then, reread this material from beginning to end.

For example, say you remember vague images of the desert. Desert becomes your primary word for association. From here the exercise could take numerous directions. For the sake of illustration, let's imagine this word sequence followed: golden, sand, sun, heat, fire, blaze, anger. Now you have something more obvious to work with. Potentially you went to bed angry, or feel like anger is being directed toward you without just cause.

4. Consider internal and external factors.

This step takes into account all the things you are coping with both internally and externally. Someone who has been sick and dreams of recovery, for example, is visualizing hope in a realized form. Someone who dreams of a particularly stressful situation may be under tremendous stress in the outer world.

These example indicators are pretty forthright, but could have revealed themselves through symbolic representations instead. To illustrate: the first person might see a withering tree suddenly start to grow and blossom after watering—an image of renewed wellness, thanks to some type of aid. The second person might see a rubber band being stretched too tightly—an image of overpowering tension that could eventually cause "snapping." As you can see, sometimes the symbolic images offer more food for thought than the straightforward ones. A lot depends on how strongly you personally relate to the symbol.

Other factors at times neglected in dream interpretation are those that come directly from our environment while we sleep. It's important to double-check your environment after recording your dream to see if anything influenced the imagery. For example, if you dream of a car's blazing headlights, you may awaken to discover that someone left on a nearby light! Or, if you dream of wearing very itchy fabric, you may get up and find several mosquito bites that you've scratched raw. When these situations occur, discount the circumstantial portion of the dream, and look to the remainder for significance.

5. Recognize patterns, cycles, and progressions.

Patterns in dreams generally develop in one of two ways. In repetitive dreaming, you may have the *same* dream that reoccurs, or you may have several different dreams that contain *similar* images.

Patterned dreams indicate a matter that deeply affects your current situation, a reluctance to accept or integrate change, or long-standing problems and concerns. This dream pattern will continue until you feel confident that the issue is settled. Sometimes the motif repeats even after this conscious juncture, indicating that some doubts still linger on deeper levels. When this happens, the dreamer needs to reexamine the entire matter and see what exactly is causing the uncertainty.

Dream progressions are slightly different. In this case, the dreamer experiences several consecutive dreams, each of which builds on the next, often by extending or changing the ending. Numerous situations encourage progressive dreams, including moving, job changes, new projects, and adjustments in relationships. Through progressive dreams, the mind examines and explores different approaches to the same concern or problem to find the best possible course of action.

6. Identify potential precognition and postcognition.

Don't automatically rule out this possibility. One step in the process of becoming an actively aware dreamer is allowing for all possibilities. Dreams work inside a framework that is more expansive than our waking reality. While we rest, the mind has far less input to deal with. This leaves it free to access latent portions believed to house psychic gifts that aren't usually triggered by normal daily activities, including those of prophesy and clairvoyance.

If you think the event already occurred, start by checking the last few weeks' newspapers. If your dream conforms to a story but contains far more details than that portrayed by the media, then there is a good chance you experienced postcognition.

Similarly, if the dream foretells the future, be aware. Remember that some people like Nostradamus saw hundreds of years into the future, whereas Lincoln foresaw his impending death only a few weeks beforehand. Therefore there is no time limit to prophetic dreams, nor must they occur with any regularity. One person may have dozens of such dreams throughout life, while another individual experiences only one or none at all.

When something confirms a prophetic or postcognitive dream, make a dated entry in your diary to build confidence in your abilities.

7. Identify memories, wishes, fantasies, and imaginings.

The importance of memories, hopes, and dreams cannot be overstated. We base many of our reactions and feelings on what has occurred in the past. Our hopes and dreams provide the motivation to face the future confidently. So, it's not surprising that memories and wishes commonly influence dream imagery.

For example, perhaps you dream of a young child gazing at a Yule tree; this is likely a flashback to your own childhood. If the child is not you, then check alternative meanings. Or, if you have wished for a life partner and begin dreaming of that perfect someone, this reflects your wishes. On a metaphysical level, this dream may also portend someone special entering your life!

With regard to the imagination, this is one part of the adult psyche that often gets pushed aside. The subconscious balances this by giving us wild, colorful, adventurous dreams from our inner child that release those creative instincts. Many writers and artists report that their dreams help them to devise new pieces.

8. Use the Dream Symbol Key.

Now that you've had the opportunity to ponder your dream without external bias, read over the appropriate Dream Symbol Key entries. First review the overall theme, and then examine the details. Some dreams have very archetypal themes—a great flood, treasure hunts, animals, or wise guides. These generally indicate a type of rebirth or fertility, self-discovery, inner nature, and the Higher Self, respectively.

Religious symbols are also archetypal, but with subtle variations depending on the culture. For example, a Christian cross and a Celtic cross carry far different emotional and symbolic values depending on who views them. Similarly, white light may be interpreted from the Christian perspective as a halo or the presence of the Holy Spirit, whereas someone involved in New Age ideology may construe the same light as energy emanating from an auric field.

Next, read through the entire list of interpretations and alternatives for the entries you have chosen. Watch your reactions as you read, and look for meanings that stir awareness on some level. Note these in your dream diary. If nothing in those entries makes sense, try the cross-referenced topics instead. Then, if you still find yourself ambivalent, make note of all the possibilities and return to the dream some other time.

You need not figure out every meaningful facet of a dream in one sitting. Stepping away from a particularly perplexing dream and returning to it later often clarifies things greatly. While you want to make notes of your dream and impressions immediately upon waking, a deeper search might be better left for improved, alert mental states, like those achieved using breathing exercises or meditation (see also step 10).

9. Evaluate personally meaningful symbols vs. given interpretations.

Dream symbols are very intimate. While all dream guides try to provide universal prototypes in their listings, this is really an impossible task. Everything that exists now, or has ever existed, can become a symbol in our dreams. Consider a person who once got hit on the head with an apple while standing beneath a tree. For this dreamer, apples might indicate a warning of impending danger, or reveal some type of physical or emotional pain. For devout Christians, this symbol engenders thoughts of broken promises and forbidden knowledge. Yet if you read many dream dictionaries, the meaning given for apple will often be health, probably generated by the aphorism, "an apple a day keeps the doctor away."

It is for this reason that I continually encourage you to return to yourself, the true expert interpreter of your dreams. While professionals may be able to help with insights, you still remain the final arbiter in what information you accept. If you blindly accept another person's words as a carved-in-stone truth, you do yourself a tremendous disservice. This discourages the development of your innate capacities and denies your place as the rightful master of your destiny.

10. Meditate and draw personal conclusions.

I recommend taking a moment to breathe deeply and evenly, allowing your tensions to flow away. Clear your mind of clutter, and focus only on the dream and the notes you have made in the diary.

Remember that your current state of mind can help or hinder the accuracy of dream interpretations. For example, a distraught individual is more likely to compile only negative meanings from the dream. Conversely, a calm, centered person will view the reflections with a more balanced, positive perspective, and therefore apply the materials more constructively.

The Human Factor

Every person is different. Individuals grow and change every minute of every day. The classroom of life just works that way. So what your dream means to a friend, and what it means to you, will differ either subtly or dramatically. Also, what you interpret in a dream today may change when you view it tomorrow. Reevaluating a dream from a year ago might suddenly inspire insights hitherto unrecognized.

I mention this to stress the vital role that intuition, instinct, and personal insight play in trying to discern the meaning of dreams. Without these factors, you might as well be reading the horoscope in your daily newspaper; it's about as personal. Please bear this in mind as you read the entries in this, or any, dream symbol book.

Finally, don't underestimate the power or importance of your dreams. Some people may say that you're chasing after rainbows, and will find whatever you wish within a dream. Even if that hypothesis is true, it doesn't undermine the usefulness of dream interpretation. Within those transitory images, you may discover solutions, valuable perspectives, answers to nagging questions, and intimate portraits of yourself. If this discovery somehow helps you live better, more happily and confidently, then it is an exploration well worth the effort.

PART TWO

The Dream Symbol Key

CHAPTER THREE

Using the Dream Symbol Key

"Up anchor, up anchor! Set sail and away, the
adventures of dreamland are thine for a day!"

—Silas Weir Mitchell, 1829–1914

The following pages list various objects, feelings, and circumstances in alphabetical order for ease of research. The main entry appears in CAPITAL LETTERS, followed by *italicized cross references* found within the book. Below this, information, potential meanings, and interpretations are given, noting any cultural, religious, historical, or situational variations as space permits. This format makes it very easy to find the information you need quickly, without a lot of page shuffling.

Due to space constraints, some less commonly seen dream objects and experiences have not received a separate entry. It would be impossible, for example, to include all the interpretive values for every known vegetable in a book of this nature. If the item you're looking for isn't classified in its own separate listing, look under a broader categorical entry. For instance, look for thyme under Herbs, doves under Birds, and lilies under Flowers. Situational and conceptual entries work similarly. For example, a flood dream can be explored by reading the entries for Water or Disasters, a huge microscope can be interpreted by reading Magnification and Size, and a dream with a pipe as a central image may be examined by looking under Smoke.

If, after following all the suggestions given in Chapter 1, you're still having trouble interpreting dreams, try the Hints for Success that follow. Beyond this, seek out someone gifted in dream interpretation, including professional psychologists as necessary. These people may shine enough light on the dream in question to illuminate the answers you seek.

Hints for Success

If you are among the group of people who do not remember dreams, sometimes a positive affirmation before going to bed helps. Say to yourself several times, "I will remember my dream." This sets up a pre-sleep program for the conscious and subconscious levels of your mind that may aid retention given enough time, consistency, and practice. Alternatively, some individuals ask for a dream guide—a spiritual partner who assists in receiving and remembering the dream.

Remember to distill your dream writings into their lowest common denominator before trying to analyze each minute detail. For example, if you dream of a field in which you are running, animals are running, and a stream is running, the predominant theme is "running."

Don't forget that dream symbols may illustrate familial lore or sayings, personal rituals, subtle humor, metaphors and similes, or even employ a symbol that is actually a pun.

Remember that the apparent length of your dream and how much detail it contains are unimportant. Even single images remembered upon waking can be significant. In fact, significance often increases because of the uncluttered impact.

If you have any type of artistic ability, try expressing your dream through that medium. Paint it on canvas, sing it, doodle, pantomime the events, or do whatever feels right. This makes the dream clearer, and also assists with the integration process.

Keep your dream diary with you as much as possible, or take along another small notebook for those unexpected moments when the details of a dream return, and you're not in bed.

Avoid interpreting dreams when you are sick, out of sorts, angry, or otherwise ill-disposed. At these moments, impartiality is often lost due to physical or mental fatigue.

In the interest of objectivity, consider comparing the entries in this book with those from other dream guides that you respect. No book or author can embrace the diversity of all humankind. Consequently, comparative reading provides a more balanced outlook and additional help in determining your dream's significance.

• ABANDONMENT

(see Desertion)

• ABBREVIATIONS

(see Punctuation, Writing)

Initials for peoples' *names* with whom you've had recent important interactions.

According to ancient dream oracles, a portent of the initials for future friends, lovers, or meaningful acquaintances. Look to the rest of the dream for more clarification on which outcome best applies.

Abbreviations for a well-known, easily recognized organization that has some symbolic import to your current situation. For example, the AMA (American Medical Association) might relate directly to your health, and possibly the need to seek a physician's advice.

A series of letters that acronymically relate to a well-known phrase or aphorism. While instances of this experience are less common, the subconscious sometimes reduces information into brief formats, akin to a mental shorthand. Even in this format, however, the dreamer usually recognizes the symbolic phrase quickly. One good example here would be the well-known "TGIF" as an abbreviation of "Thank God It's Friday," symbolizing some type of relief or jubilation.

• ABORTION

(see Baby, Embryo, Miscarriage, Pregnancy)

Stopping a project in midstream because of personal or external conflicts.

A reflection of pressures or moral struggles pertaining to this issue.

Termination of a relationship while still in its infancy.

A difficult choice from which the outcome may kill all hopes of something you've wanted to develop.

• ABUSE

(see Fighting, Running, Seduction, Sexual Encounters)

Feeling violated or exploited by an individual, a group, or a situation.

If you are the abuser in the dream, this may represent pent-up displeasure toward yourself or antagonism toward another.

A memory surfacing. Some abuse victims have uncovered their memories through dreams. However, caution must be issued here. Since this topic is widely covered by the media, what you experience in a dream can reenact some of these stories, engendered by your emotional response (fear, indignation, outrage, etc.).

•ABYSS

(see Alley, Bridge, Cauldron, Chalice, Cliff, Hole, Sky, Space)

Standing at the edge of: Your own subconscious, things you've long buried, hidden talents, or other matters that often get overlooked. The abyss goes on seemingly forever into darkness, and can be very frightening, even as discovering your own true nature can be frightening until you take the first step.

Experiencing spontaneous inspiration for a new project, as if it comes out of nowhere. Alternatively, a limitation to be overcome.

Ancient meaning: The primordial womb; a deep cavern of fertility and the gate of life through which we all pass.

Real or perceived dangers. The size of the abyss indicates how "big" you believe the hazard to be. Alternatively, following a route that goes nowhere, or one that may eventually prove self-destructive.

A bridge appearing across: Personal, dramatic changes in lifestyle or beliefs that imply some risk. For example, if you're thinking of getting married, the risk might be vulnerability or failure.

Unseen or unrealized potential. In Greek mythology, the black abyss gave birth to all cosmic matter. Similarly, in the Tarot, the Fool stands near the edge of a huge *cliff* before starting on his path toward enlightenment.

•ACCENTS

(See Announcements, Conversations, Languages)

Accents in dreams, especially those portrayed as overly heavy or nonsensical, may reflect cultural or societal prejudice of which we may be normally unaware.

The inability to communicate effectively; feeling as if people aren't hearing you correctly.

• ACCEPTANCE

(see Judgment, Notarization)

This is a very positive dream in which you welcome various aspects of self, others, or the Divine without expectation.

• ACCIDENT

Causing an accident: Guilt surrounding a situation for which you feel directly responsible, even if that feeling is unwarranted. Alternatively, working out hostility toward a person or situation through dream imagery.

Becoming seemingly helpless due to: This expresses feelings of defenselessness—as if one is totally at the whims of fate (see *Lameness, Numbness, Paralyzation*).

Being too trusting of others, or inattentive to potential dangers, causes painful results (see *Blindness*).

• ACCUSATIONS

(see Conversations)

Self-blame or guilt manifesting through the dream.

Feeling unjustly accused by others.

A moral conflict. Uncertainty over the true motivations for one's actions, or those of other people.

• ACORN

(see Nuts, Seeds, Trees)

Male virility. In ancient times, these were an emblem of the testes, and often carried as amulets for fertility among *men*.

Potential. The acorn grows into the mighty *oak*.

If a woman is eating the acorn, an emblem of abundance and fertility.

Shaking acorns from a tree: Releasing your own potential or making efforts for improved abundance in your life (figurative or literal).

In Native American symbolism, this represents the beginnings of a rigid personality developing in yourself. Take time to correct it by being more open-minded and tolerant.

• ACQUITTAL

(see Acceptance, Judgment)

Forgiveness toward self or others for behavior that's considered socially, legally, or religiously unseemly.

Discovering information about a person or situation that erased any question of liability.

If given by a judge, jury, or clergyperson, this can indicate forgiveness from others, including *authority figures*, or even the Divine regarding actions for which you are penitent.

• ACROBATICS

(see Dancing, Jumping, Running)

Balance, initiative, and sustained energy through physically trying circumstances.

Feeling as if you're jumping through proverbial hoops to please others or meet their expectations.

Walking a *tightrope*: A delicate situation with some implied danger, depending on your level of skill.

Contortionists: Having the truth or your sense of reality somehow twisted.

Tumbling: Being able to "roll with the punches" and still land on your feet. Alternatively, if being performed with another person, this may be a type of sexual dream (e.g., "taking a tumble"). Also, the ancient Minoans used tumbling as a type of fertility rite.

• ACTING

(see Costumes, Masks, Theater)

Life's roles: Shakespeare intimated that life was a stage, making dreams the theater of your mind. Here, you can act out various "parts" to literally walk in someone else's shoes, try out options, or get different perspectives.

Sensing that you, or someone you know, have been putting on airs instead of being real with people.

The various important "characters," "sets," and "props" in and around your life.

• ADOPTION

(see Baby, Orphaned)

If you see yourself being adopted by a group or family, this means *acceptance* among the people pictured, or self-acceptance with regard to your perceived roles and responsibilities to that group.

Seeing yourself alone waiting for adoption is an alternative type of *desertion* dream. Alternatively, this reveals insecurity about not being accepted or loved, or feeling totally out of place in your surroundings.

What exactly is being adopted? This symbol can represent an aspect of yourself— an idea or a characteristic with which you're becoming more accepting and comfortable, thereby adopting it into your being.

• ADULTERY

(see Sexual Encounters)

An unresolved fear that your partner is being unfaithful.

An unexpressed desire for someone outside your current relationship.

Feeling cheated by someone, or a situation, you trusted intimately.

Turning your back on something once regarded as sacred and incorruptible. This can include relationships, but may also pertain to ideals, beliefs, and work situations.

• ADVERTISEMENTS

(see Billboards, Signs, TV)

• AGATE

(see Crystals, Gems, Jewelry, Stones)

Divine favor. In the 16th century the bishop of Rennes in his book, *De Lapidum*, a treatise on the mystical uses of gems, recommended agates for attracting divine blessings.

Protection from negativity. Agates were historically favored as amulets against the evil eye. What negatives surround you right now, from which you need to be distanced?

Moss agate in the Orient represents communication, specifically verbal eloquence. If you've been worrying over your ability to get an idea across, the concern is unwarranted.

Moslems feel this stone brings improved spirits and calms bizarre behavior. So if life has been a little tumultuous lately, it should soon subside.

Among sailors, a lucky stone that ensures a safe voyage. If you're traveling soon, an excellent omen.

• AGE

Elderly people in dreams represent *authority figures*, and the accumulated wisdom that comes from living a long life. They may also represent members of your family or friends who are aging.

Seeing yourself at younger ages is likely a memory surfacing that somehow affects or taints present circumstances.

Dreaming of specific ages, like the occasion of a birthday, may be an alternative type of *number* dream.

Matters pertaining to our own mortality, like the wish to go back and relive our younger years, or a fear of growing old.

• AIR

(see Fan, Wind)

The significance of air in dreams often varies with its strength and other characteristics. For example, a spring breeze is gentle and refreshing, whereas a wind storm may energize or blow away your foundations.

Hot air represents anger and self-importance, especially in the way one speaks (e.g., "being full of hot air").

Cold air symbolizes real or perceived chilly feelings, to the point of being emotionless and stoic. Alternatively, this can indicate that a cooling-off period is necessary before reapproaching a problem will prove successful.

Humid air portends sadness by its damp nature, or a sense of discomfort that comes with nervousness. Alternatively, since humid air often precedes rain, it can reflect a forthcoming release of pain or period of refreshment.

Dry air reveals spiritual, emotional, or intellectual "dryness" manifested as droll words, tedious actions, or an overwhelming feeling of monotony in your life.

The world's soul and breath that gives life to all things. In Sanskrit, the word from which we derive "atmosphere" literally means breath.

In Native American beliefs, dreams that center on the element of air are indicating mental issues that need attending.

• AIRPLANE, AIRPORT

(see Flying)

Movement and transition, similar to other vehicles (see *Car, Horse, Spaceship*). Where the plane goes, its logo, or the other passengers on board (if any) may give you more clues here.

If you're in the plane, enroute, this can be considered a type of *flying* or *ascent* dream.

Higher ideals, due to this vehicle's movement toward the heavens. Also the courage to achieve a goal (e.g., "reach new heights").

A plane that sits endlessly on a runway indicates a life that has somehow become stagnant, or one that is being held back by outside influences. Check to see who, or what, resides in the control *tower*!

Being lost at the airport, or looking for someone there, characterizes confusion caused by getting one's signals crossed, or through poor planning. Make sure you have your information straight, get organized, then readdress this situation.

Waiting at the airport, surrounded by strangers, and never being met by the anticipated party is a type of *desertion* dream.

• ALIENS

(see Spaceship, UFO)

If the alien in the dream acts fidgety or ill at ease, ask yourself how comfortable you are with yourself and your appearance. Do you shy away from mirrors and eye contact or feel self-conscious? Also, are you intimately aware of your own inner nature?

Apprehension toward: Sometimes one must reach out and embrace the unknown to overcome fear. This includes welcoming hidden aspects of self and the Universe.

Traveling with aliens by choice: The need for a new beginning, or a wish to retreat far away from the current situation. Alternatively, someone looking for new friends, hoping to relocate, or just wanting some adventure. If so, reach for the *stars!*

In New Age ideology, potentially an emblem of our kinship with all beings within a very large and vastly unknown Universe.

• ALLEY

(see Abyss, Dead End, Path)

An unlit alley: Lurking potential for danger (see *Darkness*).

Being mugged in an alley: Unanticipated misfortune that leaves you feeling violated or out of control (see *Banking: robbery*).

Light at the end of an alley: Hope. Traversing a dark time to find renewal (see *Tunnel*).

• ALMOND

(see Eating, Nuts)

Generally symbolic of love and fertility. This association probably dates back to when almonds were a maternity charm. For example, the Greek god Attis was conceived with the aid of a magical almond.

Ancient mid-Eastern: An emblem of femininity and the womb of the world due to its shape. This effectively carried over into many arts wherein the lozenge (an almond shape) is used to represent the fullness of womanhood.

Folklore relates that dreaming of whole almonds foretells wealth, whereas those broken apart indicate problems in obtaining wishes.

Spiritual sweetness that awaits you. Just get beyond the *obstacle* or *armor* represented by its shell to savor the reward!

• ALOE

(see Healing, Herbs)

Soothing your wounds, especially those that have come from heated arguments. Aloe is nearly universally used in treating skin burns.

Fooling yourself or someone else. In Africa, aloe is used by hunters to cover up their human aroma. What are you trying to hide and from whom?

• ALTAR

(see Carcass, Church, Holy Ground, Monastery, Temple)

The meeting of two worlds: religious and mundane. This is the place where traditionally the gods are honored, offerings get made, and many rituals take place. So, look beyond the altar to see what appears on it, and what occurs around it, for more insight.

If a *sacrifice* appears before you, ask yourself what things need to be left behind so that you can get a fresh start. Alternatively, consider if you've been giving too much of yourself, and sacrificing personal needs in the process.

Approaching an altar: Acknowledging an urgent need for outside assistance of some sort. We often go to our image of the Divine when we want answers to, or help with, particularly perplexing problems. If you have hesitated to seek that help from friends or the Universe, now is the time for action.

Improved insight or visionary capacity developing. In ancient Greece, a tripodal altar was used in many divinatory efforts (see *Divination)*.

• ALUMINUM

(see Metals)

• AMBER

(see Crystals, Gems, Jewelry, Stones)

Irritating situations in which the tension is nearly audible. Amber has a natural ability to pick up static when rubbed.

Health concerns. Because of its capacity to trap insects and plant life, the ancients believed this stone could likewise entrap sickness. Look to see what the amber contains for more symbolism.

An alternative solar emblem, believed by the Greeks to have been formed in the setting *sun's* tears.

An alternative *fire* emblem. Germans called this a burning stone because it catches fire (like any resin).

In dream oracles, an omen of forthcoming voyages.

Feeling cornered or captured by circumstances over which you have no control, like the insect in amber resin.

•AMBULANCE

(see Accident)

Urgent attention to something is needed, frequently pertaining to matters of personal health.

•AMETHYST

(see Crystals, Gems, Jewelry, Stones, Purple)

Maintaining control over yourself and your situation. In the Middle Ages, this stone got the reputation of keeping people from getting drunk because whole goblets were formed from it. When filled with any substance, the effect was like looking at wine.

Religious authority in a specific area of belief. This stone appears in both bishops' and cardinals' *rings*.

Psychic energy and prophetic dreams. Pay particular attention to anything "futuristic" about this dream's story line.

In dream oracles, an emblem that assures safety from harm, or possibly a turn of events for the better.

•AMMUNITION

(see Weapons)

Gathering ammunition indicates the expectation of battle, or an upcoming undertaking that requires a show of strength (see *Fighting*).

Exhausted ammunition speaks of fruitless struggles against overwhelming odds.

Taking aim at a specific problem or situation with carefully chosen "tools" that might prove harmful if they aren't used properly.

•AMPLIFICATION

(see Magnification)

Anything in your dream that emphasizes sound or *size* should be heeded closely. For example, megaphones or microphones represent the need to communicate and be heard. On the dream plane, this can also be a message from the subconscious that is screaming for attention.

•ANCHOR

An anchor dragging through *water* or sand represents things that weigh you down, and hold you back.

An anchor holding firm in a torrential sea speaks of your personal need for security and stability. If you haven't reinforced your foundations lately, do so.

Anchors are also connected to the sea and sailing (see *Boat, Water*). In earlier times when ships carried valuable goods to port, such an arrival was heartily welcomed. So, sailors and things associated with their trade became "lucky." Perhaps your ship is soon to "come in" and stay for a while!

Safety or improved vitality. In ancient Egypt, an anchor *cross* became a variation of the ankh, the emblem of life, around 4–5 C.E. This emblem was used frequently as a seafaring amulet.

A ship that lacks an anchor represents being adrift, going from one idea or goal to another without ever accomplishing anything.

• ANGEL

(see Authority Figures, Icons)

A personal guide or guardian who either safeguards you in times of need or conveys important messages, most likely of a spiritual nature.

Divine blessings and protection, especially if one covers you with its *wings*. In Christianity, angels are servants and messengers for God, often attending and defending believers in their ministerial tasks.

What is the angel's attitude toward you? If disapproving, this is a sign that you feel negligent toward important teachings from your youth or faith. This caused guilt and inner conflict over notions of "right" and "wrong."

Recognition of bravery or honor. In Germany, winged Valkyries took great heroes to Valhalla, their version of heaven. In Persian tradition, similar beings called "houris" took faithful, courageous warriors to an erotic paradise for eternity.

Cosmic patterns and energy. In the 6th century, a monk named Cosmas Indicopleustes said that angels pushed and pulled heavenly bodies on their course. Other religious people claimed that the *stars* themselves were angels in disguise.

Cherubic angels: A type of Cupid, the Roman god of love, whose *arrow* smites humans with eros and passion.

• ANIMALS

(see by specific creature or habitat, Carcass, Fur, Zoo)

The primitive wildness within and a yearning to return to nature.

A threatening animal reveals hidden aggression or unexpressed anger toward something or someone. Alternatively, this may mean that you personally feel threatened by someone perceived as predatory.

Taming an animal: Bringing (or wishing to bring) yourself under greater control, especially characteristics like a hot temper or overly intense passion (see *Whip*).

Native Americans believe that the spirits of animals appear in our dreams as teachers and guides. In this case, read that animal's entry for more insight into its lessons.

Killing an animal: Consider what the creature itself symbolizes. For example, killing a bird signals a fear that you are somehow stifling personal freedom or vision (see *Carcass*).

Jung felt that the central self was often represented in dreams as an animal, specifically the *elephant, horse, bear, bull, fish,* or *snake*.

Consider the creature's positive and negative characteristics or integral qualities as they reflect upon the way you behave. For example, are you being bull-headed or figuratively bearish?

• ANKH

(see Anchor, Jewelry)

• ANNOUNCEMENTS

(see Amplification)

Closely heed the instructions or information given in a dream announcement. This is often a direct communication from your subconscious or Higher Self that needs immediate attention. Other factors in this dream may also prove important. Where does the announcement take place? Do other people stop to listen to it?

• ANSWERING MACHINE

(see Telephone)

Avoiding direct communication with others.

Screening or carefully recording the input you're getting from various sources.

• ANT

(see Insects)

Business concerns. What is the ant pulling or walking upon?

Tenacity. The ability to overcome insurmountable odds (note *Aesop's Fables*).

Community and solidarity. Ants live and work as a unit.

Being bitten by an ant: A Victorian symbol of quarrels or bad feelings that came out as biting words.

Divinatory insight. The ancients believed because these creatures traverse both worlds (the above and below) that they were excellent prognosticators, especially of the weather.

Moslem: A teacher of wisdom. What lesson does the ant offer you in your dream?

Chinese: A symbol of patriotism, virtue, and orderliness.

• ANTIQUES

Outmoded concepts, or overemphasizing the past instead of living in the "now."

If these are treasured possessions, this indicates you truly value your traditions, or history in general.

The question of personal value. Perhaps you are feeling old, worn, and useless, instead of cherishing the experiences life has provided over the years.

• APARTMENTS

(see Buildings, Castle)

Compartmentalization. Each *door* here represents a different aspect of self and your experiences.

Alternatives. Every door is another option waiting for examination.

Being lost in an apartment complex symbolizes having too many options from which to choose, and finding yourself overwhelmed by those options. Narrow down the field a little, then reapproach this situation.

• APE

(see Monkey)

• APPLE

(see Eating, Fruit, Juice, Trees)

Temptation to break personal taboos, or divine or societal laws.

Responsible use of knowledge, skills, or wisdom.

Matters of health: How the apple looks may have a direct bearing on how you're feeling.

Appearing abundantly on a tree: A propitious sign that speaks of realizing your hopes.

Only at the top of a tree: High ambitions that you may not be able to safely or effectively reach.

Worm ridden: If you bite into an apple to discover a worm, this means that something isn't as good as it outwardly appears, especially someone's ethical codes.

Arthurian: Longevity. King Arthur was taken to Avalon, the Isle of Apples, to live forever. Similarly, in Norse legends apples are used as a resurrection charm, and Hera's Tree of Life is filled with golden apples.

• APRON

(see Clothes)

A feminine emblem that pertains to domesticity.

A man wearing a chef's or barbecue apron signals acceptance of certain traits considered feminine, resulting in a more complete person.

Taking off: Breaking the proverbial "apron strings." This may pertain to your parents, or to any situation that has restricted you to obsolete images and thought patterns.

Turning an apron: Taking your life in hand and making a change for the better.

• AQUARIUM

(see Fish, Water)

The clear glass of the aquarium allows you to see through into your subconscious or matters of spirit. So, what's going on in the fish tank, and what creatures live there? A healthy carp, for example, symbolizes an optimistic outlook, whereas dark, murky waters indicate a soul in need of a good housecleaning.

• ARCHWAY

Victory and distinction. Archways were often built in ancient Rome to welcome back conquering heroes.

Crumbled: The destruction of hopes with little warning.

An alternative type of *bridge* dream, in which movement from one side of the archway to the other marks a transition (see *Directions*).

A guidepost to follow. Just as we use important buildings for landmarks when giving directions, our ancestors used archways as meeting and business places, often at crossroads (see *Cross*). In this case, what's below the archway or what's happening there will give you more insight.

• ARITHMETIC
(see Calculator, Numbers)

The conscious, logical self in full swing.

Look to see if the mathematics make sense. If not, check your current situation to see if things around you likewise don't "add up."

Someone with a designing, detailed personality.

• ARMOR
(see Obstacles, Weapons)

Vulnerability, or the need for protection.

Being distant and unfeeling. Putting up barriers between yourself and the world so as not to get hurt. Please note that this can pertain to anything appearing in the dream that is armored, like a truck or tank.

In Christianity, the armor of God that provides the believer with all the tools necessary for righteous living. Similarly in Judaism, a special breastplate was worn by early high priests, symbolizing their authority and connection with the Divine.

Psychically, wearing a helmet reveals the potential need for psychic or mental protection of any nature. You may be studying too hard, or be under some kind of psychic attack.

Knight in shining armor: Being rescued, or hoping for aid in time of need. Alternatively, the desire to venture forth on a quest for personal honor, or fight for a just cause.

•AROMA

(see Incense, Perfume, Smells)

•ARRESTED

(see Cage, Police, Warrants)

•ARROW

(see Weapons)

Directional guidance, like a subliminal road map showing you the way to go. Watch where the arrow lands to see if you're making or missing your mark.

Power over, or empathy with, *animals*. In Greek mythology, Artemis carried arrows representing her dominion over the animal kingdom.

Potentially a phallic symbol. The cherub carries arrows that inspire passion.

An omen or message. Arrows were used in Tibet and in the Bible (Ez. 21:21) as harbingers of truth or the future. Therefore if an arrow lands off its mark in the dream, the truth may be only partially revealed to you, or the future uncertain.

Power, strength, and possibly war. The Scandinavian god Tyr and the Roman god Mars, both of whom presided over battles, are often featured with arrows.

Being shot by an arrow: Either a betrayal of confidence or forced love.

Broken arrow: A broken vow or promise, or plans that got disengaged.

•ART

(see Canvas)

A reflection of what you hope to create with your artistic talents.

What medium does the art use, and is it one that you've tried? If not, it may be worth exploring that avenue.

In many cases, the art portrays feelings about a specific person or scenario. For example, dreaming of the Venus de Milo may reveal that while you find your current situation very attractive, it somehow leaves you feeling out of control, as if you have no arms with which to act, react, and interact.

Framed art represents your personal perception of a person or situation, whether or not that perception is accurate.

• ASCENT

(see Airplane, Balloon, Clouds, Ladder, Mountain, Stairs, Wings)

Broader perspectives and higher outlooks on any situation. If on the journey up, your head literally reaches into the *clouds*, put those flights of fancy in check and come back down to *earth*.

Emotions or memories surfacing from deep within.

Spiritually, the quest for enlightenment and reconnection with the sacred. If you climb alone, you have accepted the role of spiritual leader for your life. If climbing toward a guru or master figure, the teacher you've long awaited will soon appear.

• ASCETIC

(see Monastery, Mountain, Temple)

A life or period of serious contemplation.

Someone who denies her-/himself and worldly needs, possibly to a dangerous extreme.

A renewed religious focus growing in your life.

The need to evaluate what things or possessions are, and are not, truly important.

• ASHES

Ashes are generally a negative emblem, being all that remains of a devastating *fire*. Bitter changes, unsuccessful deals, heated emotions, and nonproductive arguments are all examples of what the ashes may represent.

Victorian: Ashes from one's hearth could be used to fertilize the land or bring love into the home. What in your life needs feeding or love?

•ASH TREES

Ancient Druids regarded ash as a tree of well-being and perspicacity, and they used it for making their magical wands. Dreaming of sitting beneath or near an ash tree can symbolize growing intuition, or perhaps a calling to follow a Druidical path spiritually.

The Norse honored the ash as being the World Tree in their mythology. If you are of Norse decent, this tree may represent your own familial lines and ties (see *Trees, Yggdrasil*).

•ASSISTANCE

This often indicates exactly what it appears to be: help freely given or offered.

Helpful *hands*, of which you may be unaware. Consider the source of aid shown in the dream for its literal or figurative meaning, then find a correlation in your life.

•ASTRONAUT
(see Space, Spaceship)

The desire for adventures, especially those into totally new frontiers.

Stretching yourself or your spirit to literally reach for the *stars*.

•ATOM

A basic building block around which your life is currently revolving.

A very simple thing, person, or situation that holds tremendous potential for both good and ill.

Pay attention to minute details; look closely and see what you discover
(see *Magnification*).

•ATTIC
(see Building)

Edgar Cayce and several other dream interpreters believed this portion of a house represents your head or the mind. So, the condition of the attic is important to the dream's overall meaning. For example, an orderly attic symbolizes well-ordered thoughts and hopes. One cluttered with *antiques* may reveal someone whose thoughts are too focused on the past. A dirty attic metaphorically indicates immoral views, or a mind that is not being used to its fullest potential (see *Balcony*).

• AUCTION

Winning a bid at an auction portends fair treatment in your business endeavors. It also shows that you feel confident about the value of something (symbolized by what you bid on). This item can represent anything from a personal characteristic to a person.

Exchanging *money* at an auction foretells plenty and luck.

Losing a bid can signify the loss of something (or someone) important in real life. Examples include an object that you treasured, a personal conviction that gets impeded, or a vision or goal being waylaid.

• AUTHORITY FIGURES

(see Angel, Icons, Professor, Priest/Priestess)

Your relationship to your boss or anyone in authority, as you perceive it.

The Higher Self or embodiment of your conscious self, and your interactions with same (or lack thereof).

How is this individual acting? If overbearing, perhaps you or someone you know is being too "bossy."

A person or situation that makes you feel childlike or out of control.

Something or someone to which or to whom you subjugate yourself. This includes belief systems.

• AUTHORSHIP

(see Books, Writing)

• AUTUMN

(see Leaves, Seasons)

• AVALANCHE

(see Disasters)

• AVATAR

(see Authority Figures, Icons)

• AWARDS

Recognition or *acceptance* that you deserve to be honored for special efforts that you've made.

A nudge from the subconscious reminding you to award yourself for hard work and unselfish deeds. Many people are hesitant to give themselves that pat on the back, but it's very healthy.

• AXE

(see Weapons)

Cutting yourself off or away from someone or something (see *Knife*).

Fear of losing one's job (e.g., "getting the axe").

Two-headed axe (the Labrys): Duality. A choice or situation that has two distinct edges, one of which may not be known. It can also be a symbol of feminine power.

Being executed by: Punishment or judgment for something about which you feel morally awkward or ashamed.

In ancient Israel, people used axes in divinatory rights. This may be how the phrase "see where the axe falls" originated. In this context, if the axe lands at your feet, or you take one in hand, it reveals a latent prophetic ability or, on a less lofty level, good instincts.

• BABY

(see Abortion, Adoption, Birth, Embryo, Miscarriage, Orphaned, Toys)

A very common dream for *pregnant women*. In this case, it needs no further interpretation.

Figuratively, new endeavors, ideals, or the opportunity to develop specific positive characteristics.

Our own inner child, who frequently gets neglected in the hectic adult world. This type of dream often comes to workaholics and overachievers who need to play more and nurture themselves.

A return to innocence. Pure trust and love without expectation.

Immature attitudes, emotions, or spiritual outlooks.

• BACKWARDS MOVEMENT

(see Clock)

• BACON

(see Eating, Meat)

Meats, in general, indicate prosperity. In earlier times, meat was an expensive commodity, so anyone who ate it regularly was believed to be wealthy.

Possibly providing for one's family and needs (e.g., "bringing home the bacon"). Along the same lines, dreaming of curing bacon may represent carefully saving for the proverbial rainy day.

Rancid bacon is considered a negative omen in dream oracles, foretelling ill motivations, bad luck, or financial problems.

• BAGGAGE

(see Clothes, Journey, Travel)

If the baggage is overly heavy, you may be carrying too great a load physically or emotionally. If the luggage is very old or worn, likely the burden is one from the past that you have never put down.

Review the size, shape, and color of the suitcase. These may be subtle emblems with deeper meanings. For example, round suitcases filled to overflowing might symbolize fertility or abundance.

The desire for movement of some kind. Possibly the need for retreat and rest.

Lost baggage: Releasing a hardship or responsibility.

Baggage left with you: The feeling that someone dumped her/his obligations on your doorstep.

• BAIL
(see Judgment, Police)

• BAKING
(see Cake, Eating, Fire, Foods by type, Hearth)

Another dream that comes to *pregnant women* due to the somewhat antiquated phrase "bun in the oven." Needs no further examination in this situation.

Simmering pots: Ideas that are "slow cooking" to perfection. Watch closely, however, so that your conceptual dish does not burn or boil over from lack of attention.

If something comes out of the oven undercooked, contemplate current plans or ideas to see if they're well thought out. Otherwise you may find the whole thing is "half baked."

• BALANCE (SCALES)
(see Dieting, Weight)

How does this tool appear? Is it lopsided? If so, consider if you have been stressing certain things too much in your life, resulting in throwing everything else off kilter.

An alternative emblem for the *zodiac sign* of Libra, whose name literally means balance. The counsel of this image is using perspective and fairness to reach a harmonious decision in whatever situation lies heavy on your heart.

The quality of living. In ancient Egypt, the souls of the recently departed were weighed for worthiness on a scale against Maat's *feather*. Maat was the Mother of All Truth. Similarly, in ancient Greece, Hermes weighed souls at the throne of Zeus, and among Christians, the archangel Michael assumed this role.

Equity especially in legal matters. In the Tarot, the Justice card carries a balance to ensure impartiality.

The amount of figurative weight you carry in terms of responsibility, burdens, etc.

• BALCONY

In dream oracles, a negative sign for lovers, probably stemming from the tragic tale of Romeo and Juliet.

Depending on your feelings during this dream, standing alone on a balcony can be an alternative type of *desertion* dream.

Because of the height and perspective offered, potentially a type of *ascension, mountain,* or *stair* dream in which you have already reached the precipice.

Due to its location, this may be an emblem of the mind or head, so check the balcony's condition for more meaning.

• BALDNESS

(see Hair)

• BALLOON

(see Ascent, Circle)

A reason for celebration.

In a bundle: An image of childhood joys and blessings.

Being lifted away by: Detachment; a type of *ascent* dream. Alternatively, burdens easing or an improved perspective that makes problems seem smaller.

Inflating a balloon represents situations that have been likewise inflated by a lot of hot *air* and heated words.

• BANANA

(see Eating, Fruit)

Traditionally, masculinity or male sexuality.

Banana peel: A slippery situation to which you should be attentive. Caution against overlooking a potential hazard.

Banana cream *pie*: From the days of slapstick comedy. Developing a good sense of humor as an ally for coping with difficult people or situations.

Protection from negativity. In Hawaii, banana *leaves* are used as a talisman for this purpose.

Heroic energy. Somewhat connected to the masculine nature. In Polynesia, legend says that bananas were born from th*e blood* of slain champions.

•BANDAGES

Covering a wound so that *healing* can begin. The caution here is to make sure the wound is not figuratively infected, in which case the bandage can do more harm than good.

•BANISHMENT

An alternative type of forced *desertion* or *judgment* dream.

Ridding yourself of an unwanted or undesirable characteristic, situation, or person.

Feelings of loneliness, displacement, or fatality that stem from others' disapproval of your lifestyle or ideas.

•BANK, BANKING

(see Coins, Gold, Money, Poverty, Silver, Stock Market)

Financial concerns, specifically with regard to savings.

A source of wealth, possibly your own hidden talents and potential.

Robbery of: Feelings of vulnerability and betrayal. Having your hard work or good ideas undermined or usurped by an opportunist.

ATM machines: Quick fixes for, or easy access to, something you need right away.

Look at the condition of the bank or where you're putting money in the dream to see if what you're "banking on" is really secure.

Without tellers: Business losses.

Tellers giving out *money*: An indication of either careless giving of yourself and your resources, or charity and generosity (sometimes to a fault).

• BAPTISM

(see Water)

• BAREFOOT

(see Clothing, Foot, Nakedness, Shoes)

Consider the context of the dream first. For example, there is nothing unusual about walking barefoot on the beach, but walking barefoot on a roadway might indicate exposing oneself to harm.

Sensitivity. Feeling the grass between your toes, and really experiencing life to the fullest.

Freedom and liberation. Tossing off your shoes is like being released from a *cage* or other material bonds.

Among *ascetics*, the ability to walk your path confidently and safely because you know it so intimately.

Fire-walking barefoot reveals an ability within to accomplish any task to which you set your mind, no matter how impossible it may initially seem.

• BARN

(see Animals, Buildings, Farm)

A barn filled with grain is an image of safeguarding resources, especially finances.

A barn with its door open reveals that you have been careless in some matter. This situation needs tending before it gets totally out of control (e.g., closing the barn door after the horses get out).

Barns painted with hex signs come from the Pennsylvania Dutch tradition, each pattern having a specific meaning. Consider the *pictograph* here as the starting point of your interpretation, then add to it other indicators like the condition of the barn. For example, if you see a circle with a heart and two *brooms*, this reflects domestic harmony and love. However, if the barn is in disrepair, this may show that your relationships at home are similarly needful of attention.

• BASIL

(see Herbs)

Love, especially if seen sitting on a windowsill. This was a way that Italian women welcomed their suitors.

An alternative *dragon* emblem, full of fire and power, having taken its name from the legendary "basilisk."

Indian: The observation of sacred *offerings* and rites. This herb is used regularly on *altars* to Krishna and Vishnu.

• BASKET

(see Bowl, Cauldron, Chalice, Circle)

The shape of a basket makes it a natural symbol of the womb, the feminine aspect, and *pregnancy*.

If the basket is full, a sign of productivity and providence. Conversely, an empty basket speaks of something in your life that is wanting for fulfillment.

What specifically does the basket contain? If it's filled with *eggs*, this can either portend productivity, or act as a warning not to "keep all your eggs in one basket."

Harvest, fertility, or unexpected surprises. Several important legends center around children found in floating baskets filled with rushes, including the story of Moses, and Romulus and Remus.

• BAT

(see Animals, Birds, Flying)

An ability to traverse "darkness" of a figurative nature, but one that may not be recognized. Native Americans believe these creatures are guides because of their uncanny navigation abilities. See where the bat is taking you, and watch closely the *path* by which you go.

If the bat is you, or you have bat *wings*, it's likely a type of *flying* dream.

In Babylonia and South Africa, bats are thought to carry souls. So, this might be an Out-of-Body Experience, or a message from a departed person.

In China, an emblem of good luck and happiness.

• BATTERIES

Carefully using your resources or energy so as to have enough left over for needful times (see *Electricity*).

Dead batteries indicate that you've overstretched yourself and now need to rest.

A source of energy or power within, of which you may be unaware.

• BAY

(see Herbs)

Victory, recognition, and success. Bay *crowns* were used in Greece to honor kings, *priests*, poets, and heroes.

Unrequited love. Daphne was changed to a bay laurel tree to keep her safe from Apollo's pursuit.

Averting emotional storms. Anciently this herb was considered a good amulet to protect the home against damage from thunder and lightning.

• BEACH

(see Sand, Seashell, Water)

• BEAN

(see Eating, Vegetables)

If seen in pairs, this represents male virility.

Lima beans specifically portend the end to a quarrel.

Among the ancient Romans and Greeks, beans were used for ballots. A white bean was a positive response; a black bean was negative. What *color* are the beans in your dream?

Eating beans may act as a humorous counsel from your subconscious not to get "puffed up" so that your words don't come out as hot air!

In the East, soybeans represent luck.

During the Middle Ages, lentils were eaten to control the temperament. How balanced have your emotions been lately?

Beans are unique in that they twine and grow counterclockwise. You may find similarly that your way of growing and changing is vastly different than those around you.

• BEAR

(see Animals)

The grizzly or domineering side of our moods (e.g., acting "bearish").

The wildness within that wishes more expression.

Heraldic: Among the medieval artisans, this creature provided the perfect vehicle for visual puns, and usually stood for for-BEAR-ance.

She-bear protecting cubs: The maternal instinct fully developed; righteous anger or anxiety with real foundations.

Hibernation: An alternative type of *death* dream. Also, resting and storing up energy for difficult times ahead (see *Cave*).

Fearlessness. The term "berserkers" among warrior clans came from "bear sarks," a shirt originated by Artemis to give strength and protection to those defending her lands.

Native American: Supernatural power and fortitude.

Biblical: The she-bear, particularly, is portrayed as ferocious (noted in Samuel, Hosea, and Proverbs). To what project or relationship are you, or should you be, applying this type of fervently protective energy?

• BED

Seeing yourself asleep in bed may indicate that you are either experiencing a great sense of weariness, or that you are disregarding the signals coming from the subconscious (see *Dreams*). Alternatively, esoterically this may be some type of Out-of-Body Experience in which the spirit hovers above the body and can see it clearly.

The bed itself may represent passion or sexual encounters. Here, the condition of the bed reflects the condition of the relationship.

If you envision the bed being made, this refers to the aphorism of "having made your bed, now lie in it." Basically, whatever situation you're currently experiencing has been brought about by your own actions or lack thereof.

Something underneath a bed symbolizes hidden matters, secrets, or fears that you're purposely avoiding.

• BEE

(see Honey, Insects)

Stinging you: An unpleasant experience that literally left a "stinger" behind, often of an emotional nature.

At the hive: Community and socialization; knowing your place and function within a specific group; harmonious teamwork.

Flying from flower to flower: Gathering life's nectar, enjoying sweetness wherever it may be found. Alternatively, a fickle nature.

Buzzing: A message; the ancients felt that bees carried missives direct from the gods themselves. The priestesses of Delphi were called "Melissae," which means bees, and they were often given honey cakes as an offering in payment for their visionary talents.

Hornet's nest: Trouble just waiting to happen. Don't aggravate this situation or you will get stung.

In China, dreaming of a bee swarm is a lucky omen.

A ghostly visitor. Both Pliny and Aristotle believed that good souls could reincarnate as a bee.

The spirit of the Muse. In Greece, eloquent people were believed to have been touched on the lips by the Birds of the Muses (bees), including Sophocles, Plato, and Virgil.

Flying down a chimney—omen of death of figurative or literal nature.

In medieval Bestiaries, an emblem of honor.

In the Koran, the symbol of faithfulness, intelligence, and wisdom.

Folkloric: A portent of forthcoming profits, especially in your trade.

Queen bees represent the ancient Mother Goddess, and as such can symbolize your own mother, your maternal instincts, or your feminine nature.

• BEER

(see Beverages, Brewing)

In Egypt, dreaming of barley beer meant longevity to the dreamer, whereas a beer made from wheat portended joyous times ahead.

Love and commitment. In old Germany, the Minne (love) cup filled with ritual beer was offered to the *bride* and *groom* at *weddings*.

Social occasions. In Norse tradition especially, and among American *sports* fans, this beverage holds the connotation of something shared with good company. As such, it may also represent the spirit of hospitality.

A sense of fitting in and being one of the "guys." Among almost all civilizations, beer was the beverage of common, everyday folk, who usually enjoyed it with each other.

• BEETS

(see Vegetables)

If you dream of *eating* beets, this foretells good news soon to follow.

Because of their color, they are an alternative emblem for *blood*. In fact, beet soup is often a part of Passover rites for this reason.

Long life that is filled with love. Aphrodite, the goddess of love, ate beets to increase her beauty. Also, in folklore, if two people eat from the same beet, they will have love eternal.

• BEGGAR

(see Poverty)

• BELLS

(see Church, Music)

Happy occasions; ringing out the old and welcoming the new.

Protection and warnings. Bells were used among the ancient Hebrews and medieval Europeans to frighten off mischievous spirits, *fairies*, and malicious *magic*.

A call to introspection: In Tibet, bowls that resound like bells are used for meditation and prayer. During the Christian era, bells announced the arrival of the Holy Spirit, and a time of worship.

Traditionally, if a bell tolls the time, listen to the hour. Midnight is the most ominous, portending an ending or *death* (see *Clocks, Numbers*).

A gong: Used in many Eastern lands to presage an announcement, gathering, or other matters of import. If you're expecting news, it is soon to come. Also, the number of times the gong sounds may be significant (see *Numbers*).

• BELT

(see Clothes)

• BERRIES

(see Eating, Fruit)

Blackberries represent the harvest. Here you reap what you sow.

Red berries portend happy occasions (see others by *Color*).

Strawberries usually symbolize matters of love or passion. They were sacred to the Scandinavian goddess Freya, who was the protectress of marriage and a wise counseling wife to Odin. Alternatively, these may represent long lasting strength, as strawberries were eaten by the Norse gods to ensure their vitality.

Profuseness in some area of your life. Berries reflect earth's bounty by their numbers and the fact that they grow wild.

• BERYL

(see Crystals)

• BEVERAGES

(see by type, Brewing, Chalice)

Situational dream caused by being thirsty during the night.

Metaphorical thirst for something or someone. In this case, what you quaff in the dream may be very revealing. For example, drinking a love potion can reflect the need to internalize self-love, or the desire to find someone with whom you can share your life.

• BIBLE

(see Books)

• BILLBOARD

(see Signage)

What does the billboard have on it? Words and images here are often messages from the subconscious or Higher Self.

Make sure you take time to notice and read the signs that life, others, or circumstances are giving you.

• BIRCH

(see Forest, Trees)

Birth and origination. This tree gets its name from the first letter of the Druidical alphabet, which also represents beginnings.

Making a mark that distinguishes your personal territory on the job, at home, or in a situation. Birch *rods* were used in ancient rites called Beating the Bounds in which people would walk and mark their lands (see *Wand*).

Sturdiness. This tree is even hardier than an oak.

Matters of communication, especially writing. Birch bark was predominantly used in the ancient world as a type of paper.

A fresh start that leads to fruitful manifestation. In many rural regions, the blossoming of the birch marks the beginning of the growing season.

As the Lady of the Woods, the birch also represents refined grace and elegance.

• BIRDS

(see by type, Nest, Flying, Wings)

A type of *flying* dream, especially if you have sprouted wings.

If the bird is carrying something to you, or away from you, what it bears is significant to meaning. For example, a bird carrying an olive branch would traditionally symbolize forgiveness and peace.

If the birds are scavengers preying on something (see *Buzzard, Carcass*), this indicates that you, or someone you know, have taken unfair advantage of a situation. Alternatively, if the birds are picking relentlessly, this may reveal inner trauma over teasing from those in your peer group.

According to Edgar Cayce, transcendental joy and beauty, especially if a bluebird. Parakeets equate to relationships on the same level. However, if the bird is confined, this is another type of *cage* dream that can reveal an inability to freely verbalize your thoughts, or a relationship in which you feel confined.

Love birds in a *cage* reveal a love that isn't totally mature or trusting, so it resorts to manipulation to keep the two parties together.

A bird singing sweetly reveals pleasure, honor, and success. Alternatively, it can indicate someone who always has something nice to say.

Birds chattering represent matters of communication, especially gossip or secrets (e.g., "a little bird told me").

• BIRTH

(see Adoption, Baby, Miscarriage, Pregnancy)

The desire to have a child, or to have something important develop in your life, be it a project or characteristic.

Memory of one's own birth, and/or unsettled psychological issues that stem from this transition, especially births that are particularly difficult. The technique of rebirthing through guided visualization and hypnosis sometimes resolves the latter matter.

Awakening potentials and opportunity. A new start.

Necessary pain or difficulties that result in something positive.

• BLACK

(see Color, Blindness, Darkness)

Mourning or depression.

Feeling lost, obstructed, blinded, or overwhelmed by fear.

In some beliefs, the color of *evil* or negativity. The source is something that you must determine here. Is it within or without?

The subconscious, or the other side of self that we have trouble facing (see *Shadow*).

• BLACKBOARD

(see School, Signage, Writing)

Life's important lessons—the ones that we return to regularly to determine our actions and reactions.

Structured learning and accumulated knowledge. A common dream appearing to students during exam time. In this case, what's on the blackboard is likely a reflection of those studies.

A formula appearing on a blackboard often refers to the solution to some conflict or problem. Try to find a way to translate the *pictographs* into positive actions.

• BLINDNESS

(see Black, Darkness, Eyes)

Entering a situation in which impartiality is nothing less than essential. In the Tarot, Justice is blinded so that she may render a fair judgment.

Not seeing something that's important, a refusal to face reality, or overlooking the obvious (e.g., "wearing blinders").

A sense of helplessness. A type of *desertion* dream.

Turning your back on the issues due to overt romanticism (e.g., "love is blind").

Wearing a blindfold: Self-imposed inattentiveness or ignorance; refusal to see things for what they are truly.

• BLOOD

(see Beet, Red)

The energy and power of life, especially if taken internally somehow (see *Vampire*).

If blood courses quickly, without regulation, this may indicate passion or other intense situations raging out of control.

If due to a sacrifice, see *altar* and *carcass*.

Female mysteries, power, and transitions. Some young women dream of blood right before their first menses.

Close ties (e.g., "blood brothers").

Christian: Sacrifice or forgiveness. The question here is what needs to be relinquished to achieve forgiveness, or who needs to be absolved and at what cost?

If the blood appears soiled in some manner, this shows that negative feelings (e.g., "bad blood") exists internally, or between you and another.

Blood appearing as covering you, or a part of the body, denotes guilt directly relating to an action, as with Lady Macbeth who could not wash the blood of *murder* from her *hands*.

Transfusions represent the need for change and cleansing. Get rid of any bad blood between yourself and others, and start fresh.

Kinship and family. It was common among Gypsies during their marriage rites to eat *bread* with a drop of their partner's blood upon it to symbolize the union.

• BLOODSTONE
(see Crystals)

• BLUE
(see Color)

Peace and happiness, especially in the form of a *bird* approaching you.

Light (*sky*) blue: The color of awakening, promise, spirituality, sincerity, hope, and new beginnings.

Dark, murky blue: Depression or weariness.

Indicative of a type of hands-on labor (e.g., "blue-collar worker").

Sea blue: Insight, emotions, and the ability to flow smoothly from one situation to another. (see *Water*.)

Faithfulness (e.g., being "true blue").

In Yoga, this is the color of the throat chakra, indicating matters of communication.

Among Hindus, the color that represents divine energy, especially that of Vishnu. Similarly, the abode of the gods is often depicted as blue.

Egyptian: The color of truth.

• BLUEPRINTS

(see Schematics)

An outline of your goals and plans for the future.

The patterns of your life, the image shown being your conception of what you have built thus far, or that which you hope to build.

Directional guidance for knowing how to proceed with a specific project or concern. Look to the rest of the dream for details that delineate this further, like any symbol key that appears on the blueprints.

• BOAT

(see Anchor, Water)

Potential and opportunity. The proximity of the ship indicates either how aware you are of the possibilities, or how long it will be before they manifest.

Your health. Like other vehicles (see *by type*), the condition of the boat may inform you about your physical status. For example, the lack of *wind* could equate to lung problems like asthma.

Adventure, and the yearning for same. In Arabia, the Corsairs were people who lived and died by the sea, and reveled in the freedom and challenges the open *water* offered.

Transitions and movement. This could indicate concern over a forthcoming change in residence or status.

Stagnant or anchored: Worry that your life isn't moving the way you feel it should. The feeling that everything is at a standstill.

Sailing without you: Either missed opportunity, or a type of *desertion* dream.

Life's voyage and new horizons. Like Columbus locating America, you are embarking on a voyage of self-discovery.

Taking a journey by boat may equate to literal or figurative death, as ferries and boats figure heavily into myths of how the spirit goes from one existence to the next.

• BODY

Each part of the body symbolizes something different. *Fingers* indicate blame or direction, arms stand for effective use of skills, and legs are grounding or support.

The *nose* reveals your instincts and level of honesty (being able to "smell out" a lie); the *mouth* indicates communicative ability or more metaphorically, tastes and preferences. *Eyes* represent your spiritual state (the *window* of the soul) and perspectives. *Ears* appear as a reminder to listen *and* hear, the abdomen has to do with birth, fertility, and nervousness (e.g., "having butterflies in your stomach"), and the back is an emblem of support or strength.

•BONES

(see Animal by type, Burial, Carcass, Cemetery, Death)

Breaking something down into the most simple, forthright form (e.g., the "bare bones").

A large pile of bones indicates contaminating circumstances that threaten to pollute your morals or ideals.

Skeletal remains often represent those things we hide from others, or even from ourselves (e.g., the "skeleton in the *closet*").

Foundational attitudes that give form and structure to all other thoughts and actions.

•BOOKKEEPING

(see Arithmetic, Books)

The tallying of your life or actions against a prespecified guideline. For example, many religions speak of a divine book wherein deeds are recorded to determine the soul's fate after *death*.

A type of *money* dream

If the *numbers* in the dream won't add up, then there is something in your life that likewise doesn't quite make sense…all the pieces don't reckon.

•BOOKS

(see Writing)

Sacred texts: Higher ideals and beliefs. Spiritual development and your relationship with sacred powers. The state of your spiritual path may be noted by the condition in which this book appears.

Matters of learning and study. Check the title for a more complete picture. Please note, however, that education can equate to "life's lessons" too.

On a bookcase: Accumulated knowledge that you have readily accessible.

A library: On the etheric plane this may represent the Akashic records that keep track of each soul and its incarnations, and all the knowledge of the Universe. If you feel this interpretation is correct, then what you read in such a book is very important—it is part of your spirit's birthright.

Closed with a bookmark inside: A momentary pause in learning that is vital so that you don't burn out or overload.

Bookstores: Acquired knowledge in a specific area. The type of bookstore or the section of the store reveals the genre after which you're seeking, or that which you already possess.

A dictionary reveals overdependence on other people's opinions and suggestions for management matters, especially in business. Give your own insight an opportunity to prove itself!

Shutting a book: Closing off a chapter of your life. Resolution of an issue, the end of a belief system, or conclusion of business dealings.

•BOTTLE (VASE)

(see Beverages, Canning)

With a note inside: A message from your heart, someone close to you, or your Higher Self that you've been trying to ignore.

Empty: Feeling drained and depleted of energy, creativity, or compassion.

Jinni in a bottle: From Arabic folklore, a potential ally or terrible adversary, which may also originate within you.

What does the bottle hold? If it is filled with *fire*, this could symbolize bottled-up anger or passion that's reaching an explosive state.

Rounded bottles and vases are an alternative emblem of the womb.

•BOWL

(see Abyss, Basket, Cauldron, Chalice)

Womanhood. In ancient Egypt, a symbol of the divine feminine principle and womb of origination.

Generative force and creativity. Babylonians regarded the cosmos as the mixing bowl of the great Goddess.

Cosmic powers and influences. Native Americans use an inverted bowl to represent the heavens, which are indirectly linked to the ancestors (see *Space, Stars*).

Consider the type of bowl for more meaning. For example, a mixing bowl might represent your need to better blend the various components of your life into balance.

• BOX

(see Closet, Wrapping Paper)

Unexpected surprises, good or bad. For example, birthday gifts are usually pleasant, whereas what awaited inside Pandora's box was not.

Gifts, talents, and abilities that exist within you, but have thus far remained "wrapped up."

Freudian: An alternative vaginal emblem.

A sense of uncertainty, source of reservation, or seed of doubt. We don't know what boxes contain until they're opened, and by that time it's too late to leave the proverbial wrappings on.

Being contained in a box is an alternative type of *cage* dream.

• BREAD

(see Butter, Eating)

The essence or "manna" of life. In this interpretation, eating bread becomes a way of accepting spiritual gifts.

Financial concerns. In most cultures, bread is a symbol of providence.

Kinship, especially if shared with another (e.g., "breaking bread together").

Miracles and divine providence: Besides the story of Jesus with the loaves and *fishes*, Moses in the wilderness, and the Christian Host, bread was involved in many types of ancient spells for continued sustenance.

Various types of bread may have specific significance as well. For example, pretzels are a solar *wheel*, unleavened bread represents haste, and hot cross buns symbolize the spring equinox, a time of renewed hope.

• BREWING

(see Beverages by type)

Dreaming about brewing may indicate the need to rise above your circumstances, like the bubbles in the *wine*.

Temporary anxiety over a situation that will have a successful outcome.

The blending of ideas (e.g., the ingredients) from two different facets of life. For example, mingling the spiritual with the mundane effectively.

Waiting for a beverage to mature symbolizes the personal development that comes only with time and patience. You cannot rush this process without damaging the quality of learning.

• BRIDE

(see Groom, Wedding, Woman)

For a woman, a straightforward dream revealing the desire to marry. For a man, wishing for a bride.

Kissing the bride in a dream foretells the reconciliation of a friendship (see *Kiss*).

Making a figurative commitment to a partnership of some nature. Note that this does not necessarily have to be between people. It can symbolize a promissory business arrangement in which the final papers haven't been signed yet.

• BRIDGE

(see Archway)

Transitions, especially if you are moving from one side to the other (see *Abyss*).

Standing in the middle of: A critical decision that is very difficult. Look to see what lies on each side of the bridge for greater detail.

Birth and *death*. Bridges span a gulf, and by so doing allow a soul to move freely from one state to the next.

Connections and communication. If the bridge reaches to someone who is far away, or someone with whom communication has been severed, this may indicate a longing or need to reconnect to that individual.

Is the bridge on *fire*? If so, be absolutely certain that whatever this overpass represents is a bridge that you really want to burn.

• BROOM

(see Dirt, Organizing)

An ancient emblem of womanhood that was later turned into a phallic symbol by the Church.

Having a bad case of the cleaning or organizational bug either at home, or toward a specific project or goal. What exactly does the broom sweep away?

Luck and friendship. According to folk beliefs, brooms found in new homes may be used to sweep out bad fortune, and sweep in good energy and warm feelings.

Jumping over a broom handle is a symbol of fertility and transition into a new life. This was part of many rural European and *Gypsy wedding* rituals.

Flying on a broom: Potentially a sexual dream in which the broom handle equates to the penis.

Woman's *magic*. Witches were sometimes called broom amazons in the Middle Ages.

• BROWN

(see Colors)

Depression and foreboding, especially if hovering around you in the dream.

An earthy color that can indicate good foundations, practicality, and the potential for growth (e.g., "being down to *earth*"). Much depends on where or how the color appears in the dream.

The color of late fall, indicating decreased initiative and ambition (see *Seasons*).

• BROWNIES

(see Fairy)

• BUCKET

Important information or truth you need to gather up (see *Water*). Remember, however, that one must go to the well and lower the bucket for it to be useful.

An alternative *cup* emblem that indicates more profuse quantities.

• BUDDHA

(see Icons)

• BUILDINGS

(see Apartments, Barn, Castle, Church, Monastery, Temple)

The condition of the building can reveal the condition of your health, a relationship, or a situation.

What does the building hold? If it is just an empty shell, consider if you're living superficially, without gaining any real spiritual substance.

Of what is the building constructed? Just like the story of "The Three Little Pigs," you want your hopes to be based on good foundational material if they're ever going to materialize in reality.

Are the *doors* and *windows* of this building open and accessible? If so, this shows a very open-minded person who may be too exposed. Similarly, a building that appears locked up tight indicates narrow views and large *obstacles* to intimacy.

What type of building is it? Certain structures carry fairly direct meanings. For example, hotels, motels, and mobile homes represent temporary conditions, change, movement, and transition, sometimes literally in our living space.

• BULL

(see Animal)

A potent masculine nature evidencing itself.

Stubbornness (e.g., being "bull headed").

Fertility. The Sumerians believed that the stomping hooves of a bull could bring nourishing rain to the land. Minoans also used bulls as a fertility emblem.

Inventive inception. Zoroastrian priests (the Magi) taught that a slain bull's soul became the germ of creation.

Leadership skills, or their development. In Egypt, the kings and Pharaohs were often called bulls. Among the ancient Israelites, Yahweh was called the Bull of Israel.

Buddhist: The ego and mortal self.

Taming a bull: Bringing your anger or masculine side under control, or taking control of a situation (e.g., "seize the bull by the horns").

A situation that was handled clumsily (e.g., a "bull in a china shop").

Sacrifice of one valued thing in the hopes of obtaining another. Bulls were regularly used as offerings to the gods, like El in Phoenicia, Attis and Mithras in Rome, and the Oak god of the Druids (see *Altar, Carcass*).

• BURIAL

(see Bones, Cemetery, Death, Dirt, Holy Ground, Tomb)

Some type of cover-up, or a hidden matter. Look closely at what's being buried here for more interpretive value.

Putting something totally to rest and leaving the past behind where it belongs. Again, what's being buried will provide more clues.

Seeing someone walk on a new grave reflects feeling ill at ease with your own or someone else's actions to the point of anxiety.

Digging your own grave represents being your own worst enemy in the current situation. Try another approach.

If you believe in reincarnation, this might symbolize the chance for a totally fresh start.

• BUS

(see Vehicles by type, Highways, Travel)

Taking indirect routes with frequent stops to obtain your goal (see *Velocity*).

Choosing a course of action that you perceive as safe and fairly dependable.

Depending on an *authority figure* to determine the best course of action in a situation, especially scheduling.

• BUTTER

(see Bread, Eating)

A favorable sign of accomplishing your goals and having continued good health.

Selling butter portends small gains in business (e.g., making your "bread and butter").

Spreading butter may indicate that you are somehow trying to "butter someone up" instead of taking a more direct tact.

Worship and *sacrifice* given to the Divine. In Mesopotamia, Tibet, and India, butter is considered a seemly offering.

Among Tibetans, also an emblem of prosperity soon to follow.

•BUTTERFLY

(see Flying, Insects, Wings)

Personal growth, especially spiritual. In classical Greek and Roman philosophy, the butterfly's transformation mirrored that of the ever evolving soul.

Esoterically: Reincarnation, which may be literal or figurative. If you see yourself emerging from the cocoon, this speaks of a new, beautiful beginning, and astounding positive changes.

The question of personal identity and uniqueness. In China, there is a story of the sage Hsuang Chou who dreamt of being a butterfly. During the dream, he had no awareness of Hsuang Chou, only the butterfly. When he awoke, this experience left him wondering. Was he really Hsuang Chou, or actually a butterfly dreaming of being Hsuang Chou?

In China, the butterfly also symbolizes a happy union, usually a *marriage*. An excellent portent for any type of partnership, especially if the butterfly is formed out of *jade* (see *Gems, Jewelry, Stones*).

Missives from beyond: The Hopi Indians believe that butterflies carry the souls of the departed.

Swallowing a butterfly: In Ireland and ancient Greece, this signified *pregnancy*.

The ability to rebound and rejuvenate after a major setback.

If seen in its caterpillar form, it means you're entering a stage of positive transformation.

If the creature is *flying*, you may soon receive news from friends afar.

For a young woman, this foretells happy love.

• BUZZARD

(see Birds)

A very negative emblem, being that this is a scavenger bird. Often it reveals gossip or scandal afoot.

If the bird is sitting nearby, it portends some type of loss caused by an opportunist.

If the buzzard flies away from you, then you will be able to avoid reproach in the matter lying heavily on your mind.

A buzzard picking at a *carcass* reveals incessant needling from those around you, to the point where the sacredness of self seems lost. Alternatively, some type of violation of your body (see *Abuse, Sexual Encounters*).

Among certain Arizonian, Mexican, and Californian Indian tribes, the *feathers* from this bird create the clothing for their medicine man. In this setting, consider if you are being called to a *healing* vocation, or perhaps are yourself in need of seeing a "medicine man."

• CABBAGE

(see Eating, Vegetables)

Because of its color and shape, this is an alternative *moon* or *circle* emblem.

Moodiness. In earlier days, eating this item was believed to cause sullenness or irritability. However, the Greeks reversed this concept and claimed eating cabbage could cure this problem. The rest of the dream will have to delineate which interpretive outlook is correct.

As an omen, this portends decreasing finances. Historically, cabbage was often the food of peasants.

• CACTUS

(see Desert, Sand)

Metaphorically, prickly situations that require careful handling.

Protection and safety. The *needles* on this plant may speak of your own need for protection, or possibly they represent the *armor* you place between yourself and the world.

Unexpected refreshment from an equally unexpected source. In the *desert*, cacti are an alternative source of *water*.

Because of the cactus's natural ability to safeguard its nourishment, this symbol can also reflect a wise, frugal attitude.

• CAGE (JAIL)

Escaping from a jail: Freedom, liberation, and self-expression. Also moving into a new stage in your life.

Punishing yourself or someone else for something you perceive as going against personal, societal, or divine law.

Cabin fever. Feeling cooped up with no place to really stretch your skills.

Restraint. What's inside the cage that you're not letting out? Or, what's holding you in?

Having your rules set by an *authority figure* who makes you feel boxed in.

Prisons represent the inability to regain control. Also having limited options or confinement within a specific societal boundary.

An expression of claustrophobia.

• CAKES

(see Baking, Eating, Frosting)

Labors that result in favorable outcomes, especially if the cake rises.

Something that's easy, possibly too easy (e.g., a "piece of cake").

Eating cake alone can reveal selfishness, or being out of touch with the needs of others (e.g., "let them eat cake").

Eating cake with others may be a type of initiation, or another sacred ritual. Specially prepared cakes feature predominantly in many such pagan observances.

Birthday cakes are an emblem of celebrations and wishes. This may be an actual memory surfacing, so look to see who else appears in the dream. Count the *candles* on the cake for numerical significance, and see who is joining in the festivities.

• CALCULATOR

(see Arithmetic, Numbers)

Accurate determination of the correctness, or incorrectness, of your thoughts and actions (e.g., does everything "add up"?).

Mental determinations and subsequent reckoning either to yourself or a situation.

• CALENDAR

(see Numbers)

Systematic approaches and arrangements that maintain a steady flow of work, creativity, etc.

The date that appears on the calendar is usually of great import. Pay attention to it, and check its numerological significance, if you don't immediately recognize the meaning.

Each month and day of the week has special significance, some of which can be discerned by their names or at what time of year they occur. For example, Monday is the Moon's day, and reveals your intuitive, emotional nature. April occurs in spring, and is a month signifying opportunity knocking (see *Seasons*). Try looking at a good astrological calendar for other ideas along this line.

•CAMEL

(see Animals, Desert, Sand)

Being a desert creature, camels often represent a dry spell in our lives when we must have patience. Additionally, there is a subtle caution here not to drink any figurative "*water*" too quickly during this drought, lest you run out or get sick.

In Africa, a symbol of obedient service.

In Arabia, camels are the guardians of the waters, which in this case reflects the intuitive or emotional nature of the dreamer. Are you safeguarding your heart or throwing caution to the winds?

Some important biblical figures are also associated with this creature. John the Baptist was clothed in camel hair (again relating to *water*) as a symbol of his temperance, and the Magi rode camels to Christ's birth, making this a creature of dignity and stamina.

•CANDLE (LAMP)

(see Fire, Light, Torch)

Illumination, understanding, or enlightenment. The quest to understand spiritual matters.

The soul. As the Bible says, "let your light so shine among men."

A candle being lit represents a new beginning, whereas an extinguished candle symbolizes the passing of the old.

Fear of an early death or growing old (e.g., having your candle "snuffed out").

Spiritual presences. A winding sheet or *blue* flame on the candle, according to folklore, speaks of ghostly company. This might be a departed loved one, an *angel*, or even your Higher Self trying to communicate (see *Ghost*).

Energy levels. Are you burning the candle at both ends?

Hope and protection. In the Middle Ages candles were not only a source of light, but were placed near beds to safeguard the sleeper from wandering spirits.

Ideas or ideals. Suddenly experiencing comprehension (having the proverbial "light bulb" go on).

An alternative phallic symbol. Pagan folk dances often included candle *jumping* for fertility.

A clear burning flame on a candle indicates the presence of devoted friends, or constancy in yourself.

• CANDY

(see Eating, Food)

If you've been *dieting* lately, this is likely a circumstantial dream that requires no further examination.

Things in life perceived as sweet to obtain, even though not necessarily good for you. For example, success can be quite sweet, but at what cost?

Because candy is strongly connected with dental work, this may be an indicator that your words are either too sugary, or not amiable enough, depending on what's happening to the candy in the dream (see *Teeth*).

A happy portent of social pleasures on the horizon.

• CANNING

(see Eating, Fruits, Vegetables)

Setting aside some type of resource for a time when you feel it will be needed.

Hiding something; what's getting locked away in that can?

Alchemical: Canning as an art mythologically owes some of its beginnings to Hermes Trismegistus, a legendary author of alchemical doctrines sometime in the first three centuries C.E. (e.g., Hermetic seals), and the god of communication. The implied symbolism here is that something is "bottled up" or "airtight," often pertaining to discourse.

• CAN OPENER

Opening up yourself and letting out all the accumulated knowledge and experience stored within.

Getting past a tough barrier to gain something with substantial sustenance. This includes breaching any *obstacles* you've placed between yourself and the world, or those behind which other people hide (see *Armor*).

• CANVAS

(see Art)

This represents the blank slate of life upon which our experiences, cultures, families, and personal dispositions paint the mural of our being. Look at the image closely. It will tell you how you perceive yourself. Also check the easel on which the painting rests to be sure your foundations are secure.

• CAR

(see Airplane, Horse, Spaceship)

If you are behind the *wheel* of the car, this shows self-control and the ability to steer your own fate.

If someone else is steering, and you're in the passenger seat, consider if you allow other people to manipulate your decisions too much. Alternatively, there may be parts of yourself over which you have little mastery.

Travel, movement, and activity, as common to many vehicle emblems (see *Highway*).

A literal reflection of your current driving habits.

Parked: Halted momentum, or temporary waylay of plans, usually of your own making, whereas a traffic jam indicates external forces stopping your progress.

Your body's condition: According to Edgar Cayce, each part of the car may correspond to a *body* part. For example, wheels are legs, and therefore a flat tire may indicate regional circulation problems. Note that this is also true of buildings and other vehicles (windows = *eyes*, paint = skin, roof = hair or head, engine = heart or emotions, etc.). In this case, seeing a mechanic in your dream might be a gentle nudge to go to a doctor.

Speeding: Reacting quickly without real thought. Slow down, then decide the best avenue for approaching this situation.

Slow moving vehicles: The propensity for procrastination or delaying the inevitable.

Driving a standard in your dream shows how well you handle the constant changes that life hands you. Consider whether the gears grind or if the clutch sticks. If so, get out some elbow grease and work on being more flexible and prepared.

Missing your ride indicates a failed attempt to forward current prospects. It may be necessary to wait a while before trying again (see *Bus*).

•CARCASS

(see Altar, Bones, Animals, Death)

Appearing on an *altar*: The hope of blessings from a "higher" power, including *authority figures*. The Mesopotamians, Babylonians, and Hebrews all had religious sects that offered animals to their gods and goddesses to gain favor. Alternatively, guilt feelings related to something perceived as a sin, for which you wish to atone through an offering.

Partially eaten flesh: Exposure; feeling like you're at the whims of some predator in your "territory." Also a painfully blunt reminder of mortal limitations. Likely, your emotional state is jagged, torn, and overly agitated by these sensations. You need to regain some stability.

If more than one *animal* devours the carcass, this signifies someone being pulled in two distinct directions, both of which seem unhealthy. Two or more forces are fighting for dominion in your life, and none has your best interests at heart.

For people considering becoming vegetarian, a disgusting carcass may signal your readiness to start heading in that direction.

Turning away from a carcass signals a change from mundane outlooks to an increased focus on metaphysical or religious matters.

•CARDS

(see Games)

A deck of cards: Is the deck complete with 52 cards? If not, you may have fragmentary information about a person or situation.

Playing cards: Consider if you're gambling on something or someone, or taking an unnecessary risk. Alternatively, having your attention diverted from more legitimate, and worthwhile, endeavors.

Playing an ace: Successfully and confidently making your move, or having an alternative plan of action on which to fall back (e.g., having "an ace in the hole"). In terms of omens and signs, this is considered a very positive dream denoting victory (see *One*).

Potential mental instability, or lacking thorough information or tools with which to handle a situation (e.g., "not playing with a full deck").

If the hand you see is filled with jokers, this reflects your own sense of humor. Is it a healthy one, or do you make jokes and laugh to cover up insecurity? Also if you're the eternal prankster, this dream acts as a gentle warning that someone might get hurt as a result of ill-conceived shenanigans.

Tarot cards in dreams should be interpreted according to their layout and images. For more information, consult a classical Tarot deck with interpretive guide like the Rider-Waite Tarot.

Business cards may have symbolic words and phrases upon them to consider. The *names* and phone *numbers* can also have interpretive value. Consider each separately, and the card as a whole unit, when trying to understand this emblem.

Greeting cards in dreams reflect matters of communication, particularly those missives coming from other people. Look at the card's message (see *Writing*) or its *art* for more meaning here.

• CARNATION
(see Flowers, Gardens)

In the Victorian language of flowers, this represents pride and beauty.

Elizabethan: Preventing an untimely death on a scaffold. If you've stuck your neck out lately, you may want to reconsider this course of action.

Happy celebrations and/or some type of promotion or public recognition. Carnation gets its name from "coronation," because it was used so often in ancient times as a festival flower.

• CARNELIAN
(see Crystals, Gems, Jewelry, Stones)

Because of its *red* color, this is an alternative *blood* emblem.

Among Moslems, a symbol of perfect happiness, effective speech and depression's abatement.

In ancient Greece, this represented having one's wishes satisfied.

Arabian: Take care, someone is trying to trick or deceive you.

In dream oracles, this stone warns of forthcoming misfortunes for which you should begin to prepare.

•CARPET (RUG)

Feeling stepped on or ignored.

Red carpets: Special treatment or well-deserved honor.

Sweeping beneath: Hidden matters or things you're trying to conceal (see *Broom*).

Flying carpet: Another type of *flying* dream, but one that also denotes a sense of rescue, maneuverability, and safety. Aladdin's carpet aided him in times of great need.

Buying a rug in dreams is a good sign that foretells gains and financial help that's available from friends.

Wall-to-wall carpeting reflects an attempt to try and cover up some type of flaw in your character instead of fixing it.

Tapestry rugs often have *pictographs* or whole scenes that reflect prevalent matters in your life. Look at the whole image first, then each object or person shown, for significance (see *Fabric*).

•CASTLE (HOUSE)

(see Apartment, Buildings by type, Cave)

Physical matters, as with any structure. Note the condition of each portion of the castle and its relationship to your body (see *Body, Car*).

According to Henry David Thoreau, the image of our highest hopes and aspirations that may or may not have any foundation to uphold them (e.g., building "castles in the air").

Matters of honor or chivalry, going back to medieval tradition.

A place or situation that seems safe and secure, as if surrounded by an impenetrable mote. The mote, however, may also represent *obstacles* or *armor* that you place between yourself and others.

Being locked in the *tower* or dungeon of a castle: A type of *cage* dream.

An old, vine-covered castle represents romantic idealism that may not have any footing in reality. Take care not to get locked into this vision without being aware that the "here and now" cannot always meet up to lofty expectations.

• CAT

(see Animals, Lion, Tiger)

With a *mouse:* The power of good over evil. In ancient Egypt, the great God Ra was sometimes depicted as a cat slaying a *snake* with similar connotations.

The ability to land on your feet, even in difficult circumstances, and remain independent.

An emblem of rebirth and new beginnings. Cats have *nine* lives, upon which one are you now embarking?

If seen on a sailing vessel, very good luck and health (see *Boat*). Cats eliminated mice from ships on long journeys, thereby decreasing disease.

Magical or mystical energy. The cat was a sacred creature to the Greek goddess Hecate, and the Roman goddess Diana, both patronesses of witches. Additionally, it was the most commonly mentioned familiar for witches in old Grimoires, medieval books of practical magic that included spells, herbals, and folk wisdom.

An alternative symbol of feminine, lunar characteristics.

Hissing and scratching: A "catty" nature rearing its ugly head, or withheld aggression toward women.

The Cheshire Cat is an emblem of haughty or arrogant attitudes (see *Laughter*).

• CAULDRON

(see Abyss, Basket, Bowl, Chalice, Circle, Forge, Water)

The symbol of the triune, primordial Goddess and birth giver (because of its shape and having three legs).

Fertility, femininity, and procreativity.

Magical power. In Indian mythos, Indra drank from three cauldrons to empower himself with mystical energy.

Wisdom, insight, and knowledge. According to Teutonic stories, there are three great cauldrons in the earth's center containing beverages that impart these beneficial characteristics. Odin, the ruler of the gods, was believed to have drunk from all three.

Creativity. Among the Celts, the Cauldron of Cerridwen dispensed the muse to any who partook of it.

• CAVE (CELLAR)

(see Darkness, Underground)

The subconscious or hidden nature within.

Archetypal: The womb of the earth—e.g., *Earth* as our mother who gave all humankind birth and nourishment. Also an emblem for a woman's womb. In Hebrew tradition, Abraham was born in a sacred cave, as was the Persian savior Mithra.

Fears: If *monsters* or other terrible things lurk within the cave, this reveals unresolved phobias and apprehensions.

A retreat, *sanctuary*, or place of hiding. Many notable figures went to secluded areas to find themselves or the Divine. In this instance, what you seek is probably more intuitive in nature (see *Desert*).

Damp caves represent fertility.

An archetypal *sanctuary* eluding to humankind's earliest dwelling places where communities began to form. Here the subconscious may be relating your need for a safe haven, or joining a friendly group within which you feel comfortable.

• CAVE IN

(see Disaster)

• CELLAR

(see Cave, Underground)

• CEMETERY

(see Burial, Death, Holy Ground, Tomb)

Death, endings or conclusions, in literal or figurative terms.

If any of the headstones had *writing*, what did they say? Any messages here could prove quite helpful with your interpretation.

Being lost in, or terrified by: The fear of death, or the unknown.

Being buried in: Symbolic opportunity in disguise for resurrection and a new beginning. Burying in soil or mud was used in folk medicine as a sympathetic cure that fooled the spirits of sickness and death into believing they'd won.

Dreaming of a *tomb* represents a metaphorical opportunity for rebirth and a fresh start. The word tomb actually means "tummy," being the womb of the *earth* from which we are all born and return. Alternatively, a well-kept, elaborate tomb may reflect achievements and honors accumulated during your life.

• CENSORING

(see Movies, TV)

Limits or boundaries that are set by an outside source, some of which may hamper free expression of ideals or beliefs.

Oppressive moralism from others with regard to your lifestyle and its outward representations.

Not getting complete information; having the truth clouded for the sake of political correctness.

• CHAINS

Restraint or control. Dependency or addictions. What exactly is being chained and by whom or what?

Alternative type of *cage* dream.

Rattling: *Ghosts* of a figurative nature. What are you trying to hide or avoid?

Security. Chains can be protective, keeping safe something or someone you perceive as being in peril.

Restrictive relationships (e.g., "the old ball 'n' chain").

• CHALICE (CUP)

(see Abyss, Basket, Beverages by type, Bowl, Circle, Cauldron)

Alternative womb and fertility symbol, especially if filled with liquid (see *Milk, Juice, Water, Wine*).

Arthurian and Druidical lore identify this emblem as the grail, the cup that signifies humankind's connection with nature and each other.

Christian: The sacredness of life and the quality of forgiveness (the cup of Christ's blood). In this case, do you drink freely of what's offered you, or pour it away?

Unity. In *Gypsy*, pagan, and Hebrew *marriage* and courtship rites, people drinking from one cup link their destinies and become as one.

Refusing: Wishing to avert a personal trial that is really unavoidable (note the story of Christ in the *garden* of Gethsemane). Alternatively, rejecting an opportunity for friendship or camaraderie because of suspicious motivations.

In Eastern philosophy, a cup is shaped by what it contains. What metaphorical beverages do you incorporate into yourself by drinking of this cup?

• CHAMELEON
(see Animals, Color)

Inconsistency to the point of losing all focus of the self and one's sense of identity apart from a group or situation.

The ability to change or blend in when necessary for self-preservation.

Pliny attributed this creature to the element of *air*, saying it lived on this etheric substance.

Because the chameleon's eyes see independently of each other, it also represents awareness, specifically of the past and future.

• CHANTING
(see Incantation, Languages)

Dedicated religious observance. Numerous civilizations recognized chanting as a viable expression of veneration, or a means of communing with greater powers.

The Om chant from Tibet acts as a creative spell that reaffirms the self and the Source. In a dream this reflects the birth of a more aware, actualized person who has discovered the Divine within.

Among the Greeks, Mesopotamians, and Egyptians, sacred sounds and words symbolized the originating force within all things, including you!

• CHARGE CARDS
(see Bank/Banking, Money)

Obtaining something that will carry a very high *price* over the long term.

Overextension of resources, and being impatient for material things.

What is being paid for? Is it something for which you should work instead of taking the easy road?

•CHEESE

(see Eating, Milk)

Matters of love and commitment. In ancient Greece, cheese was used as part of traditional *wedding* cakes.

As a visual pun, this may reflect a "cheesy" attitude or outlook.

Consider the type of cheese for more potential symbolism. Swiss cheese represents plans that have lots of holes in them, whereas Roquefort stands for something not smelling quite right (see *Smells*).

In Switzerland, a cheese fondue portends unexpected guests, because the food is so tasty that it inspires visits!

Longevity of your achievements or ideas. According to Pliny, Zoroaster lived for 30 years on cheese alone.

•CHICKEN

(see Animals)

Fear and timidity (e.g., being "chicken").

Running aimlessly around: Lacking personal direction, racing from worries or doing so much that everything loses focus (e.g., "like a chicken with its head cut off").

An omen or message. Among the Romans, chickens were used to foretell the outcome of battles by observing their movements and clucking.

Health matters (stemming from the idea that chicken soup is a panacea of sorts).

In a roost: Good planning and foresight; preparing for an arrival, sometimes that of a child.

Appearing on a doorstep: A portent that foretells the arrival of guests.

•CHOKING

Someone who is not being totally candid and honest (e.g., "choking back words").

Having your own words return to haunt you.

Something that is so sugar coated that it is impossible to swallow. Look further here and uncover the truth.

•CHRIST

(see Icons)

•CHURCH

(see Altar, Bells, Holy Ground, Monastery, Priest/Priestess, Sanctuary, Temple)

Sanctuary, safety, privacy. A place within which secrets remain concealed except to the Divine. If you entered the church and sat down, this shows a personal need for seclusion or security. Alternatively, perhaps you feel as if someone has betrayed a trust, and seek alternative sources in which to place your faith (see *Religions*).

Your health. We often hear the aphorism that the "*body* is the temple of the soul." In what condition do you find your *temple*? If the church appears run-down, get some rest and take better care of yourself.

Seeking the sacred powers or a desire to give that portion of your life more attention. It may also mark the beginning of a spiritual ideology unfolding, especially if the church is of a specific tradition with which you feel affinity.

•CINNAMON

(see Herbs)

Prosperity, or something for which you would pay highly. In ancient Rome, this was one of the most highly valued imports.

The expanding of human consciousness to more universal horizons. Cinnamon was one of the spices that helped spur world exploration in humankind's early history.

Cleansing and purification. Cinnamon has natural astringent properties.

•CIRCLE

(see Abyss, Balloon, Basket, Bowl, Cauldron, Chalice, Coins, Satellite Dish, Zero)

Wholeness, totality, centering. Halos, for example, symbolize spiritual wholeness and focus (see *Light*).

Pictorially, an alternative emblem for either the *sun* or *moon*.

Freudian: A vaginal emblem or symbol of femininity due to its shape.

Equality and unity. The round table of King Arthur's court gave everyone an equal voice and symbolized the solidarity of Britain.

Protected or sacred space. In the first century B.C.E., magicians were sometimes called "circle drawers" because ritual *magic* uses this emblem to contain power. Similarly, a *fairy* ring safeguards its residents from mortals.

Going around in circles: Being trapped in progressively worse cycles, outmoded ideas, or a static lifestyle with little achievement.

A circle with a point in the center is a type of *mandala* emblem representing personal wholeness, order, harmony, and healing.

God or divine influences and protection. There is a Hindu saying that God is an unbroken circle without a circumference, being nowhere and everywhere.

• CIRCUIT BREAKER

Being overloaded with too much information or too many ideas, and consequently unable to integrate them effectively.

Advice from your subconscious to take a break from the potent forces around you before you burn out (see *Electricity*).

Self-regulation, especially with regard to personal energy.

• CITIES

(see Locations)

• CLAY

The loam of creation from which characteristics can be formed and molded. In Genesis, Adam was formed from clay in God's image (see *Earth*). Similarly, the Mesopotamian Armaiti and Sumerian Nammu created humankind from clay.

Too much emphasis on trying to change yourself just for the sake of appearances and fitting in.

Flexibility. The ability to temporarily remold yourself to fit into different situations and settings.

•CLIFF

(see Abyss)

A crucial turning point in life that requires a decision, especially one pertaining to polarities, such as "good" versus "evil" or action versus waiting.

Real or perceived danger that exists in your current situation. Are you about to dive into something without really looking first?

Falling off of: A type of *falling* dream in which it's important to figure out exactly what the cliff represents.

•CLIMBING

(see Ascent, Ladder, Mountain, Stairs)

Ambitions and the desire for success.

If you dream of a very long climb, potentially the desire to retreat or escape. Alternatively, this can portend a lengthy period of hard work before you reach your goals.

To a platform: A type of ivory *tower* from which it is easy to fall. Alternatively, a place where you can get a better outlook.

Over a wall: Anxiousness, or the need to escape from a restrictive situation imposed by your family, society, religion, or whatever. Alternatively, overcoming an *obstacle*.

•CLOCK

(see Bells, Hourglass, Numbers, Time)

Standing still: Impatience for some event soon to come, or feeling spiritually, emotionally, or mentally paralyzed.

Hands or *numbers* moving counterclockwise: Ask yourself if you're going against a personal taboo or taking a step backward toward obsolete habits and thought patterns.

Punching a time clock: The danger of becoming a slave to schedules and the agendas of other people.

Is the clock digital, electric, a wristwatch, wind-up, a cuckoo clock, or perhaps even a sundial? Each of these has different associations. Digital clocks show that you are living in the present. Electric clocks and wind-up versions are more antiquated, revealing a stronger focus on times past. The cuckoo clock expresses craftsmanship. Have you been giving enough time to your arts lately? Lastly, the sundial represents our ancient roots when humans were more intimately aware of nature. How much time do you spend outdoors just appreciating the *Earth*?

Look at what time the clock gives, and check the numerological significance.

•CLOSET

(see Box, Clothes)

In children, often a reflection of their fears. What exactly is the closet hiding?

If the door is ajar, perhaps you are thinking of coming out of the closet with some controversial aspect of your life or beliefs.

If a skeleton is in the closet, consider what you might be hiding from others, or even from yourself (see *Bones*).

How does the closet appear? Is it orderly or messy? This organization, or lack thereof, can be a reflection of your own thought processes, or the orderliness of your lifestyle in general.

•CLOTHES

(see Apron, Closet, Costume, Hat, Jewelry, Mask, Shoes, Tie, Veil)

How do the clothes feel? Are they itchy or uncomfortable? If so, this reveals discomfort with yourself or a situation in which you've been placed.

Old or tattered clothing indicates self-neglect or feelings of inferiority.

Changing clothes: A transition in status, jobs, *relationships*, and the like.

A statement of individuality and how you see yourself (e.g., "clothes make the man").

Rejecting or throwing away out-of-date clothing: New enterprises, loves, characteristics. Forsaking outmoded ways of thinking and living.

Each *color* of clothing has different oracular value. *Yellow* indicates financial progress, *blue* portends success from tenacious efforts, *red* reveals a timely deliverance from a difficult situation, *green* is prosperity and happiness, and mixed hues foretell swift changes.

Each item of clothing also has slightly different meaning, much of which is dependent on your perception. For example, a businessman dreaming about tying his tie again and again might interpret this as too much attention to his appearance at work instead of the work quality. Dreaming of tightening your belt probably relates to financial struggles.

Dirty clothing sometimes represents the soiling of someone's virtues.

Cross-dressing represents a figurative "trying on" of masculine or feminine attributes that you wish to develop. This can also reveal a greater balance of the Yin-Yang energies within you (see *Hermaphrodite, Homosexuality*).

• CLOUDS
(see Ascent, Fog, Rain, Snow)

Storm clouds gathering equate to similarly stormy times, especially on an emotional level.

Dark clouds reveal depression, melancholy, and sadness. Alternatively, dark clouds moving toward you may be some type of warning.

Moods and feelings. Does your cloud have a *silver* lining?

Obscuration of a situation. Clouds can hide the *sun* and *moon*, temporarily removing them from sight. What are your clouds concealing?

Youthful imagination. Remember finding shapes in fluffy *white* clouds as a child? Try it again and see what meanings those shapes have for you.

In China, an emblem of sexual union and fertility, especially gently pouring rain clouds.

• CLOVER
(see Flowers)

Much depends here on how many petals the clover has, or what color it is in the dream. Two portends love and good partnerships, three is a protective emblem, four means luck and *money*, five represents prosperity, white clovers safeguard you from negative *magic*, and red ones indicate lust and passion.

• CLOWNS

Insincere or immature emotions, specifically false gaiety (see *Costumes*).

Imprudent beliefs or foolish ideas disguised by amusing wrappings.

Hiding your feelings behind a smiling *mask*.

A reflection of the quality of your sense of humor especially as perceived by others. How funny is the clown?

• COCK

(see Birds)

As the greeter of dawn, this was an alternative symbol of the *sun* in many cultures, especially that of Greece and Rome where many central gods were associated with solar imagery. Therefore, a cock crowing at dawn in a dream is a very fortunate sign of new beginnings and renewed hope.

The vigilance and courage necessary to experience a real awakening of mind or spirit.

In Japan, the cock represents a call to prayer. Perhaps this is a message to focus on spiritual matters for a while.

Buddhist: Passion and pride.

• COCKROACH

(see Insects)

Hiding yourself to survive.

The presence of cockroaches can reveal physical or psychological *dirt* that needs to be cleaned up.

Durability. These insects have the capacity to mutate against many *poisons*. Metaphorically, this may relate to societal poisons to your self-image.

• COCOON

(see Butterfly)

• COFFEE

(see Beverages)

Perky, energetic attitudes.

The need to be more alert (e.g., "wake up and smell the coffee"). In Arabia, this beverage is revered because it allows people to stay awake during long prayers. It is often served to guests with toasts honoring the name of God.

Something important that's currently *brewing* in your life, which must also be watched so that it doesn't boil over.

•COINS

(see Bank/Banking, Circle, Gold, Silver)

In the Tarot, the emblem of earthly concerns—e.g., *money*, jobs, possessions.

An alternative *circle* symbol due to their shape.

Improved luck or finances. Found pennies, and coins with the date of your birth are tokens of good fortune. Similarly, in Old Europe turning a pocketed coin by the light of a crescent *moon* or burying a silver coin beneath your doorstep encourages fortuity and prosperity.

A positive change in the weather (literal or figurative). When sailing ships were a predominant mode of transportation, found coins would be tossed on deck or imbedded in the masthead to ensure fair weather and good winds.

Spiritual protection and well-being. Ancient Egyptians placed coins on a mummy's eyes so that the deceased could pay the ferryman and move safely into the next life.

Each coin may have more than one connotation. For example, pennies are lucky, but in modern society they are also regarded as somewhat worthless. So, a dirty old penny bearing the year of your birth being passed by in your dream could expose poor self-images, for example.

Flipping coins: Choices to make, or the interaction of fate and "chance" in your life.

•COLD

(see Ice, Snow)

•COLOR

(see by specific hue, Clothes)

Generally, dark or murky colors indicate somber feelings, seriousness, or depression, while lighter, sharper ones are upbeat, positive, and cheerful.

Mixed hues, especially those that swirl without form, reveal confusion, a lack of direction, or mixed feelings.

•COLUMN
(see Pillars)

•COMB
(see Hair)

Having the proper tools or wherewithal to smooth out a tangled situation.

Magical control, especially over the elements. Hair combing was once used as a spell component, predominantly for bringing *rain*.

Motherly concern and protection.

•COMET
(see Stars, Space, Meteorite)

•COMPACT DISCS
(see Computer, Music)

Because of its shape, a compact disc may be interpreted as an alternative *circle* emblem.

Information crunching. Perhaps you've been studying too much, or trying to integrate too much data too quickly.

Technological advances and their influence in your life.

Having a lot of talents or knowledge right at your fingertips—all you need do is access it!

•COMPASS
(see Directions)

•COMPOST
(see Garbage)

• COMPUTER

The logical, analytical, rational, conscious self (see *Calculator*).

Technology and how much of a role it plays in your life.

Problems with: Disorientation, confusion, or communication difficulties.

Blank computer screen: The need to exercise your mind and get some "brain food." Alternatively, hitting a dry period in the creative process in which your mind feels blank.

• CONCRETE
(see Dam, or other objects formed from)

Foundations and security. Is the concrete fresh—or crumbling?

If your feet or other *body* parts are encased in concrete, this is a partial *cage* or other burden that needs to be released so that you can move freely.

• CONNECTING DEVICES (STAPLES, PAPERCLIPS, ETC.)
(see Knots, Ties)

Security and safety. Tying up loose ends and knowing that everything is in its place.

Connections and networks. Maintaining those ties you perceive as important.

Relationships. Binding yourself to someone or something (e.g., the "ties that bind").

Note that if the connecting device is being taken off or opened, the above symbolism is reversed.

• CONTROL TOWER
(see Airplane/Airport)

Because of its location and function, this may be the workings of your mind in symbolic form, especially the higher functions (see *Attic, Balcony*).

Carefully controlling and evaluating ideals, and integrating them one at a time so that they are properly understood and applied.

• CONVERSATIONS

(see Counseling)

A dialogue between the subconscious and conscious, or Higher Self and conscious, either of which should be closely heeded.

Communications from other beings, such as spirits, Devic entities, *angels*, *icons*, or divine figures. Again, take careful note of what gets said.

A discussion within your own mind examining various options through the dialogue.

• COPPER

(see Metals)

The emblem for copper is the same as that for the *planet* Venus, giving this metal strong associations with love and passion.

The use of copper wire for electrical purposes endows copper with conductive symbolism. In this case, what shapes it forms and to what it's connected will provide more clues for interpretation.

Improved *balance*. This substance is sometimes used in polarity healing to bring the energy patterns in the body back into symmetry.

An omen of prosperity soon to come. In Victorian days, copper pennies were placed in kitchens for just such a purpose (see *Coins*).

• CORAL

Because of its connection with the sea and *water*, coral is a fertility emblem.

Mediterranean: Safeguarding your children. Note that this "*baby*" can be anything to which you creatively give *birth*, like a piece of *art*.

If washed to shore in the dream, this represents a treasure from the Mother Goddess of the sea. Look at its color and shape and other elements in the dream for more insight as to Her message.

In dream oracles, coral predicts recovery from sickness or a loss.

• CORN

(see *Eating, Vegetables*)

Gathering corn represents rejoicing in the prosperity of friends and relatives.

A rich harvest of corn speaks of prosperity. Since this was a popular early grain crop, the presence of corn on the land directly reflected the wealth of a farmer. In your dreams, the condition of the corn or how it's taken to market may hold more significance here. For example, if the corn is transported via *horse* and buggy, maybe you need to update your outlooks to experience success.

The cycle of life, death, and rebirth. Egyptian, Christian, and Celtic traditions often draw parallels between corn's cycle and that of the soul. A popular pagan song tells of corn and grain, adding that "all that falls shall rise again."

Passing through a field of corn symbolizes harmony in the home and figurative wealth that comes from having true friends. It may also portend a temporary increase in funds.

A newly planted corn field is an omen of forthcoming success.

Popcorn is an emblem of excitement from an unexpected gift or some good news. Among Native Americans, it may also represent divinatory skills "popping" up.

• CORNERS

(see *Alley, Buildings, Cage, Dead End, Obstacle*)

Feeling trapped, especially by others' rules and practices.

Punishment or chastisement with parental overtones.

Turning corners: Modifications, corrections, and improvements; finally being able to find a "better way" to achieve your goal.

• COSTUMES

(see *Clothes, Masks*)

A facade or charade. Things are not as they seem.

Various roles we play in life. For example, someone who is an *authority figure* may be seen in a costume depicting a famous leader like Julius Caesar (see *Icons*).

Mimicry of various real-life scenarios as if in a play. This provides a safe medium for the expression of your perceptions.

Sustenance and support. Among ancient tribal cultures, costumes and masks served as a vehicle for sympathetic *magic*. For example, if they needed crops to grow, they might dress as vegetation and perform a *jumping dance* to encourage that growth. So, what facet of your life does this costume represent, and how does it accent that facet?

•COUNSELING

Observing or taking part in a counseling session in your dreams often shows that you feel uncertain or guarded about your ideas and judgment with regards to a specific set of circumstances or people. The counselor may represent your Higher Self, the subconscious, or some other type of guide who can offer you insight in this situation (see *Conversation*).

•COUNTRIES
(see Locations)

•COWS
(see Animals)

Red cows appearing in a dream are a positive, hopeful omen of peace and plenty. In Persia, these represented the spirit of dawn, which is filled with renewed vitality and courage.

In Greece, an all-white cow was an alternative symbol for the *moon*.

A natural source of nourishment (see *Meat*).

Among the Celts and people of Scandinavian heritages, an emblem of continued provision.

A sacred animal in India, representative of life itself. The milk from cows is used to nourish kings and *priests*, so this dream may represent self-nourishment.

Among ancient Egyptians, Indians, and Scandinavians, the cow was an emblem of the Great Mother, and some psychological schools still ascribe this image as possibly being linked to your own mother (see *Women*).

• CRAB

(see Fish, Zodiac Signs: Cancer)

Scuttling about, carrying half truths with you wherever you go.

The hard shell of the crab equates to *armor* that you may use for protection.

Metaphorically, a crabby or grabby personality manifesting itself.

A life in limbo. Among Buddhists, a crab is used to represent the time between *death* and the next incarnation. Perhaps you feel like everything is on "hold" right now. If so, just be patient. A fresh beginning is around the corner.

• CRANE

(see Birds)

A messenger from the Divine, who bears intelligence and discipline on its *wings*.

According to Pliny, because this bird stands on one leg when it sleeps, it is actually standing watch. As such, it represents vigilance.

In Japan, this is the teacher of law, specifically governmental, mundane law.

In China, the crane intercedes between heaven and *Earth*. What messages do you wish for it to take back?

Longevity for yourself or a personal pet project. In the East, this bird is thought to live for 1,000 years, so the *seeds* you're planting now will have lasting effects long into the future.

• CROCODILE

(see Animals)

Vicious, snapping words spoken in haste; treachery or hypocrisy without thought to the consequences.

Falsehood, insincerity, and deception (as in crying "crocodile tears").

As the guardian of the gate to the underworld, the crocodile also represents an *obstacle* to the threshold of the subconscious.

• CROSS

Something coming to an end or a crossroad.

The Celtic or Greek equidistant cross: An elemental balance and wholeness (see *Pictographs*).

Carrying a cross: Burdens that may not be yours to bear. Self-imposed martyrdom.

Protective energy. Carrying or wearing a cross was long considered a potent safeguard from evil, especially from *vampires*.

A Red Cross: Take special note of your health, as this suggests you may be overlooking a problem that could become serious with time.

According to Jung, other items that are symbolic of crosses include the *ace* of spades (see *Cards*), forked branches, *anchors*, and four-armed *wheels*. If any of these appear in your dream, consider both entries for interpretive value.

A Saltire Cross (one rotated halfway) creates an X, marking the spot under which you should look for more answers, or to discover the *treasures*.

• CROWD

Each face in a crowd dream can represent different facets of yourself.

People with whom you regularly interact. Potentially a Karmic circle that exists to help you learn and grow.

Feeling lost in a crowd: A sense of insignificance, of not knowing the power of the individual to make a difference. Alternatively, a type of *desertion* dream.

• CROWN

(see Gold, Jewelry)

Is the crown being put on or taken off? If accepted, this reveals your acceptance of responsibility for your life. If removed, perhaps you're trying to set aside culpability for your actions (or lack thereof).

Greco-Roman: Hospitality. It was a common practice to present guests with crowns of decorative *leaves* so that they would be treated like kings while in the host's home.

Developing leadership qualities, skills, or higher ideals (see *Authority Figures*).

What type of attitude does the person with the crown portray? Is it dictatorial or fair? This attitude reflects the way you treat yourself or others—either overly harsh, or fairly.

• CRUMBS

Receiving less than you deserve in a situation, particularly emotional or financial sustenance (see *Bread, Eating*).

Literally not getting enough nutrients in your diet.

A frugal nature evidencing itself, sometimes to an extreme.

• CRUTCH

Leaning on someone or something for support. Depending on the other symbols in the dream, this may be hindering personal growth (see *Lameness*). If so, stand up and take responsibility!

Being emotionally or spiritually "disabled" to the point where you constantly look to other people to supply ideas or motivation.

• CRYING

Dreaming of crying or moaning is usually a straightforward release of some type of pain, regret, guilt, or sadness. If it is the cry of an *animal*, the emotions are likely tied to whatever that creature represents.

The cry of a child can represent your own inner child trying to get attention (see *Baby*). Alternatively, for new *parents* this is a circumstantial dream caused by normal concerns, and by being woken up so frequently by the newborn.

• CRYSTALS

(see by type, Gems, Jewelry, Stones)

Clear crystals: purity, refinement, and accuracy.

A single crystal: The core of self, our identity and existence. Look at how the crystal appears for more interpretive value. Is it clear, multifaceted, cloudy?

Clear vision, discernment, or foresight. Smooth crystal surfaces were used for scrying throughout history, in numerous cultures including that of Medieval Europe and Victorian America. Watch and see if any symbols or images form in the sphere, and use those as a starting point for interpretation (see *Divination*).

As with *gems*, each crystal has different interpretive value and represents various omens. *Agate*, for example, portends positive business ventures, while *amethyst* reveals contentment with your work. Conversely, dreaming of losing an amethyst signals the loss of love or self-control. Here is a brief list of other common crystals and their interpretations. Note that many meanings correlate to the crystal's *color*:

Beryl: harmonious relationships
Bloodstone: wish fulfillment
Carnelian: luck and safety
Garnet: faithfulness
Hematite: charm and grace
Jet: sadness and mourning

Lapis: psychic awareness
Lodestone: enticement
Malachite: peaceful rest
Onyx: discord
Opal: change, bad luck
Quartz: energy, strength

What happens to the crystal in the dream will alter the interpretation. To illustrate, having a bloodstone shatter probably indicates that you feel as if your hopes have been dashed, whereas receiving the gift of a *lapis* might indicate an openness to develop your latent psychic abilities.

• CUP

(see Beverages, Chalice)

• CURTAINS

(see Door, Fabric, Obstacles, Veil, Windows)

Differences in, or separations between, groups of people, ideals, and dimensions. In the Old Testament, a veil or curtain separated the outer court and the Holy of Holies.

Privacy; having something that ensures a quiet, personal *sanctuary*.

Closing yourself off (especially if you see the curtains being drawn). Not wanting people to see you as you truly are; hiding from yourself or your feelings.

Torn curtains reveal quarrels and reproach within the home. The rifts caused by this discord need to be mended.

Changing curtains discloses similar transformations within you or your home. For example, a change to loud, vibrant hues might indicate increased energy and an outgoing nature.

• DAGGER

(see Knife, Weapons)

• DAISY

(see Flowers, Garden)

The daisy got its name as a combination of "day's eye," making this an alternative *sun* emblem.

Innocence and fidelity, especially when covering a *field* or lawn. The blissful simplicity of your youth.

If the daisy is worn, it portends love.

• DAM

(see Concrete, Water)

Pent-up emotions or energy that need some form of release.

Holding back information, or refraining from a course of action.

Putting a finger in a leaky dam: Temporary solution for a very big problem that threatens to overwhelm you.

Steady control over your spiritual or emotional nature, as represented by the regulated flow of *water*.

A person or situation you find invigorating and refreshing.

• DANCING

(see Drum, Foot, Music)

A type of passionate, sexual dream, like the Dance of the Veils in Arabia.

The act of courtship.

Joining a dance equates to integrating with a new group or situation. Watch to see how smoothly this dance progresses.

The dance of life. Consider if you are standing at the sidelines here, being a wallflower, or if you participate fully in what the music offers.

Ecstatic dance: In places like Africa and Arabia, this type of dancing reflects religious zeal and acts as a vehicle for divine possession. So, ask yourself how much you wish to be controlled by faith, lead by convictions, and influenced by creeds.

Dancing without a partner: Either reveling in self-fulfillment, or wishing for someone with whom to share the dance floor of your life.

A representation of the universal feminine aspect through movement. In many ancient cultures, dance was part of fertility rites. In Asia, specifically, the art of belly dancing developed from this idea.

Each form of dance has specific implied or symbolic interpretive value. For example, tap dancing can equate to side stepping the issues, whereas ballet reflects either a graceful demeanor in difficult situations or walking on tiptoe around people.

•DANDELION

(see Field, Flowers)

Folkloric: Hospitality. It was once believed that rubbing your *body* with the *juice* of a dandelion would ensure your welcome anywhere.

Victorian: In the language of flowers, this blossom represents ancient oracles and messages. Review the missives you've received lately. They may have greater meaning than you suspected.

Male fertility. The white juice of this plant was often used to represent abundant semen.

The amazing potential in simplicity. This pesky weed has a variety of uses, including salads from the leaves, coffee from the roots, and wine from the flowers!

•DARKNESS

(See Black, Blindness, Night)

Mysteries, the unknown, hidden matters, elusive truths, and the subconscious.

Oppressive darkness: Depression, gloom, or despair.

Being lost in: Frustration from the lack of direction, or a fear of *death*.

An alternative womb emblem (see *Abyss, Space*).

A *light* in the darkness: Hope, troubles coming to an end, truth being revealed.

• DEAD END

(see Alley, Corner, Highway, Path)

A futile path, which, if pursued, will only result in wasted energy.

Feeling trapped and unable to move. As such, an alternative type of *cage* emblem that offers at least one way out, namely, the way by which you came.

• DEATH

(see Bones, Burials, Butterfly, Cemetery, Ghost, Tomb)

Endings and beginnings of a literal or figurative nature. This may indicate death of the "old self," or a relationship, for example.

A wish for, or fear of, death. An awareness of your mortality.

Closing off your feelings from someone, thereby killing the relationship. Also, becoming reclusive or introverted.

Repressed hostility or wrath, especially if someone living is presented as dying in the dream. Note that this includes anger toward yourself.

Paracelsus felt that dreaming of people who have been dead for 50 years was a way of receiving knowledge from the other world, and that any messages received in these dreams should be closely heeded (see *Ghost*).

• DEER

(see Animals)

Swift, agile movement. The deer is an excellent guide through any figurative *forests* in your life.

Buddhist: A representation of the *Wheel* of Law in action. Also symbolizes meditation and gentility.

A stag specifically is regarded as solar and masculine in aspect, banishing evil by symbolically trampling snakes under its swift, strong hooves.

• DESERT

(see Camel, Oasis, Sand)

Spiritual dryness.

A retreat to find and understand the sacred, as both Moses and Jesus did in the wilderness.

If you are alone or lost in the desert, a type of *desertion* dream.

A very dry *abyss* wherein one may either lose or find oneself.

An unforgiving situation over which you'll have little control once you've entered into that domain.

• DESERTION

(see Banishment, Desert, Island, Separation)

Recent emotional traumas like divorce or the *death* of a loved one. In this case, the dream expresses repressed sadness and fear.

Childhood fears. Latchkey children who came home to an empty house, for example, sometimes have residual apprehension about finding themselves alone.

A sense of loneliness or emptiness. Feeling lost in a sea of humanity, or neglecting to care for yourself properly due to poor self-images.

A portion of self that you've outcast or rejected for boon or bane. For example, it's not healthy to push your emotions aside regularly, whereas rejecting prejudicial outlooks is a positive thing.

• DEVIL/DEMON

(see Evil, Hell)

• DIAMOND

(see Crystals, Gems, Jewelry, Stones)

The diamond's durability makes it a natural symbol of tenacity and strength through trying times. It takes tremendous pressure to turn coal into a diamond— perhaps you are the diamond in the rough here!

Among Hindus, an omen of success and youthful energy.

In Arabia, Persia, and Egypt, the diamond foretells a period of good luck.

Diamonds can also be symbolic of greed's curse that slowly eats away the beauty and goodness within. Many famous diamonds were thought to carry curses, probably because of the number of times robbery was attempted, with often deadly results.

• DICE

The laws of probability, or the powers of chance and fate.

The *numbers* shown on a roll of the dice may prove more significant than the dice themselves. Check the resulting numbers herein. Also consider common gambler's symbols. For example, snake eyes can be considered an ill omen of trouble or loss ahead.

Taking a risk or a gamble where the stakes may be quite high.

• DICTIONARY

(see Books)

• DIETING

A situational dream that comes to those who feel they need to lose *weight*, or who are already dieting. In this case, probably needs no interpretation.

A metaphorical representation of other types of intake, including emotional and spiritual "foods." Is your body-mind-spirit receiving the nutrients it deserves and needs?

• DILL

(see Herbs)

Heroic energy. This herb was hung in Greek and Roman feast halls to welcome back victorious heroes.

A period of well-deserved rest, or a temporary decrease in activities. Dill takes its name from the Norse word *dilla*, which means to lull.

Protection and safety especially against magic and negativity.

• DIRECTIONS

Movement or guidance to the left, in most cultures, is regarded as a negative sign. In medieval times, for the purpose of heraldry, left was called "sinister," reflecting the overall negative feelings toward this side of the body. Similarly, in *crystal* gazing, wisps of *color* moving to the left indicate a negative answer. This feeling may have developed because left-handedness is recessive, and therefore an oddity not easily explained by earlier peoples.

Right is a beneficial direction (note the term righteous), generally revealing positive actions and motivations.

Movement upward may be a type of *ascension* dream that shows your personal progress, hopes, and improvement.

Downward movement may show dissension, fatality, or pessimism that leads to feeling literally "down." Alternatively, this can signify a new focus on your internal nature—an exploration that often proves very useful to personal growth.

When two directions are featured at the same time, this symbolizes harmony and balance between opposites (see *Cross*). Conversely, this can also indicate an internal tug of war between two facets of your being.

Being shown directions by a compass or a map reveals feelings of being somewhat lost or out of place in your current situation (see *Blueprints, Schematics*).

Each direction on a compass has slightly different meanings. North is cool, denoting frozen movement and frosty emotions. East is the point of the rising *sun*, bringing hope and a new beginning. South is for *fire*, which can warm, energize, or consume depending on its potency, and West is the *water* or emotional center where fountains of creativity or floods of feeling may originate.

•DIRT (DUST)

Anything you regard as ugly, foul, or repulsive, especially in a moral sense.

Gossiping (e.g., "having the dirt on something").

Guilt or negativity that tarnishes an otherwise lovely thing.

Lack of use (something getting dusty, or having to be dusted off, like an artistic talent).

Dirt appearing on a specific part of the *body* can warn of an undetected malady.

•DISASTERS

(see Accident, Lightning, Storms)

Warning or fear of danger. Alternatively, consternation over your ability to survive upheavals.

Avalanche: Feeling trapped, frozen, or unable to act. Or, an overwhelmingly heavy burden that you feel was thrust upon you unwillingly (see *Ice, Snow*).

Cave in: The crumbling of foundations or an insecure position. Also a type of *burial* dream.

Earthquake: Something is shaking your foundations, potentially to the core of what you regard as truth. Alternatively, breaking up with, or away from, a person, organization, job, or situation.

Flood: Feeling swept away by uncontrolled emotions or overpowering circumstances. Alternatively, a thorough cleansing before a new start (see *Water*).

Hurricane or tornado: An alternative symbol of the *air* element, which relates to the mind, voice, or breath. In this case, however, the element is destructive, probably revealing ill-health or an overly active conscious mind that does not allow the intuitive self through. If related specifically to speech, this symbolizes an individual whose loudmouthed nature destroys much of what it contacts.

Landslide: Backward movement or retreat. Returning to old thought forms and behavior patterns.

Oil spill: A renewed awareness of personal responsibility toward nature. Alternatively, a defiled trust, the adulteration of an ideal, or a slippery situation.

Volcano: These are Earth's cauldrons that stir up your temper or other hot feelings that have already been building to the point of violent eruptions (see *Fire*). Find a safe outlet before someone gets hurt. If the volcano exhibits a slow lava flow, this represents a gradual venting of emotions.

• DISOBEDIENCE

Having an independent, rebellious spirit that may not always express itself positively.

Purposely not heeding the voice of reason, especially your own intuitive nature, Higher Self, or subconscious.

• DIVINATION

(see Arrow, Axe, Crystals, Dice, Feather, Gypsy, Hand, Hazel, Tea, Writing, Zodiac Signs)

To dream of fortune-telling indicates a dependence on the opinions or ideas of others when making decisions, especially those of a spiritual nature.

The reading received in such a dream may be a prognostication of forthcoming developments in your current situation.

Each type of divination system has a specific theme that can add dimension to your interpretation of this dream. For example, Tarot entails dispensing *cards* and accepting or rejecting the hand fate deals. *Dice* speak of taking risks, and *crystal* balls rely on vision, thereby putting the dreamer on notice to open her or his eyes fully!

Divinatory abilities and interests developing, or latent talents coming to the forefront.

• DIVORCE

A separation from a negatively influential person or bad situation.

Potentially a dream that considers this option in your current *relationship*.

Separation from distinct elements of self that you perceive as holding you back, or with which you've been unhappy.

• DOG

(see Animals)

If belligerent or barking, this dream shows personal aggression and hostility.

Sleeping at your feet: Service, good friends, and gentle companions.

Good instincts. Dogs are believed to have a kind of second sight in judging people, or discerning spiritual presences (see *Ghost*).

Being bitten by a dog reveals quarrels between friends or family members.

Dreaming of a purebred dog, especially at a dog show, indicates a personal love of performance, possibly to the point of putting on airs.

Growling dogs warn of being surrounded by designing or unpleasant people.

A Cerberus (many-headed dog) counsels that you are trying to maintain too many loyalties, interests, or friends. When you spread yourself too thin, quality suffers.

Zoroastrian: Sagacity, vigilance, and fidelity. Consider how the dog is treated and where it's seen for more interpretive value.

The afterlife: In Babylon, Greece, and Persia, dogs attended aspects of the great Goddess to the underworld where human souls slept, awaiting their next incarnation. This close affinity to *death* is why dogs are often credited with the ability to see spirits.

The ability to sniff out honesty and good character. In the Tarot, dogs sit at death's *gate* to be sure the soul is properly prepared. Similarly, Egyptian mythology speaks of Anubis, the jackal-headed god, waiting in the underworld to judge newcomers with his nose. This is why the Egyptians packed their mummies in sweet spices!

• DOLPHIN

(see Fish)

According to Pliny, this creature represents the need for swift movement with regard to a decision or opportunity.

A guide. Many *fables* tell of dolphins aiding shipwrecked sailors. From what reef is this creature offering to liberate your mind, body, or spirit?

Native American: A messenger between the worlds, dancing above and below the waves (see *Water*). The dolphin is the essence of the Great Spirit and the *wind* of life itself. Breathe deeply of its symbolic messages.

Playfulness. Dolphins speak directly to the child within and urge it to come out more regularly.

• DOORS

Options under examination (see *Buildings*, *Windows*).

An invitation to explore aspects of the self from the past, present, or those reaching to the future.

Revolving doors: Going in *circles* and getting nowhere. Being stuck in a pattern or cycle and not knowing how to break it.

Glowing doors: Spiritual opportunities.

Back door: hidden things, sneaky motivations.

New phases or openings. If the door remains firmly locked, you might not be ready to take this step.

An entryway into the subconscious.

Hospitality offered or given.

Standing in front of, but not entering: A reluctance to actively pursue present options.

A missing door reveals tremendous openness on your part, or that of another person or situation.

Stone doors often stand in front of important revelations or bits of knowledge, like those that were frequently used in *tombs* (note the story of Christ's resurrection).

Doorbells: A sign of forthcoming unexpected news, guests, or messages.

• DOVE

(see Animals, Birds)

Someone with gentle, loving words.

Peaceful offerings and reconciliation, as in the Biblical story of Noah and the Ark.

A common emblem of the Holy Spirit among Christians.

Cooing: A Victorian emblem of love or romance.

In Asia Minor, these birds represent the fertile, feminine aspect of our personality or the Universe.

Among Slavic peoples, doves bear the souls of the departed. As such, this may be an alternative *ghost* dream.

• DRAGON

(see Animals, Fables, Lizard, Monsters, Snake)

The guardian of great power, *magic*, and wisdom. If you can befriend this aspect of yourself, many new talents and abilities will open to you.

Among Taoists, the dragon represents eternal change, and the part of the *path* that we cannot as yet see. Consequently, you must perfect the spirit and trust that your road is sure.

In China, the highest spiritual Yang (masculine) power attainable. On Earth, this was embodied by the power of the Chinese emperor.

Slaying a dragon: Overcoming negative traits. Alternatively, cutting off the feminine aspects of self (see *Sword*).

Fire-breathing dragon: An overbearing person with strong words.

Procreative power of nature. In Assyrian and Babylonian mythology, Tiamat was a half-dragon, half-human (to show higher and lower self) Goddess who gave birth to all things.

Archetypal: The primordial consciousness and psychic transformation.

The ongoing struggle of light versus darkness, and good versus evil, that is always with us. Here you become the hero who preserves your vision of virtue.

•DRAGONFLY

(see Insects)

If hovering near water, this represents the cooperation between your mental/conscious self and your emotional nature.

Dragonflies are very adaptable, but also territorial. Have you been hovering around your domain too much? Or perhaps you've been too flexible in a specific situation.

Dragonflies need warmth and sunlight. On the dream plane, this may represent a similar physical need that manifests as depression or restlessness. Alternatively, it may symbolize the need to be more aware of the conscious, masculine, solar self.

In Japan, these are emblems of happiness and good fortune.

Among Native Americans, the souls of the departed may reside in these creatures. As such, they may be messengers from other realms communicating through your dream (see *Ghost*).

•DREAMING

A type of lucid experience or an OBE. (See Part One: Programmed and Lucid Dreaming).

A memory. Dreaming that you're dreaming can be an alternative way of recalling images from past dreams. Watch, and let this vision play itself out like a good movie, then recall the details like any ordinary dream.

•DRUM

(see Music)

Communication. Among tribal cultures, drums were not just used for rhythmic accompaniment, but to send messages across long distances.

Intense emotions like passion (the drumming of your heart).

Imminent war (or quarrels) being fought on a personal front.

A spiritual summoning to native or shamanic ideals.

Muffled: Missing an important call for aid from yourself, a situation, or another person.

•DUCKS

(see Birds)

Chattering: Deceitful conversations.

Flocking: Moving with a group mind toward a common goal.

In China and Japan, an emblem of conjugal joy, and a fortuitous omen for young couples.

The seasonal movement of these creatures speaks to us of learning to listen to our instincts for well-being and safety.

Possibly an alternative type of *swimming* dream.

What are the ducks doing and how safe do they appear in their habitat? If there is a hunter nearby, consider if you have likewise become a proverbial sitting duck for someone's aim. If so, then duck!

•DUNGEON

(see Cage, Castle, Underground)

•DYNAMITE

A sudden, and rarely pleasant, revelation or shaking of your foundations.

Anger or other emotions that threaten to blow up if not properly redirected.

What does the dynamite demolish? This may be a symbol of something within of which you wish to rid yourself. Due to the potency of dynamite, however, caution is indicated here. Don't go after this ideal or characteristic so forcefully that you destroy something valuable in the process.

Do the initials TNT mean anything to you? This abbreviation for dynamite has been used for a long enough time that the subconscious may use the abbreviation as a vehicle for its message.

Unanticipated personal expansion or exposure.

• EAGLE

(see Animals, Birds, Wings)

American: Freedoms and liberties in which everyone deserves to share.

Soaring with an eagle: A type of *flying* dream.

Many solar gods are equated with this symbol (see *Sun*), giving the eagle associations with the lifting of depression or a more conscious awareness.

Lofty ambitions that require great skill to achieve.

Jungian: Your father or another masculine *authority figure*.

Leadership skills. Among the Romans, this bird became a kind of totem for the emperor, who was thought to reincarnate as an eagle. Alternatively, this may also symbolize traditionally masculine characteristics like pride and fierceness developing.

An alternative *lightning* emblem. In ancient Greece, people placed eagles on temple rooftops to protect the building from lightning, as they felt this creature controlled the *fire* from the *sky*.

Riding on the back of an eagle represents a spiritual voyage, possibly an astral journey or OBE.

• EARS

(see Body, Face)

A direct reflection of your listening skills, or lack thereof. The size of the ears here might help interpret the dream further, large ones being more open but also less discreet.

The need to listen more closely to your inner self, or the messages from those who care about you.

Earrings represent decorating or exaggerating the facts of a story to make yourself look better (see *Jewelry*). Alternatively, this may be a warning from your own conscience to stop listening in on private conversations. In folklore, the ear originally got pierced as a chastisement for such impropriety.

• EARTH

(see Clay, Globe)

Being grounded or having solid foundations (e.g., being "down to earth").

Earthly or mundane matters. The physical plane.

Plowing and planting: Efforts toward acquiring or accentuating positive attributes (see *Garden, Farm*).

A place of emergence, especially for magical power. In the Middle Ages, it was widely believed that witches gained energy from the earth, and could disappear if they touched soil. Alternatively, this can imply positive energy directed toward developing personal traits and characteristics.

A period of peacefulness. Teutonic tribes would often put down their weapons of war during the season of the Earth Goddess.

Groveling in earth: Debased morals or ideals, or possibly begging for forgiveness.

Mud: Ambiguous circumstances; things getting botched (see *Dirt*). Alternatively, malicious gossip meant specifically to make a perceived opponent look bad (e.g., "mud slinging).

Among Native Americans, the earth element represents the physical nature, so if the land in your dreams is rich and fruitful, you are likely quite healthy, as is any effort that requires "hands-on" attention.

• EARTHQUAKE

(see Disasters)

• EAST

(see Directions)

• EATING

(see Food by type, Beverages, Candy, Fasting, Hunger)

If you have been *dieting* lately, this is likely a circumstantial dream that needs no further explanation.

The ideas, concepts, or beliefs currently being internalized (e.g., "you are what you eat").

In esoteric traditions, eating is a way to ground energy and reestablish foundations in the material world. Consider if both feet have been on terra firma lately.

Metaphorically, is there something for which you *hunger* in your life, physically, mentally, or spiritually? If so, find the right food to fill that hunger so that strong, healthy growth may begin (or continue).

A representation of your current eating habits. Are you eating well-rounded meals—or too much junk food? Consider what the dream shows you in terms of how you've been feeling lately, and make appropriate adjustments in your diet.

Eating a celebratory feast represents sampling a little from many different aspects of life, and enjoying each fully. It may also portend a period of abundance and pleasant surprises soon to follow.

Arriving late for a feast indicates the presence of many pressing personal matters that often detain social interactions.

Reviewing a *menu* in a dream signifies life's decisions and how metaphorically "good" they are for you. Consider what types of foods were chosen, and if the choices were costly, for more specific symbolism.

Leaving a table *hungry* represents being dissatisfied by the results of an effort, the answer received from a question, or a situation that is less fulfilling than you might wish.

• ECLIPSE

(see Moon, Sun)

Being in between two phases; a momentary limbo.

Temporary concealment of the truth.

Lunar eclipse: Hiding from, or trying to ignore, the feminine aspect of self (see *Women*).

Solar eclipse: Hiding from, or trying to ignore, the masculine aspect of self (see *Men*).

Being devoured or obscured by something or someone that seems larger than life. Several myths from various lands tell of great creatures, like *dragons*, who eat the sun or moon, thereby causing its disappearance.

•EGG

(See Basket, Chicken, Eating)

Cracking open: Coming out of a shell and enjoying a more social existence. Alternatively, the birth of new ideals or abilities.

Potential and fertility just waiting to be liberated from within.

Rotten: Something about this predicament "smells" bad, even though it may outwardly appear quite good.

A fragile or delicate situation requiring diplomacy (e.g., "walking on egg shells").

The creative force of the Universe becoming actively expressed in and through your life. In several mythological cycles including those of Egypt and Greece, the primordial cosmic matter is represented by an egg.

Folk medicine: If placed in the ground or broken into soil, this represents the waning of sickness.

•EIGHT

(see Numbers)

The number of integration and eternity, indicating that whatever you put effort into right now will have lasting effect. Note that the number eight turned on its side becomes the infinity symbol.

In Egypt, the number symbolizing rebirth. Watch for a window of opportunity to open, offering you a new beginning.

Natural cycles (see *Seasons*). The *wheel* of the year is generally depicted as having eight spokes. What cycle or *season* are you in now?

•ELDER

(see Field, Forest, Trees)

Increasing personal energy and zeal for a goal or project. Frequently elder is used to bolster fires because it has hollow branches that catch well.

Some type of ending or *death*. Elder is a traditional funerary wood.

In Serbia, this is a symbol of fortune and luck smiling upon you.

Carrying an elder branch in a dream represents devotion in your relationships.

Among Celtic tribes, elderberry *wine* was used to inspire divinatory visions, and was only drunk by the initiated. As such, this dream may reflect a personal initiation into the psychic realms (see *Beverages*).

• ELECTIONS

In an election year, this is a situational dream wherein you mull over the present candidates from a new vantage point.

Choices that we all must make, especially those that affect your interaction with the community or those associated with legal matters.

Political game playing at the office or in other circumstances.

• ELECTRICITY

(see Circuit Breaker, Light, Lightning)

Shocking changes.

A sudden increase in personal energy. Look to see what the source of power is for further insight.

The driving force within the dreamer. Where the electricity originates should shed more light on the meanings here.

Being a "live wire" or knowing someone who fits this description. The counsel here is to maintain a good sense of grounding so that the energy doesn't go to waste or become harmful.

• ELEPHANT

(see Animals)

Elephants exhibit many positive attributes, including affection and loyalty. Consider how much of both you have given to yourself, or to those around you, and vice versa.

These creatures also have a strong sense of smell that affords discernment. How does your present situation smell? Is something amiss?

An affinity for nature worship. According to Pliny, this creature worships the *sun* and *stars*, and invokes the heavens.

In ancient Rome, this image appeared on coins representing the power of charity. Does someone around you have a need that you've overlooked?

Among Hindus, the elephant symbolizes wisdom. Ganesha, the god of sagacity, is an elephant, often portrayed dancing.

Buddhists regard the *white* elephant as emblematic of compassion, love, kindness, self-restraint, and patient endurance, revealing the emergence of such positive traits within you. Note, however, that Western society transforms this image's meaning to that of useless decoration (e.g., a "white elephant sale"), which might reflect a lack of self-worth or feeling ineffectual in a specific situation.

Chinese: Prudence and independent authority over self, others, or a situation. Don't be afraid to take charge!

In modern aphorisms, a *pink* elephant represents being deluded by your own senses. Such delusion usually comes by your own hand (as happens when one drinks too much alcohol).

•ELEVATOR

(see *Ascent, Ladder, Stairs*)

•ELVES

(see *Fairy*)

•EMBROIDERY

(see *Fabric, Needle*)

•EMBRYO

(see *Baby, Birth, Miscarriage, Pregnancy*)

For a pregnant woman, or her partner, a situational dream that requires no further interpretation.

A period of gestation and waiting that may actually span 40 weeks. This is not a situation that can be rushed or forced.

A new beginning or opportunity that has just been recognized, or is just starting to develop.

•ENGAGEMENT

(see Bride, Groom, Relationships, Wedding)

A commitment of some nature, but it is not permanent yet. This is a good time to reexamine your thinking and make sure this is a decision about which you feel confident.

As a play on words, social commitments that you may, or may not, have any time to enjoy (e.g., "pressing engagements").

What are your feelings in this dream? Are you happy and content about the pledge made? If not, this can reflect anxiety or anger over someone else's upcoming nuptials, or second thoughts about a responsibility you've recently taken on.

•ERASER

(see Writing)

Wishing to negate something as if it never existed, or correct a mistake totally.

Your own ability to rectify a situation that has been haunting you. Look to see what words or *pictographs* get erased for more interpretive value.

•ESCAPE

(see Cage, Separation)

A very favorable omen marking the beginning of better times.

Feeling trapped, but not without some course of action that will lead to liberation. Pay close attention to the details of this dream to see if it offers the solution you have sought.

Distraction that allows temporary escape from whatever's on your mind.

Purposefully separating yourself from a situation that you perceived as unhealthy or unhappy.

•EVIL

(see Black, Darkness, Monsters)

Your personal shadow; negatives to overcome within.

Metaphysically, the dark forces that exist in all things, maintaining the balance (see *Hell*).

Demons and other malevolent creatures represent fears and anxiety that manifest through these images. If very threatening toward the dreamer, this can reflect self-hatred or guilt. Alternatively, this can indicate dangerous companions whose immorality is disguised by flattery.

•EXCAVATION

Hunting for something that seems elusive or hidden from direct view. Due to the soil involved, this may have something to do with personal foundations.

Metaphorically digging up the *dirt* on someone or a situation.

Uncovering *treasures* that are just waiting for your persistent efforts to discover them.

Digging through your own past to discover the worth of experiences, and how they have made you what and who you are today.

•EXPLOSION

(see Disasters, Dynamite)

Disapproval or dissatisfaction with a particular idea, person, or situation that is reaching a critical point.

Indiscreet action or abused confidences that resulted in very explosive emotions.

An alternative symbol for an extremely passionate sexual encounter.

Destroying *obstacles* that threaten to impede your *path* or goals.

•EYES

(see Body, Face)

As the *window* of the soul, these reveal truth to us. So, how do the eyes appear? Are they fully open to see things as they are really?

Judgment from others, or judging yourself for specific actions or words. In Hindu tradition, the Goddess could create or destroy the Universe with a blink of her eye. Similarly, in Syria and Mediterranean regions, the all-seeing eyes of the Goddess symbolized truth and the universal laws from which no one could hide.

The shape and size of the eyes may hold import. For example, very small eyes that appear closed in the dream indicate someone who is small-minded and unwilling to look at alternative viewpoints.

Various conditions in eyesight also have specific meanings. Being nearsighted indicates the need to extend your perspective, whereas farsightedness suggests that you should take a closer look at things. Tunnel vision equates to being so focused on a goal that you neglect to see other potential opportunities and angles through which you might succeed. Finally, having cataracts is a kind of *blindness* dream, where vision is partially or totally impeded.

Eye of Horus: Wisdom within the mind, and the power of knowledge to help us see and understand things more clearly.

Third Eye (center of the forehead): The psychic nature and transcendent universal awareness.

If you see only the right eye in your dream, this represents the *sun*, whereas seeing only the left represents the *moon* (as is seen in the eyes of Mithras).

Squinted eyes represent avoiding the *sun*—the logical, rational, conscious mind and thought processes. Alternatively, this can symbolize looking at something very closely.

Pop-eyed visages: Abundant surprise, excitement, or fear.

Two different-colored eyes: In earlier times a person with two differently colored pupils was thought to be able to administer the *evil* eye. Is there someone looking at you with malicious intent, or perhaps selfish motivations?

Wearing glasses in your dream indicates impaired vision that has somehow been corrected. However, if the glasses are tinted, check to see if you aren't looking at a situation or person through "rose-colored glasses."

• FABLES

(see Dragon, Monsters, Phoenix, Storytellers)

Characters or themes from the fables of our youth commonly appear in dreams as archetypes of personality traits or prevalent situations. Normally, the subconscious tries to illustrate a key that will help you develop those traits, overcome negative habits, or succeed in your present circumstances. For example, the tale of Goldilocks and the *Three Bears* could be counseling you to be less selfish or bearish in the way you act toward strangers.

The hero or heroine reflects your Higher Self, and the best personal characteristics you hope to eventually develop. Pay close attention to what these people do (see *Icons, Men, Women*).

Kings and queens reflect *authority figures* (or situations, belief systems, etc.) to whom you subjugate yourself. The question here is whether such service is beneficial to you as a whole person. Alternatively, these can be *icons* of gods and goddesses.

Fantastic creatures represent your ability to imagine and reach beyond surface reality. Each creature also has a unique symbolic message to consider. For example, dreaming of a Lilliputian might indicate that you feel very "small" about something right now, or that you lack self-confidence.

• FABRIC

(see Clothes, Needle, Sewing, Wool)

The metaphorical fabric of time, space, and dimensions in which your life represents one strand. Note, however, that each strand touches the others within this *web* directly or indirectly.

The substance of your foundational belief system. How does this fabric appear? Is it finely woven or full of *holes*?

Patterns in the fabric represent the cycles and patterns within your own life. For example, regular geometric imprints can indicate a personality that is very ordered and constant.

Frayed fabric is symbolic of something coming apart, but you still have time to stop this progression. Find the loose ends and sew them up!

• FACES

(see Body, Masks)

People you know, or with whom you interact regularly.

Different facets of the self.

Reflective of prevalent moods and emotions. A smiling face indicates joy, for example, while a scowling one reveals worries or anger.

Two faces or heads on one body indicates either a split personality or betrayal (e.g., being "two faced"). Alternatively, if one face is male and the other female, this represents an integrated balance between the sexes (see *Hermaphrodite*).

• FAIRIES

The unseen world, our imagination, and the spirit of the inner child that awaits acknowledgment or expression (see *Fables*).

Brownies: Tiny, ragged men who symbolize matters of *hearth* and home, especially keeping things orderly and well run.

Elves: Thin, fair-skinned, pointed-eared, *forest*-dwelling Devas, these represent your magical or mischievous side.

Gnomes: As squat earth-dwellers, these creatures symbolize earth-related concerns.

Goblins: Green-skinned impish creatures that usually equate to our fears, malevolent prankishness, and, potentially, thievery.

Leprechauns: *Shoe* makers and the eternal *gypsies* of the fairy folk, these represent good luck, improved wealth, and a rogue-like personality.

Pixies: Being lead astray by something that looks quite innocent.

Salamander: A spirit who embodies a single flame, this Being knows how to live life to its fullest, and suggests you do the same (see *Fire*).

Sylph: Joy, laughter, carefree existence. Possibly a type of *flying* dream, as these fairies have gossamer *wings* (see *Air*).

Troll: Something or someone that prohibits a change or movement that you're trying to make (see *Bridge*), at least not without exacting a *price*.

Undines (Merpeople): Essential emotions, and things you regard as wholly lovely (see *Water*). Alternatively, your idealized image of masculinity or femininity, depending on the sex of the creature (see *Men, Women*).

• FALLING

(see Abyss, Cliff, Climbing, Ladder, Stairs)

The need for improved *balance* and control; feeling helpless.

Going beyond safe boundaries and losing yourself; overextension.

A phobia: The fear of falling (or fear of heights) may manifest in a dream to help you overcome the anxiety.

Letting go of something you perceived as an important foothold can cause falling dreams, like the first time a young person moves into her/his own *apartment*.

Lost status or the proverbial "fall from grace."

• FAN

(see Air, Wind)

A type of *air* or *wind* dream that offers more personal control because you know where the "off" switch lies.

Handheld fans may symbolize secret communications. In the Victorian era, when propriety would not allow lovers to outwardly speak of their feelings, fans were used to convey those desires. Also, handheld fans placed before the *face* obscure the words or expressions behind them.

Causing trouble (e.g., "fanning the flames").

Attempting to keep yourself cool despite heated emotional, physical, or spiritual matters.

• FARM

Rural life, simplicity, and a strong connection to nature. Farmers live by the land and nature's whims.

Figurative *death* (e.g., "it bought the farm").

The type of farming shown in the dream may also have meaning; consider the *animals* and crops that reside thereon to expand your interpretation. For example, farming *corn* can represent your tenacious efforts to improve finances, and how well the efforts are faring.

• FASTING

A dream that sometimes marks the beginning of a vision quest or other important religious sojourn. Moslems, Christians, Native Americans, and Jews alike use fasting as expressions of faith, or in the hopes of receiving divine missives.

An unsatisfied *hunger* within. The question then becomes for what are you hungering?

A temporary abstinence from something meaningful in order to obtain something even more precious.

• FEAST

(see Eating, Food and Beverages by type)

• FEATHERS

(see by type, Birds, Flying, Wings)

Spiritual purity and truth: In ancient Egypt, the soul was weighed upon death against the Plume of Maat, whose name means truth. Similarly, the Hopi regard the gift of an *owl's* feather as a means of helping the recipients be true to themselves. Less directly this may pertain to honesty in communications.

Lifting of guilt or burdens, or someone who is a truly free spirit (e.g., being "light as a feather").

Changeability: Feathers equate to the *air* element that shifts directions without any forewarning.

A prognostication: In ancient Greece, people used found bird feathers as portents of their travels and the future. Consider the feather's color, where it lands, and the type of bird from which it comes for expanded interpretations.

• FENCE

(see Obstacles)

• FENNEL

(see Herbs)

An alternative emblem for *fire*. According to Greek mythology, Prometheus bore a burning fennel stalk to earth when presenting humankind with this gift.

Clear vision and defined goals. In folk remedies, this herb is used to aid eyesight.

Folkloric: The natural cycle of *death* and rebirth that may be allegorical or situational. *Snakes* are said to shed their skin after eating this herb.

The ongoing battle between dark and *light*, good and evil within or without. In the Strega tradition (the Witches of Italy), symbolic battles are fought between good and evil sorcerers using fennel stalks for *weapons*. The goal of this enactment is to ward off negativity and ensure a good crop.

Digesting recently received information. Historically, fennel was favored to aid indigestion.

• FIELD

(see *Animals and Flowers by type, Forest, Trees*)

If this is an open meadow, it can represent the open expanses of the mind. Alternatively, it can also represent exposure and unseen hazards that lurk just beyond the peaceful greenery, like a hunter watching for *deer*.

A field of *daisies* reflects youthful, innocent, and carefree outlooks.

Consider other fields according to what they contain, like a barren field equating to emotional or spiritual dryness, or one filled with seedlings as emblematic of fresh growth or new beginnings.

• FIG

(see *Fruit, Tree*)

Ancient Greeks considered this a fruit that offers strength and endurance during trying times.

In Egypt, the fig was sacred to Thoth, making it an emblem of wisdom, learning, and the *moon*.

Spiritual awakening. Buddha is said to have been enlightened while meditating beneath this tree.

Dreaming of a fig plant growing in a kitchen is an omen that you will never want for food or, more figuratively, spiritual sustenance.

Fertility. Women used to carry figs to ensure conception. In a figurative sense, this may mean conceiving good ideas or receiving bountiful inspiration that spreads into something remarkable.

• FIGHTING

(see *Abuse, Armor, Weapons*)

Conflict or clashes with social strictures, other's ideals, or your own sense of right and wrong.

Jungian: Self-conflict between what we wish to be and what we truly are or how we perceive ourselves.

A battle raging between the conscious and subconscious, between thought versus emotion, masculine traits versus the feminine, etc.

Releasing anger and related emotions that otherwise get subdued, or for which we do not have an adequate avenue of expression.

• FILING CABINET

(see *Doors, Organizing*)

Each drawer or file in the cabinet represents a memory, bits of knowledge, experiences, or other parts of yourself that you have neatly sequestered away for future reference or use.

Take note of the condition of the cabinet and files. Are they orderly and well maintained, and do they appear as if they're regularly used? If so, then this dream indicates that you apply all your experience and knowledge in daily living. If, however, some of the files (or drawers) appear locked, are marked "confidential," or are laden with heavy dust, this shows that there is something unconfronted in your past. Now might be the time to open that folder so that it doesn't become a skeleton in your *closet*, waiting to appear at the worst possible moment.

• FINGERS

(see *Body, Hand, Rings*)

Pointing at someone or something represents an *accusation*. Alternatively, in a magical setting this may symbolize directing power toward an intended goal.

A finger to the lips indicates silence as the best course of action right now. Hold your words and use this time to think things through.

Raising the two central fingers is a protective emblem from classical times, averting the influence of the "evil *eye*." Consider from what or whom you feel the need to protect yourself and why.

Clenched fingers reflect tension or anger that has not been directed constructively.

The central finger of the hand is an emblem of the phallus, which actually dates back to Rome when prostitutes used it to beckon their customers. This usage slowly changed to our modern insult. The question here is to whom is the insult directed and why?

Crossed fingers symbolize your wishes and hopes.

Fingernails have several implications. First, they were a common component for magical spells to gain power over another. Second, depending on how they're used in the dream, these can be a kind of *weapon*. In addition, fingernails over a *blackboard* reveal irritations.

• FIRE

(see Baking, Candle, Disaster, Forge, Hearth, Hell, Red, Sun, Torch)

A predominantly masculine symbol associated with the *sun* and intense passion. Native Americans additionally believe the condition of the fire appearing in the dream reflects your emotional nature. Is it burning out of control—or neatly tended?

Goodness over *evil*. Fire illuminates the *darkness* and chases away frightening *shadows*. Upon what areas of your life does this light shine?

Drastic transformation. This is the flight of the *phoenix* who must die in a *nest* of flame to be renewed.

Emotional devastation or a burning obsession. Look to see what exactly you perceive as burning.

Awareness and vision. Besides shedding light, fire was used as a divinatory tool in cultures ranging from ancient Greece to Tibet. Known as pyromancy, seers would stare at a flame source, watching for symbolic images to appear in answer to questions posed.

Elemental forces that must be tempered and controlled or they will destroy instead of empower.

Dramatics (being full of "flash and fanfare").

Squelching: Ignoring or turning your back on the masculine nature, or resentment toward *men*. Alternatively, having a source of personal energy taken away.

Walking through a fire: Your reactions in the dream to this experience indicate how you are coping with a particularly heated situation.

Sitting amidst a fire: Being on the proverbial "hot seat." Alternatively, a type of *death* dream in which the fire relates to the ancient pyres upon which bodies were burned to release the spirit.

Campfires: Simple pleasures, reveling in nature, remembering stories and experiences from youth (see *Fables, Storytellers*).

What's burning here can be vitally important to your dream's meaning. For example, seeing a *building* on fire might indicate that you're burning up your body's resources/energy. An *attic* fire can reveal someone whose mind is totally consumed by one topic. Dreaming of burning *clothes* symbolizes the desire to do away with societally designed images for a more honest self-representation.

Dreaming of a fire whose coals have grown cold is a very negative image. It represents trouble, despair, and possibly the loss of love among those people close to you due to a misunderstanding. Try to find a way to put a fresh warm ember into this situation.

• FIREFLY

(see Insects)

A small spark that leads to illumination and awareness.

Potentially a spiritual guide or elemental visitation (see *Angel, Fairy*).

• FISH

(see Animals, River)

Miracles, especially those of providence, as portrayed in the story of Christ and the loaves and fishes.

Determined procreativity. Some fish, like salmon, fight their way against *water* currents to mate.

According to Edgar Cayce, ugly fish represent *evil*.

Hooking a fish: Seizing a spiritual or personal quality.

Hindus regard fish as representative of charity and timely rescue, especially from the emotional nature. The first incarnation of Vishnu was a fish that saved humankind from the flood.

In China, this symbolizes prosperity, renewal, and peace. The word for fish in Chinese is actually a homophone for abundance.

An alternative *icon* dream, because fish coincide with many savior figures, including those of ancient Babylonia and India.

Among Buddhists, the symbol of separation from desires and attachments.

In Japan, the carp specifically is an emblem of the masculine nature (see *Men*).

Potentially a play on words that warns against a "fishy" situation.

Seeing yourself fishing indicates a search. Watch your catch, however, as your hook can snag an old shoe as easily as it might the prize you seek!

Casting nets for fish reveals a person who is liable to accept all received information as truth, without discriminating good information from bad (see *Webs*).

Each type of fish can become a distinct symbol within your dream. For example, a flounder indicates someone who is constantly wavering and unable to make a decisions (e.g., "floundering around"). On the other hand, a piranha reveals a biting personality, or one that is anxious for success at any cost.

• FIVE

(see Numbers, Pentagram)

Emotional, mental, spiritual, or physical transitions.

Protection and safety. The pentacle of the Knights Templar is illustrated as a five-pointed *star*. This was used regularly to shield people from the evil *eye* or malicious *magic*.

Ancient Roman: An emblem of love and commitment. The Roman *marriage* rituals featured five burning *candles* throughout the ceremony.

Islamic: The number of sacred tasks: regular cleansing, offerings, fasting, prayers, and taking a pilgrimage.

In some dream oracles, this number portends the restlessness that accompanies change. Listen to your inner voice, and let it steer you in the right direction.

• FLAGS

(see Locations, Pictographs)

A means of self-identification. What image appears on the flag, and what does it say about your true self?

Battered flags indicate some type of war being waged, often on an emotional level.

Raising flags represents honor and remembrance of traditions.

Flags flying at half-mast represent a literal or figurative *death*, or some type of memorial. This can be circumstantial too, like the death of a relationship, or the ending of a job.

Allegiance and devotion. In what condition does the flag appear? If torn in two, this can represent divided loyalty or a conflict of interest. Also note the country, state, or city the flag represents for more insight.

• FLINT

(see Metals)

• FLOOD

(see Disasters, River, Water)

• FLOOR

(see Buildings)

As with any part of a *building*, this can represent our body's floor—the *foot*. The condition of the floor then becomes the dream key. For example, a cracked floor could indicate skin conditions or fungal growths on this part of the *body*. Or, metaphorically, this dream reveals that you may not be looking where you are walking, thereby putting yourself in danger.

Your foundational belief systems. How does the floor appear? One that is highly polished shows someone who has refined an external spirituality to appeal to others' expectations. A rotten floor reflects a negative *path* that will eventually lead to downfall. Uneven floors reveal someone who has trouble maintaining a *balance* between faith and fact, the mundane and the esoteric.

• FLOWERS

(see by type, Field)

Fulfillment and maturity in yourself, a job, or a relationship.

Research the specific flower for other more detailed associations. Most have correlations with divine beings, historical figures, and folkloric attributes. For example, the *lily* is often an emblem of Christ, the *rose* is often a symbol of Mary, the Mother Goddess, and of England, and *lavender* portends renewed happiness.

Personal values, morals, and characteristics budding to the forefront.

Appearing as an offering: See *Altar, Sacrifice*.

Gathering in a *garden*: A delightful surprise, depending on the flower. Buttercups portend successful business, *carnations* foretell love, irises predict communication from someone you miss, and primroses are an omen of new friendship.

Dying or wilting: Personality disorders, physical maladies, or decreased energy that erodes inner beauty.

Alchemically, an alternative emblem for the soul, as the petals radiate from the center, like the *body* around the spirit.

Opening flowers represent potential, hope, and the first evidence of manifestation with regard to your goals.

Victorians used flowers to communicate messages and for a special petaled *divination* system in which each blossom meant something different. Consider if your words are being directed with flowery sentiments that may or may not be appreciated and understood by the recipient.

• FLYING

(see Airplane/Airport, Birds by type, Butterfly, Bat, Fairies, Insects by type, Wings)

Liberation or freedom. Overcoming a difficult situation and transcending limitations. If you fly alone, this represents a personal journey filled with positive realizations. If flying with others, this indicates the support of family, friends, or acquaintances, especially for a new endeavor.

An Out of Body Experience (OBE): Esoterically, flying through the air is sometimes interpreted as an OBE. Christian figures like Elisha and St. Anthony were believed to have this ability. The ancient Egyptians called the astral body the *ba*, and in Germany the astral figure was sometimes likened to a doppelgänger. No matter the name, the purpose of such travel is to edify and educate the spirit, or potentially aid someone that you could not reach by normal means (see *Bed*).

With wings: If you have the wings of a bird when flying, check mythical or folkloric information on that bird for possible clues to your dream's meaning. For example, having the wings of a *dove* reveals nonviolent intentions or resolutions.

Wishful thinking (e.g., "flights of fancy").

•FOG

(see Clouds, Rain, Storms)

Disorientation and confusion.

Hidden or concealed matters.

Being figuratively "thick," that is, naive to the point of stupidity.

•FOOD

(see by type, Eating)

•FOOT

(see Barefoot, Body, Shoes)

Your sense of mobility and spiritual or emotional balance (e.g., "footing").

Taking a new step or direction with your life.

Jungian: Our connection with the *earth*; our foundations in materiality.

Kissing or washing of the feet represents humility and service, as Mary Magdalene with Christ.

Footprints: Leaving behind a waymark that others can recognize, respect, or follow.

Aching feet may represent trying to move too far too fast. All of life's journeys have an optimum pace. Try and find that pace before you wear out.

•FOOTNOTES

(see Books, Writing)

• FOREST

(see Animals by type, Field, Trees)

Obscureness (e.g., "not seeing the forest for the trees").

Dark and filled with *animals*: Personal instincts and drives, reflected in the type of animals or their activities.

Freudian: An emblem of the vaginal region (more specifically, bushes).

A sacred space. The first *temples* to the ancient gods and goddesses were *groves* of trees, often those that formed a natural protective *circle* in which to worship.

• FORGE

(see Fire, Hammer)

This *cauldron* of flame hones and refines your skills or characteristics.

Because of the fiery element, an alternative type of *fire* or *sun* dream, but with more implied regulation.

Smith at a forge: Control over the masculine nature, and knowing how to use its attributes effectively. Also, magically speaking, an improved skill with fire as an empowering element. Look to see what shape or object the smith works on for more symbolism.

Metal sitting in a forge: The metal represents an aspect of an individual that is undergoing a fiery time. This experience tempers and shapes that characteristic.

• FORGIVENESS

(see Acceptance, Acquittal)

• FOUNTAIN

(see River, Water, Well)

Refreshment for the spirit.

An outflowing of creativity, or the surfacing of new talents.

Vitality and longevity, like Ponce de León's fabled Fountain of Youth.

If the fountain is dry, consider whether or not you've been attending to the needs of your body-mind-spirit effectively. If you give too much of yourself on any level, the inner reservoir goes dry and will need refilling.

If the *water* in the fountain is cloudy, this indicates insincerity in your associates. It can also reveal a lack of clarity regarding your own creative ability, or a pending decision.

•FOUR

(see Numbers, Square)

An ancient Babylonian and Egyptian emblem for wholeness and fulfillment.

A number representing the divine spark or source. Many languages depict God with a four-letter name, including French, Latin, Greek, and Sanskrit; the cabalistic name for god is YHWH.

The movement of time or changing cycles. The *calendar* has four major points: spring, summer, fall, and winter (see *Seasons*).

In some metaphysical traditions, this number represents physical conditions, so seeing it frequently in dreams may be a signal to take better care of yourself or get a checkup.

•FOX

(see Animals)

Shrewdness, especially in the way you handle other people.

In its den, the fox symbolizes a wise retreat into safety.

Transformation or clever adaptation. In Eastern lands and among Native Americans, this creature is considered a shape-shifter.

Foxes live in borderlands and usually come out at dawn or dusk. This activity provides the symbolism of being in between stages, places, or worlds.

Camouflage and blending in. How exposed are you right now?

Using charm to get what's desired. Foxes play with their prey using elaborate or funny gestures to distract the animal while they move in closer.

Having been defeated by trickery (e.g., being "outfoxed").

In *relationships*, this speaks of monogamous territoriality. Take care that you are not holding on so tightly here that you actually push the one you love away.

• FRACTIONS

(see Arithmetic, Calculators, Numbers)

• FRAME

(see Art, Canvas)

• FROG

The shape of the tadpole looks similar to a young fetus, thereby symbolizing fertility and fecundity.

Egyptian: Rebirth or figurative renewal in some area of your life.

Shamanic: A messenger regarding matters of health. Alternatively, a charm against any figurative bad weather coming your way.

Transformation and perspective. The frog prince of fairy tales reminds us that things are not always as they seem.

In China, frogs represent the ultimate Yin principle, *healing*, and business prosperity.

Ancient Greece: A portent of harmony between lovers.

• FROSTING

(see Baking, Cake, Eating)

Glossing over the surface of a matter without really digging down to get the full story.

The little serendipitous bonuses in life, like the icing on a cake.

The sweetness of the frosting gives it some meanings similar to *candy*.

A decorative facade that won't hold up under detailed scrutiny.

• FRUIT

(see by type, Field, Grove, Trees)

Fertility (e.g., the "fruit of one's loins").

Distinctiveness. On the Tree of Life, each fruit was grown by its own design. Similarly, *fruits* have *colors*, shapes, and *smells* that set them apart from one another.

In oracular dream books, *figs* symbolize wealth and wisdom, *melons* indicate travel and adventure, golden *apples* express financial opportunities, and pears indicate improvements at work. Cherries may portend a loss of love, *lemons* reveal growing relationships, *oranges* promise devotion from one adored, and strawberries foretell a rural adventure.

Harvesting fruit equates to cultivating talents, characteristics, or spiritual gifts. Be sure, however, that you wait to pick these fruits when they are fully ripened for the most pleasing personal results.

Forbidden fruits, like the *apples* in Eden, equate to taboos—things, people, situations, or material desires that entice you to stray from a belief.

•FUN HOUSE

(see *Mirror*)

Distorted images of reality.

Having inaccurate perceptions based on superficials, especially in regard to self-image.

An expression of your inner child who is seeking some attention.

•FUR

(see *Animals, Carcass, Hair*)

Shamanically, a representation of an animal spirit with which you wish to connect.

A disguise or ruse used to fool a perceived enemy, or one that helps you better integrate with new surroundings.

Either attempting to internalize the positive attributes and characteristics of the creature featured, or presently bearing the negative traits of that animal.

If the fur in the dream is standing on end, this is a visual metaphor for having your "fur up" over a situation, or perceiving danger therein.

•FURNACE

(see *Fire, Hearth*)

• GALAXY

(see Space)

• GAMBLING

(see Cards, Games)

• GAMES

Each game envisioned in a dream has different meanings, depending on its focus. For example, chess stresses logic, forethought, and strategy as a key for victory, roulette *wheels* reflect gambles and uncertainty, word jumbles symbolize the need for ordered communications, and Monopoly might represent cautious use of money.

Figuratively, playing games with people instead of being forthright.

• GARBAGE

Having too much mental clutter, or scattering attention in too many directions.

In a dump: Feeling literally "dumped on" by others or circumstances. Alternatively, being surrounded by scandal.

A desire for orderliness and organization that's generated by having your sense of structure dismantled.

Things in your life of which you need to rid yourself.

Counsel from your subconscious that you figuratively need to socially, mentally, or physically clean up your act. What exactly needs to be thrown away so that you can grow and change?

A poor self-image that manifests in treating yourself like worthless garbage.

Ecological concerns displaying themselves through your dream.

Garbage trucks represent personality types that tend to accumulate possessions to assert their security, instead of developing personal qualities.

Finding something valuable in: An alternative type of *treasure* dream ("one person's trash is another's treasure"). Also, an optimistic outlook.

Compost heaps represent the need to nurture and fertilize your ambitions. A compost heap is also an emblem of taking a negative and finding a creative means of making it a positive (e.g., recycling garbage so that it nourishes the land).

• GARDEN

(see Farm, Flowers, Fruit, Herbs, Seeds, Vegetables, Weeds)

The condition of the garden can indicate the condition of many things, including your health, a *relationship*, or a business venture. So, a weedy or barren garden isn't a good sign, whereas a flourishing garden is very positive.

Planting a garden: Seeding the soil of self with specific virtues that you hope will grow to fullness.

Weeding a garden: Ridding yourself of things that entangle and deter real maturation.

Tilling a garden: Preparation and readiness. Putting things in order so that your goals have good ground on which to develop.

An alternative type of *island* or *oasis* dream in which a blossoming garden equates to your image of paradise, or the attainment of some spiritual goal portrayed by what's growing.

• GARLIC

(see Herbs)

Talmudic: An emblem of increased fecundity. Among Hebrew men, it was customary to eat garlic before intercourse to ensure fertility.

Protection: Garlic was used regularly in spells and charms for safety, especially against spirits and *evil* creatures like vampires. You may want to consider this dream more metaphorically, like safeguarding yourself against the spirit of the *vine*, or people who "suck" your energy dry.

Vows, commitments, and promises. The ancient Egyptians swore oaths on garlic, rather like we swear on the Bible.

Strength during trying times. Ancient Egyptians, Israelites, and Romans ate garlic for this purpose, especially before battle.

The pungent flavor and smell of garlic makes it an alternative *fire* symbol.

Passing through a *field* of garlic portends increased prominence and a better financial outlook.

Eating garlic represents having sensible views of life, and well-rounded ideals.

Being able to endure a time of difficulty and still land on your feet. Seamen and mountaineers alike carry fresh garlic to protect them against wreckage and foul weather, respectively.

• GARNET

(see Crystals, Gems, Jewelry, Stones)

• GAS STATION

A strong indication of your energy level. Are you filling up the tank regularly? If not, consider taking some time to rest and recoup your inner resources.

If the vehicle at the gas station has its gas gauge on empty, you've probably felt unproductive lately due to overexpending yourself. Conversely, an overfilled tank can reveal a hyperactive personality who never seems to run out of energy (see *Bus, Car*).

• GATE

Gates have associations similar to *doors* and *archways* with some minor variations. For example, if the gate has a keeper, this person may symbolize your Higher Self or a guardian figure (see *Angel*) waiting to help you traverse this *obstacle*.

Gates have strong correlations with fertility and productivity, being that the womb is sometimes referred to as the "gate of all life."

The barrier between worlds, in this case the conscious and subconscious. Many mythologies speak of the gate that leads to paradise in the afterlife. Once the spirit passes this juncture, there can be no return to mortality.

• GEMS

(see by type, Crystals, Jewelry, Stones)

Something precious, to be cared for and guarded with due diligence.

The gem of truth. Facts revealing themselves.

Commitments and devotion. Precious gems, especially *diamonds*, are exchanged as part of engagement or *wedding* rites.

In a *ring*: Authority. Popes, kings, and other *authority figures* often wear *gold* rings mounted with precious gems as a sign of office.

Metaphysically: Assisted health, protection, or improved personal characteristics. People in nearly every ancient culture carried or wore precious gems as amulets, charms, and talismans for a variety of positive purposes.

Each precious or semiprecious gem carries different meanings within a dream. *Amber* equates to feeling trapped, *diamonds* are for love, emeralds represent resourcefulness, and garnets portend the end to a period of questioning. Additionally, *jade* indicates health, moonstone stands for foresight and all things feminine, opal represents financial situations, ruby is a type of *fire* dream, and sapphire shows faithfulness on your part. For more ideas along these lines, try reading my book *Folkways* or any book that includes the lore of gems.

Faceted gems represent different aspects in something or someone, including the Divine and yourself.

•GHOST (SPIRIT)

(see Death, Séance)

Residual feelings or uncertainties that you haven't totally dealt with honestly or recognized.

Esoterically, the disembodied spirit of a person who has returned with a message for you, or to ask for your aid.

Something perceived as remote or unlikely (e.g., "ghost of a chance").

Memories of deceased friends, *parents*, and loved ones.

Undiscovered talents or portions of the self, especially those of a psychic nature.

Jungian: Uncontrolled psychic forces or complexes.

Being possessed by a spirit: A neurosis or psychosis that overrides your normal actions and reactions. Alternatively, this dream may occur to someone who has a drinking problem as a warning not to let this spirit possess them.

A ghost town: This symbolizes a penchant for living in the past instead of fully handling the present. The counsel here is to keep the good memories, let go of the rest, and start living fully again.

An omen of unexpected confrontation or trouble.

• GINGER

(see Herbs)

If you've dreamt of ginger recently, you may discover that your zest for life and passionate interests are increasing.

Faithfulness: In the Koran, only the steadfast believers enjoy ginger-flavored *beverages* in paradise.

Honoring the gods. In China ginger was used as part of offerings, and in the Middle East it was favored for communing with the Divine.

Affection. When consumed, ginger generates a warm, cozy feeling within.

Assimilating new ideas or becoming more comfortable with a situation. Medicinally, ginger is an excellent aid to digestion.

If the ginger is consumed in the dream, this may represent purging figurative poisons from your system. Pythagoras recommended ginger for similar medicinal uses long ago.

• GIRAFFE

(see Animals)

Because of the giraffe's extended neck, this animal often symbolizes someone who take unnecessary risks and put themselves on the line for other people (e.g., "sticking your neck out").

The height of the giraffe affords it a unique perspective. The caution here is not to become meddlesome in this investigation. Use your heightened awareness discreetly and wisely.

The long legs of this creature provide swift movement (see *Velocity*). Just take care where you step along the way.

If gathering *water*, this represents counsel from the subconscious to keep your eyes on the horizon when it comes to emotional or intuitive matters. Giraffes are most vulnerable when they drink, as it sets them slightly off-balance. Raising your sights back up may avert an unanticipated problem that could likewise set you off-kilter.

• GLASSES

(see Eyes)

•GLOBE

(see Earth)

The World Card of the Tarot, representing fulfillment, a well-rounded outlook, and having the "world" at your doorstep.

A more universal, one-world mind-set developing.

•GLOVES

(see Clothing, Hand)

During the Middle Ages, an emblem of approval and honor. To take up a glove was to accept a challenge, and giving a glove indicated respect.

Victorian: Propriety and manners, especially among women. In this setting, the glove might indicate a refined outlook, gentility, and the graces associated with fine Victorian ladies.

White gloves: Focus on neatness and cleanliness, often in a critical manner. Don't expect other people to live up to your expectations of what constitutes good housekeeping.

Boxing gloves: Someone who is ready, willing, and able to *fight*, if need be.

Rubber gloves: Insulating oneself from perceived dangers, especially of a physical nature.

•GNOMES

(see Fairy)

•GOBLIN

(see Fairy)

•GOLD

(see Colors, Coins, Sun)

Rulership or leadership. Taking control of your life or a situation. Note that this is the predominant *metal* historically used for *crowns*. Similarly, in Incan myth the Sun God gave the first created man and woman a golden staff with which to civilize a savage world (see *Rods, Wand*).

Financial matters—as such, a type of *money* or *treasure* dream.

Pyrite (fool's gold): A disappointing gamble, or something that looks too good to be true.

New life, renewal, and the happiness that follows same.

An alternative emblem for *light*. In Hindu beliefs this metal is formed underground by trapped sunlight.

Long lasting happiness and love. The preferred metal for *rings* at marriage ceremonies is gold because it doesn't tarnish.

•GOLDENROD

(see Flowers)

Something or someone really getting under your skin and making things itchy or uncomfortable, like hay fever.

Folkloric: Discovering the hidden treasures within yourself. This flower marks underground springs, which on the dream plane equates to creative flow or the subconscious (see *Water*).

Healing your wounds. In China and among Native Americans, this plant was used regularly as a curative. What's ailing you?

Growing near a home, goldenrod portends good fortune for the family therein.

•GOOSE

(see Birds, Swan)

The creative principle. In Egypt, a goose laid the cosmic *egg* from which the Universe sprang.

India: Representative of freedom, eloquence, and learning.

Easter: A bringer of good news, especially for lovers. Geese mate for life.

An alternative *wind* emblem, having associations with Boreas in Greek mythology, the god of the north wind.

In the form of Mother Goose, an alternative goddess symbol, or reminder of youthful imagination and fancy.

Modernly, a symbol of foolish behavior (e.g., someone acting like a "silly goose").

•GRAIN

(see Corn, Farm, Field)

•GRAPE

(see Fruit, Vine, Wine)

Eating grapes is supposed to increase the frequency of oracular dreams. Alternatively, according to folklore, eating grapes or raisins aids concentration and conscious alertness. In a dream this may mean improved prophetic abilities or an increased need to focus on studious matters, respectively.

Fertility. The abundance of grapes on the vine shows that the positive energy put toward your goals will reap rewards.

Fortitude shared with those around you. In a *garden*, grapes strengthen the hardiness of most nearby plants.

An emblem equated with Bacchus or Dionysus, both of whom had rather roguish natures, being fond of wine, song, and laughter. For the dreamer, this can reflect more social times or an improved sense of well-being accompanied by playfulness.

If the grapes are tart, this reflects a similarly caustic attitude (e.g., being full of "sour grapes").

•GRASS

Foundational ideas from which you are either nourished or weakened. Look at the condition of the grass for more indicators.

Mowing grass symbolizes ideas or situations that get cut short before they have the chance to grow naturally into maturity.

Where do you see the grass in your dream, and what color is it? Depending on the answer here, you may discover a yearning for, or jealousy of, another's perceived success, thinking that the "grass is greener on the other side." In this case, the dream reminds us that what's "*green*" and what's not is purely a matter of personal perspective.

•GRAVE

(see Bones, Cemetery, Death, Tomb)

• GRAY

(see Colors)

Old age and the sagacity that comes with long life (note the gray *hair* on elderly people).

Finding yourself in between stages, or having qualms and misgivings (e.g., "gray areas").

The subconscious or the substance of the mind itself (e.g., "gray matter").

The cabalistic color of wisdom.

• GREEN

(see Color)

Growth, health, and rejuvenation, as the color most strongly associated with the *season* of spring. Take care, however, that growth is always tempered with conscientious pruning to yield more *fruit*.

A need to emphasize, or reconnect with, the natural world regularly in your life.

A manifestation of jealousy or spite (e.g., the "green-eyed *monster*").

Feeling that it is the right time to move ahead with your plans (e.g., "getting a green *light*").

Moldy, rotting green represents the things you've neglected in your life.

If a light green color is dreamt of in a *stone*, this symbolizes having strong faith and godly devotion.

• GROOM

(see Bride, Engagement, Men, Wedding)

For a man soon to marry, or his partner, a situational dream that needs no further interpretation.

In earlier times, it was the groom's responsibility to protect his lady. On the dream plane, this may equate to a guardian of some type who watches over you (see *Angel, Ghost*).

• GROVE

(see Field, Forest, Trees)

• GUIDE/GURU

(see Angel, Ascetic, Authority Figures, Icon)

• GYPSY

(see Divination, Storyteller, Travel)

Latent psychic abilities or unexplored occult interests (we often equate Gypsies with fortune-telling with *cards*, *crystal* balls, and palmistry).

Having a free spirit, adventurous heart, and a slight disdain for definite rules (e.g., having "gypsy blood").

Matters of sensuality or sexuality may be worked out through the image of a Gypsy, who is stereotyped as being more liberal in such matters.

Possibly a false guide or teacher who gives misleading information to gain adoration or money.

• HAIR

(see Body)

Personal strength (as with Samson).

Long hair: Equates to the wisdom and sagacity that comes through a long, well-lived life, especially if the color is *gray*. Alternatively, prosperity. In Asia, long hair was so valuable that it was used as currency.

Cutting: Drastic life changes. Many religious orders mark initiation rites through the cutting of hair, notably of monks and nuns (see *Religions*).

Power: In Tantric Oriental traditions, undoing the hair was a way to access the forces of creation and destruction. Also, in European folklore it was believed that a witch could increase the power of her spell by letting down her hair during its casting (see *Incantation*).

Consider the texture and style for further symbolic clues. For example, hair brought up in a very tight bun reveals someone who is prim, sometimes to the point of restrictiveness. Disheveled hair, on the other hand, exposes confusion and a flurry of activity. Dyed hair reveals someone concealing true thoughts, and greasy hair suggests a person with a "slick" disposition.

Baldness: Too much thought, or possibly a visual metaphor for "pulling your hair out."

Being cut by a barber: Attention to details, and being meticulous in your efforts especially with regard to personal appearances.

Wigs: A false line of reasoning.

• HALL

(see Alley, Highway, Path)

• HALLUCINATION

(see Dreaming)

To dream of someone, or yourself, hallucinating indicates some misconception or misperception of reality. Whatever situations exist right now, everything is very unclear and uncertain, and caution is called for.

• HAMMER

(see Nails, Tools)

Stamina and courage during times of conflict. In Teutonic tradition, this was an emblem of Thor, the god of war and thunder, whom warriors called upon for strength.

Building or repairing something, often the self or a relationship (see *Nails*).

Tempering a situation through diligence, as a smith carefully tempers *metal* (see *Forge*).

Making, or wishing to make, an ardent point (e.g., "hammering it home").

The desire for security; knowing that everything you have built is going to hold together.

• HAND

(see Body, Fingers, Gloves)

Healing (e.g., the "laying on of hands"). In many cultures, hands are a predominant tool as a healer's conduit for divine energy.

A token of friendship, especially if extended toward you.

Good intentions. In some tribal societies, people greeted each other with upheld hands to indicate the lack of *weapons* and a mutual wish for peaceful discourse.

Help or service (e.g., "many hands make light work" or "lend a helping hand").

Surrender. Two hands held high in the air indicate giving yourself over to some *authority figure* or letter of the law.

Tied: A situation over which you have no direct influence or control (see *Knots, Ties/Tying*).

Clenched hands reveal a lot of tension and anxiety present in the dreamer.

Upturned hands are a sign that some comprehension is lacking. Alternatively, you are constantly asking for help, like a beggar, but not necessarily helping yourself.

Missing: To dream of not having any hands means that you probably feel helpless or ineffective in your current situation. You need to find an alternative tool or approach that's productive.

The palm of the hand represents life's road map—the directions one has taken or is soon to take (note that the divinatory art of palmistry is based on the secrets that lie literally in the palm of your hand).

Callused or chapped hands equate to hard work that has questionable rewards.

• HARE
(see Animals, Rabbit)

• HAT
(see Clothes)

Antiquated methods or approaches (e.g., something is "old hat").

Involvement or interest (e.g., "tossing your hat into the ring").

The mind: Keeping ideas "under one's hat."

Top hat: A refined, classy approach to a situation.

Jester's hat: Clowning around. Possibly using humor as a communication tool, or to cover up insecurity.

Changing hats: Transitions or additional responsibilities especially in a work-related situation (e.g., "wearing many hats").

• HAWK
(see Birds, Feathers, Wings)

Having keen eyesight, or the ability to quickly recognize, and react to, opportunity (e.g., being "hawk-eyed").

Hawks are very able hunters, so the question is, what do you seek?

Maneuverability; rising above problems. Hawks are also very powerful fliers.

The red-tailed hawk specifically represents *healing* in Native American traditions, and the spirit of life-giving *water*. Should one appear in your dreams, it signals the end of weariness or sickness, and renewed hope.

• HAWTHORN
(see Field, Forest, Trees)

If the hawthorn appears in bloom, this represents happiness.

In Europe this tree has somewhat divergent meanings, being both chastity and fertility. For the purpose of dream interpretation, this might mean maintaining your devotion to someone or something for a productive outcome.

Along with the *oak* and *ash*, this is a sacred *fairy* tree, and may represent a subconscious connection to Devic realms and messages.

•HAZEL

(see Field, Forest, Nuts, Trees)

Victorian: Assured devotion. Hazelnuts were predominately used for love divination to determine if one's mate was true.

Among the Celts, the nut of this tree represented wisdom, being something sweet that is buried beneath a sturdy *obstacle*.

Psychic abilities, specifically object location. Hazel branches were favored for *water* witching and *treasure* finding (see *Rods, Wand*).

•HEALING

(see Salve)

Historically, receiving such a dream on *holy ground* was believed to foretell recuperation from whatever sickness was depicted (see *Church, Monastery, Temple*).

A pressing need for physical attention. Take note of what type of healer is pictured here to better discern where to seek aid.

The person or *animal* receiving healing in a dream can represent a situation, relationship, or condition of the soul or mind that needs gentle care.

•HEARTH

(see Baking, Cauldron, Fire, Foods by type, Forge)

Focus on, or the condition of, home and family. Traditionally, the hearth was the heart of a *house* in Europe, where all important family activities took place. How does the hearth appear? An evenly burning hearth with good coals indicates consistent love and tending. One that is artificial or bricked up reveals pretense or blocked emotions, respectively.

An alternative type of womb emblem, in which the masculine element (*fire*) burns.

Fertility, kinship, and love. Old folk spells regularly recommended *ashes* from the hearth fire as a component for these purposes.

Depending on its configuration, this may be an alternative *altar* dream, in which the food becomes a kind of *sacrifice*. In the Orient, especially, there are gods and goddesses who preside over, and are honored in, the kitchen.

• HELL

(see Evil, Fire, Monsters)

An alternative type of *cage* or *judgment* dream.

Reexamining or finally recognizing faults and failures, to the point of feeling guilty.

Negativity or bitterness growing within that can destroy your sense of harmony or wholeness. You need to get these fires under control.

A situation or relationship that you regard as hellish to endure.

• HEMATITE

(see Crystals, Gems, Jewelry, Stones)

• HERALDRY

(see Signage, Pictographs)

In the Middle Ages, a person's coat of arms revealed a great deal, including family lineage, trades, and characteristics. These often appeared on *armor* so that honors won in battle could be properly attributed (and so you didn't accidentally kill an ally). For your dream, consider first what appears on heraldry for more clues. Each item and *color* symbolizes aspects of you, your relationships with others, your profession, and how all these facets of your life intermingle. Additionally, having an item like this show up in your dream may represent an unfulfilled need to set yourself apart somehow, and make your mark.

• HERBS

(see by type, Field, Flowers, Gardens)

The smell of a plant, and the feelings or memories it engenders, may be more important here than the herb itself (see *Perfume*).

Because of their long association with folk medicine, herbs in your dream may reveal matters of personal health, or concerns about same.

If a kitchen spice, this may be a figurative symbol for needing to spice things up in your life or home.

• HERMAPHRODITE

Balanced sexuality; comfort with both sides of the soul (see *Men, Women*).

An attempt to eliminate real or perceived gender-specific limitations.

Hiding your true sensual or sexual nature behind an ambivalent *mask*.

• HERO/HEROINE

(see Fables, Icons, Men, Women)

• HICCUPS

Being in a bumpy situation, or a circumstance that gets disrupted with petty annoyances.

Minor technical troubles that seem to keep popping up.

Interrupted communications that will eventually abate.

• HIGHWAYS (ROADS)

(see Bus, Car, Path)

Highways carry you toward, or away from, someone or something. Other parts of the dream are important to meaning here, such as *billboards, buildings*, and people or vehicles that are traveling on the same highway.

Being lost on the highway: Needing to make a decision, but not having a clear picture of what all the options offer. Alternatively, feeling as if you have lost your faith or spiritual focus.

Stranded on a highway: A type of *desertion* dream. Also, a need within to reach out and ask for aid, otherwise the vehicle of your life may remain stalled.

Hitchhiking down: Wanderlust; the desire to release all responsibilities and experience some adventure. Alternatively, riding on someone else's talents, abilities, or finances, instead of being independent.

Fork in the road: A determination that must be made fairly quickly or the opportunity may be lost. Two vehicles taking separate parts of this fork represent individuals or situations moving away from one another.

• HILLS

(see Mountains)

• HOLE

(see Abyss, Cliff, Underground)

Freudian: A vaginal emblem.

Jungian: The subconscious, or an opening to this realm.

Aspects of the self that you've hidden or fear.

Manholes represent pitfalls and traps that can be plunged into, often without noticing the danger beforehand.

Falling into a hole symbolizes a hazard that was either unforeseen or underestimated. This can also be a descent into the subconscious, or a deepening depression.

• HOLIDAYS

(see Calendar)

Each holiday has a unique ambience that depends on your family's culture and *religion*. Consequently, any holiday celebration that appears in your dream must be considered with that background in mind. For example, Christians celebrate Easter as the resurrection of Christ, and might therefore interpret this holiday in a dream as significant to personal restoration. To a modern pagan, however, this date honors the spring, fertility, and earth's renewal, the implied symbolism being productivity, hope, or healthful rejuvenation.

Consider the name of the holiday in a metaphorical context. For example, dreaming of April Fool's might reflect feelings of foolishness that stem from ill-considered actions, words, or pranks.

The need to honor and remember one's family traditions.

A memory from previous holidays that somehow reflects, or affects, current situations.

• HOLLY

(see Herbs, Trees)

Heroism. In the Druidical alphabet, this bush is represented by the tau *cross*, often equated with the Tree God, whose strength and endurance stands for all to see.

The *red berries* of this bush are an alternative *blood* emblem.

Long lasting results or impressions from your efforts. Ancient people associated this plant with longevity, immortality, and the immutable soul due to its ability to stay *green* through the winter.

If seen as planted around a home, this represents safety to all who dwell within.

The well-being of a newborn child. This plant got its name from the Teutonic goddess Holle, whose dominion is protecting *babies*.

• HOLY GROUND

(see Church, Cemetery, Monastery, Sanctuary, Temple)

Something inviolable, which you will honor at all costs.

Respect for higher powers, both human and divine.

A place or situation within which you feel completely safe and unafraid.

Retreating a safe distance from a person or situation perceived as risky.

• HOMOSEXUALITY

A fear, misunderstanding, or disapproval toward this lifestyle.

Latent tendencies expressing themselves.

An intimate exploration of the masculine or feminine nature, depending on which gender is seen in the dream (see *Men, Women*).

The need to focus on your own gender for a while to achieve greater understanding, "brotherhood" or "sisterhood," and empowerment from same.

• HONEY

(see Bees, Bread, Eating)

Fertility and productivity. In Egypt, honey was offered to Min, the goddess of productivity and abundance, to help people conceive children. Note, however, that fertility can apply to any project in which you're currently engaged.

Youthful outlooks and energy. The ancient Greeks ate honey believing it would extend life.

Creative inspiration. In Rome, this was an emblem of poetry and eloquence, especially with words. For a writer or speaker, this is an excellent omen.

Honey also has strong associations with the *sun*, having mythologically been formed by the tears of the Egyptian sun god Ra, and therefore represents strength and authority.

Love, romance, and commitment. The term honeymoon comes from the Teutonic tradition of celebrating *marriage* with a month of mead drinking; mead is a wine made with a base of honey.

• HORN

Sounding: A type of announcement or *judgment* dream. Note that the angels of heaven often presaged major matters with horns, as did court musicians (see *Music*).

Animal horn: A masculine symbol, usually denoting the penis. Note the sexual energy associated with the bull, ram, stag, and goat gods of ancient times.

Drinking horns: A type of *chalice* dream in which the masculine nature, or other qualities, as represented by the *beverage* in the horn are internalized.

Fertility or abundance, as with the legendary cornucopia.

Lust, especially if you sprout the horns yourself.

• HORNET

(see Bee)

•HORSE

(see Animals, Farm)

In earlier times, horses equated to movement and transition much as modern vehicles (see *Airplane, Bus, Car, Spaceship*) do now.

Burdens that come from labors. Horses were often work animals on farms, and were highly valued. In what condition does the horse appear? If run-down and abused, this represents feeling unappreciated no matter how much you do. On the other hand, if the horse is well fed and groomed, it symbolizes a kind "task master" who really values your efforts.

Ancient Greeks revered the horse as a sacred creature to Artemis, the goddess of the *moon* and *forests*. Consequently, this may also be an alternative *earth* or *tree* dream.

Spiritual sojourns. Mohammed rode a horse on his mystical journey from Mecca to Jerusalem and then on to heaven.

Galloping: Ecstasy, ambition, and the emotional self. Conversely, a tethered horse reveals one of these things being restrained.

A stallion: Male virility.

Look to see who's got the reins in this dream—the creature or its rider. If the creature, it's time to reclaim your control!

Finding a horseshoe: A nearly universal emblem of good luck.

White horse: In German and English traditions, this is a harbinger of *death*.

If the horse is happily cavorting, this may be a visual pun for horseplay. Take care that no one accidentally gets hurt by your current jovial outlook.

Psychic powers emerging. Folklorically, horses are said to sense or see spirits and have foreknowledge, similar to *dogs*.

Seahorses represent being transported into the *waters* of intuition or the subconscious with significant insight resulting.

Winged horses symbolize fame, eloquence, poetry, and the muse. Let your imagination fly on its *wings*.

•HOTEL

(see *Buildings*)

•HOURGLASS

(see *Clock*)

Time management. Is time slipping quickly away from you, or are you seizing the day? Alternatively, consider if you're pacing yourself well.

The sands of time in a more universal context express the nearness of beginnings and endings. For this dream, how much sand is left in the timer is important to interpretational value.

•HOUSE

(see *Apartments, Buildings, Castle*)

•HUMMINGBIRD

(see *Birds, Feathers, Wings*)

The energy of pure joy to keep you aloft the *flower* of the world, extracting the nectar of life wherever you go.

This is the only bird in nature that can fly backwards. As such, consider what part of the past you're retrieving for productive review.

Love. In folk *magic*, hummingbird feathers were a common component in love charms. Just take care that this is not forced or manipulated. Such a *relationship* will not last.

Among the Native Americans and Basque people, this represents total honesty. They believe that hummingbirds cannot tell a lie.

Reveling in freedom and playfulness. Scientists have shown that these birds seem to enjoy both tremendously. How much free time or play time have you had lately?

•HUNGER

(see Candy, Dieting, Eating, Fasting, Foods by type)

A situational or circumstantial dream resulting from going to bed hungry or having an unsatisfied craving.

A symbolic manifestation of desires for things like achievement, adventure, passion, etc.

Essential portions of the self that are being neglected, and therefore metaphorically hunger for your attention.

•HUNTING

(see Animals, Weapons)

A desire for conquest. For what are you currently hunting, and is it truly something over which you should try to take dominion?

Is the creature used as food, or is it being hunted in sport? If for food, this may be a type of *hunger* dream, or representative of your need for fulfillment. If being hunted in sport, the *animal* may symbolize a coveted object or person that remains elusive.

• ICE

(see Snow)

A potentially hazardous situation. Watch your footing.

The cooling of emotions or a *relationship*. Frigidity.

Halted movement, feeling frozen and unable to act.

Being frozen in ice: A type of *death* or *cage* dream.

An icicle: The masculine nature.

Making an ice carving: Chipping away at the walls that disguise the true self. Alternatively, a subliminal wish that the object portrayed (or its symbolic meaning) would either manifest or halt completely.

Hail: This ice falls from the sky and barrages the dreamer's landscape, symbolizing a torrent of personal, social, political, or religious dogma that seems to overshadow simple, straightforward faith.

• ICONS

(see Ascetic, Authority Figures, Parents, Religions)

A god or goddess: Each varies here by the specific visage seen, but ecumenically any such appearance indicates a higher consciousness, morality, and the divine spark within each of us.

Christ: An image of healing, forgiveness, protection, and renewal. If crucified, an emblem of martyrdom, or giving too much of yourself (see *Cross, Sacrifice*).

Buddha: Introspection. The path of positive speech and acting in accord.

Gandhi: Empowerment that comes from knowing your own mind. A just cause fought for without violence. Peaceful negotiations.

A guru: Looking for, and dependence upon, spiritual insights from other people. Remember that your own heart is the best guru to guide your life.

Mother Teresa: The highly underestimated power of gentility, kindness, and compassion.

Moses: Redemption that first requires the trying of your beliefs.

A wizard: Mastery over the elements, and the ability to foresee the consequences of actions. Alternatively, a stage magician represents trickery and illusion meant to fool people.

King Arthur: Wise and peaceful leadership. Having a real understanding of equity.

Merlin: A tutorial image from your Higher Self who helps you see things differently, from a more metaphysical perspective.

Kings and queens: People, situations, or ideals in your life that have some authority over you. The questions to ponder here are how much control do they have and how healthy is it for you? Look at other elements in the dream to determine this. Alternatively, these may be reflections of your own Higher Self, and self-rulership.

Mary: An alternative image of the primordial goddess, who through obedience and faith gave *birth* to the Messiah.

•IMMOBILITY

(see Lameness, Paralyzation)

•INCANTATIONS/INVOCATIONS

A type of *magic* that employs spoken words to express and manifest personal will, or words to encourage divine assistance, like a prayer. In a dream, this can reflect your desire to reconnect with metaphysical energies, or your own Higher Nature, and take greater control over your fate.

•INCENSE

(see Fire, Perfume, Smells, Smoke)

Because of its nearly universal use in ancient *temples*, incense has strong correlations with life's rituals and conventions, especially of a religious nature. If you have recently reached a special crossroad in your life (like *engagement*, *pregnancy*, or retirement), consider honoring and better integrating this new experience through a ceremony shared with family and friends.

Religiously symbolic of the sweet prayers of the faithful rising to the gods. How long has it been since you reconnected with those sacred powers?

Overwhelmingly potent incense represents unnecessary trappings and embellishments to your faith. This dream acts as a counsel to get back to the core of your beliefs, instead of focusing on the externals. No amount of dressing can hide your heart and motivations from the Divine.

•INDIGESTION

The inability to internalize or accept what's been presented to you, at least in its present form. What causes the digestive trouble here will provide more meaning.

A line of reasoning that you just can't swallow (see *Eating*).

A situation, person, or belief system that causes a negative reaction within, once you've taken your first taste.

•INITIALS

(see Abbreviations, Names)

•INK

The power of words (e.g., "the pen is mightier than the sword").

Permanency of a decision (e.g., "putting it in writing").

Communication.

Red ink symbolizes harsh, critical language, like that delivered by a "poison-pen press."

Inking something out represents corrections, alterations, and revisions of a permanent nature (see *Eraser*).

•INSECTS

(see by specific Insect, Wings)

If a single creature, this may be a communication from your inner self. *Bees* were considered divine messengers by several ancient civilizations.

Revulsion: Sickness, decay, corruption, or filth. What the insects are flying around should provide more insight as to the source of these feelings.

If you are an insect with wings, possibly a type of *flying* dream.

Feeling as small and insignificant as an insect.

Petty annoyances. Usually manifested in the dream as buzzing or flying insects from which you cannot rid yourself.

• IRON

(see Clothes, Fabric)

Working out a difficult situation by diligently applying a little pressure.

If the iron appears at a dry cleaners, this indicates that you're hoping for someone else to straighten things out. The advice here is not to pass the buck on a problem that is best handled yourself.

An unattended iron symbolizes a potential hazard resulting from misapplied energy, often of an emotionally heated nature. Take care right now that you're paying attention to those who care about you, and their feelings. If something's amiss, iron it out!

• IRON ORE

(see Metals)

Since *meteorites* often supply one of the few sources of pure iron, this is sometimes called the *sky* stone and can herald a reconnection with more "cosmic" awareness.

Everyday life, and how effectively you use the simple *tools* you have available. In ancient times, iron was rarely used magically or religiously. People believed the metal would hinder metaphysical energy. Instead, iron became a favored metal in hand tools.

Because of its metaphysical neutrality, iron did find its way into amulets and talismans to protect people against *fairies*, *jinni*, *ghosts*, and *dragons* (China). Consequently, dreaming of it may portend a visitation from or the need to safeguard oneself from the Devic realms.

Roman: Strength and health. Athletes carried iron for endurance, and if worn as a ring or bracelet, they believed it could draw out maladies (see *Jewelry*).

Have you been daydreaming a lot, or are your goals too lofty? Iron reminds us to keep at least one *foot* in reality.

• ISLAND

(see Desertion)

Isolation and solitude, sometimes by choice. In these moments remember that even Moses had to spend time alone to find his destiny (see *Desert*).

Being shipwrecked by, or stranded in, life's storms, without emotional support (see *Boat*, *Water*).

An archetypal Paradise or Eden where one strives for wholeness. In the myths of the Russians, Norse, Danes, and Hindus, islands are places filled with magical creatures and idyllic peace (see *Garden*).

Unshakable resolve and strength (e.g., being the "island in the *storm*").

• IVY

Ivy *leaves* on or near your head reflect being overly intoxicated by an idea or dream without any firm foundations upon which to build.

Ivy is an emblem of striving for notoriety and honor, such as the "ivy leagues."

Among Druids and the ancient Greeks, this symbolized blessings for a union, specifically used during *weddings*.

The evergreen nature of ivy implies that your efforts will be long lasting.

•JADE

(see Crystals, Gems, Jewelry, Stones)

Your station in life. In China, jade was used to indicate a person's rank.

Love and commitment. The Chinese also felt jade was the perfect stone for lovers, ensuring their happiness (see *Butterfly*).

Among the Hopi Indians and Africans, Jade was fashioned into musical instruments, and as such becomes an emblem for harmony and creative use of what's available.

Jade worn or carried in the dream represents increased mental faculties that also result in good business sense. If you've been pondering a new venture, now's the time to act.

•JAIL

(see Cage, Dead End)

•JAM/ JELLY

(see Eating)

A play on words indicating that you feel like you've gotten yourself into a "jam."

Lacking form in your thoughts, or concrete convictions.

If being spread on *bread*, the need to apply a little sweetness to a situation or *relationship*.

Eating jellied bread in a dream foretells of pleasant interruptions.

•JAR

(see Bottle, Canning)

•JESTER

The original clown, the jester represents the important things that get overlooked or ignored while absorbed in silliness.

Speaking or acting in "jest," but not necessarily having people interpret this correctly.

In the Middle Ages, jesters relieved people from their worries for a while, and often kept royalty happy so that less severe judgments got handed out. In a modern setting, this reflects taking much needed time to relax and enjoy life, and stop being such a difficult task master to yourself.

•JET

(see Crystals, Stones, Gems)

•JEWELRY

(see Clothing, Crown, Gems, Metals, Stones, Rings)

Meaning may sometimes be determined by where the jewelry is worn. For instance, necklaces lie near the throat, the center of communication. So, if a necklace felt very tight in the dream, this may indicate swallowing your words, or having communication strangled (see *Choking*).

Overly large or small pieces: Exaggerated senses. For example, big earrings might reveal a propensity for eavesdropping, while tiny ones indicate underdeveloped listening skills (see *Ears*).

The finer things in life; luxuries.

Wearing excessive jewelry in a dream indicates that the individual envisioned tries to impress others with wealth or possessions.

Jewelry that is not worn, but seen as a central image in a dream, should be reviewed for its component parts, like noting the significance of *gems* or *metals* used in its construction. Or, if a specific image appears as the jewelry's focal point, that can also have meaning. For example, seeing an Egyptian ankh could represent renewed health or improved courage, whereas a pin depicting the zodiac sign Pisces might reflect a personal focus on productivity.

In the 2nd century C.E., Artemidorus wrote that women dreaming of fine jewelry would soon marry, have children, or increase their wealth.

•JINNI

(see Bottle, Fables)

The manifestation of wishes on the dream plane through a mythical figure.

The tendency to want (or expect) instant gratification in certain situations without really working for that goal.

Heeding universal law. Despite the jinni's power in ancient tales, they had specific restrictions with regard to life and love. So, if the jinni does not grant your wish in the dream, it may be time for some soul searching about your motivations.

Restricted power. Even the jinns answered to a greater authority—they each had a master. Know your own limits and observe them wisely.

In a bottle: Feeling *caged* or "bottled up" and limited by some authority over which you have no control. Alternatively, a power or talent within yourself that you have hesitated to release.

•JOBS

(see Professions, Workers)

Concerns over your current work situation (or lack thereof), sometimes also related to how others perceive your performance on the job.

Unemployment: Seeing yourself unemployed in a dream has several potential interpretations. You may feel as if your professional skill or performance is somehow lacking. If so, find productive ways to improve your confidence, like getting extra training. This can also be a type of *money* or *poverty* dream, as jobs and financial security are so closely related. Or perhaps something is happening that makes you feel uncertain about the future of your career. If so, try to find the source of that apprehension.

Seeing yourself working can reveal that you are striving toward self-improvement. Look to see on what exactly you are working for more symbolism.

•JOKES

(see Clown, Laughter, Jester)

As is often the case in waking reality, jokes often cover up something far more pertinent in your dreams. They are also a way of calling attention to things that you might otherwise overlook. Consider the subject of the joke, and the peripherals in the dream, for more insight.

•JOURNEY

(see Travel)

Esoterically, the development of the soul through a spiritual sojourn.

Transitions in life, from one phase into another.

Situational dream caused directly by pondered or forthcoming travel plans.

A renewed focus on life's lessons. In the East, the importance of a journey is not determined by the path taken, or the destination, but by what you learn along the way.

Seafaring voyages represent diving into the subconscious or reconnecting with your Higher Self (see *Boat*).

Mountain journeys symbolize concentrating on the mind and intellect (see *Climbing*).

Also consider your mode of travel in these dreams for more insight. For example, a journey by *train* affords time to take in the scenery, thereby also allowing you to take in what's happening along the way.

• JUDGMENT

(see Acquittal, Authority Figures, Police, Warrants)

Feelings of guilt playing themselves out before the judge and jury of your Higher Self.

Examining the facts of a particularly perplexing problem in an alternative format in which you remain impartial.

Judges represent the law, in all senses of the term. This includes those guidelines imposed by family, culture, *religion*, and personal experience.

Juries symbolize impartiality and the chance for a more balanced opinion.

Obtaining bail is indicative of a temporary reprieve; not having to face the consequences of your words or actions immediately, or being given more time to assemble the facts that prove your innocence in a matter.

Judging yourself using the conscience as a guide for personal development and eventual wholeness.

• JUGGLING

Having too many responsibilities and too little time, or so many options from which to choose that you become indecisive.

What is the juggler juggling? *Knives*, for example, may indicate the need for extreme care and caution to avoid being hurt in your current situation. Juggling hearts could represent being torn between two or more lovers.

An extreme focus in your life on precision and timing. This focus may act as a coping mechanism during particularly trying times so that tasks get accomplished effectively (see *Acrobatics*).

•JUICE

(see Beverages by type, Fruit)

Vitality and health.

The life force, especially if the juice is *red*. Energy that is flowing within you. Consider the *fruit* from which this juice comes for more symbolic meaning.

The proverbial "nectar of life" which, once internalized, supports joy, well-being, and the path to wholeness.

•JUMPING

Joyfulness and glee.

Successfully overcoming an *obstacle* (see *Acrobatics*).

Nervousness and anxiety (e.g., "being jumpy").

Leaps of faith.

Avoidance or hasty movement ("jumping bail" or "jumping on the bandwagon").

A visual representation of life's ups and downs, some of which you may presently be experiencing.

•JUNGLE

(see Creatures by type, Forest, Trees)

The chaotic world (e.g., "it's a jungle out there").

The wild, untamed *animal* nature within each of us that desires a place where it can run freely.

Filled with vines: Entangled situations in which almost every movement makes things worse.

Hidden hazards despite overwhelming appeal.

The heat and humidity of the jungle can metaphorically relate to feeling pressured or nervous (e.g., having "sweaty palms").

• KEY

(see Locks)

Solutions to problems, especially ones that seem puzzling (e.g., "the key to the matter").

Opportunity unfolding.

Lost keys: Losing your way, or feeling unable to find the right resolution to a situation.

Using the wrong key in a dream signifies approaching a problem in the wrong way, with a solution that doesn't really fit the situation.

Breaking a key means that a good idea got bungled somehow, probably by someone becoming too enthusiastic or pushy. If this is the case, just start again with a calmer, paced approach.

• KINGS

(see Authority Figures, Fables, Icons, Men)

• KISS

(see Bride, Engagement, Relationships, Wedding)

Bodily fluids have long been considered very magical, including saliva. Consequently, kisses appear in a diversity of fairy tales and myths. For example, Snow White receives a kiss of resurrection and love. In Christian tradition, there is the kiss of peace. Today, bad behavior or ill-conceived actions are called the "kiss of death" for in-progress proposals or projects. How to interpret the kiss in your dream, therefore, will depend much upon the setting in which it's received, and from whom.

• KITCHEN

(see Baking, Eating, Fire, Foods by type, Hearth)

• KITE

(see Air, Wind)

A kite that cannot get off the ground represents a project that seems doomed to stagnate or fail. Wait for a better wind and try again.

A kite soaring high in the *sky* reflects ambitions and lofty goals. Take care, however. From this height the wind can easily snag the kite out of your hands, and all control may be lost.

A kite that is flying firmly controlled from the ground symbolizes goals that have good foundations. With continued management, this effort should prove successful.

•KNEE

(see Body)

Flexibility. Learn to bend so that you don't break.

Kneeling represents humility or subjugation, usually with religious overtones.

A fast response that wasn't necessarily well considered (e.g., a "knee-jerk reaction").

•KNIFE (SCISSORS)

Alternative phallic symbol, with its sheath being feminine, similar to a *sword*.

Cutting something out, or away, as one cuts the proverbial *apron* strings to discover independence.

Brutally harsh words that carry a sharp edge upon delivery.

Placed openly on a table: Peaceful intentions. This was a common practice in the Middle Ages, akin to how we shake *hands* today.

Pointed toward you: Enmity or threats coming from others, directed specifically at you.

•KNOTS

(see Connecting Devices, Rope, Ties)

Feeling bound or obligated to something or someone.

Security in relationships (e.g., "tying the knot").

Nervousness (e.g., a stomach "tied in knots").

Being tied up with: A type of bondage fantasy or *cage* dream.

Problems and delays that have to be untangled (see *Red: Red tape*).

Slip knot: Something that's transitory and offers little security. Alternatively, wrangling your way out of a tight situation, akin to slipping out the back *door*.

The return of health. In ancient times, knot *magic* was used as a kind of folk *medicine* wherein a person's ailment was bound in a knot, then tossed away.

Being untied: Restrictions and tensions easing. Liberty.

•LABOR

(see Baby, Birth, Miscarriage)

For a woman nearing the end of a *pregnancy*, or her partner, this is a situational dream that needs no further interpretation.

Figuratively laboring over a project or relationship in the hopes of bringing it to fruition.

If a breach birth, ask yourself if you might not be approaching things from the wrong direction, making the obtainment of your goal all the harder.

Induced labor represents feeling like you're being forced into starting something too soon, for which you may not be totally prepared.

•LADDER

(see Ascent, Climbing, Mountain, Stairs)

Mystically, the ascent to a higher spiritual plane. In ancient Egypt, the ladders of Set had *angels* on each side that helped the Pharaohs reach heaven.

Communing with spiritual powers (note Jacob's ladder in the Old Testament).

The quest for, or achievement of, enlightenment in Asia and China.

Going downward on: Deep introspection and internalization.

Getting dizzy on the *ascent* upward represents intoxicating ambitions that may lead to a hard fall.

•LAKE

(see Water)

•LAMENESS

A fear of being hampered physically (see *Crutch, Paralyzation*).

A subconscious concern that you are ineffectual in your present circumstance.

The dread of impotency.

Having an obstacle that slows your progression with a person or situation.

• LAMP

(see Candle, Light, Torch)

• LANDMARKS

A memory resurfacing of a place or *location* that you visited before. Ask yourself if there was something about that region or experience that pertains to your present situation.

If you have never traveled to this place before, consider its name, location, and the landmark itself for more interpretive value. For example, seeing "Old Faithful" might speak of your own timeliness or dedication (see *Water*).

Possibly the manifestation of a memory from a past life experience. Even so, there is something important about this experience that directly relates to your circumstances now.

Monuments appearing at the landmark show your loyalties to someone, something, or a situation. Such loyalties can be good or bad influences, so check the condition of the monument for further insight here.

• LANDSLIDE

(see Disasters, Earth)

• LANGUAGES

The origin of the language, if known, may have import here. For example, if your family originated in Italy and you dream in Italian, this may be a subconscious desire to learn more about your heritage.

The letters in some languages, like the Norse and Germanic runes and certain Hebraic characters, have very specific symbolic values. For more insight, peruse a book on the appropriate language at your local library, or ask someone who is familiar with the tongue (see *Pictographs*).

If the language is unrecognized, write it phonetically in your journal for future reference. This may be a past life memory, a spiritual message, or a type of glossolalia (speaking in tongues) that can be interpreted later.

Communication difficulties (e.g., someone who is not "speaking your language").

• LAPIS

(see Crystals, Gems, Jewelry, Stones)

Divine favor, and the God-self within. Kings and queens regularly wore lapis to encourage blessings and as a mark of divine right.

Asserting your independence. In Sumer and other parts of the ancient world, lapis was used as a signature stone not unlike *heraldic* emblems were later, or our modern seals.

The *color* of lapis makes it a symbol of the psychic nature, peace, and uplifting emotions.

If worn by lovers in a dream, this portends devotion and fidelity.

• LAUGHTER

(see Clown, Jester, Jokes)

What type of laughter is it? Joyous laughter reflects happy occasions in your life. Mocking laughter, on the other hand, may be that which you perceive as coming from others, or from within yourself.

Figuratively, the best medicine to lift melancholy and aid motivation. If one can remember to laugh with life, almost everything becomes easier.

• LAVA

(see Disasters, Fire)

As the child of a volcano, this stone represents creative eruptions of some type. This is a flash of insight, bridging artistic *obstacles*, and resulting in true genius.

Hawaii: Health and well-being, especially if someone is seen in a circle of lava stones. More drastic *healing* and cleansing is symbolized by being within hot, flowing lava.

Reciprocity with nature. Hawaiian lore claims that the goddess Pele does not allow anyone to take lava stones without leaving a small offering first that acknowledges the gift of the *earth*.

Flowing lava becomes a *river* of *fire*, indicating a similarly fiery course for your life right now. However, lava does cool eventually, as will circumstances. With the settling, new foundations will develop.

•LAVENDER

(see Flowers, Garden, Herbs)

Love and passion. During the Middle Ages, this was commonly used as an aphrodisiac or addition to love potions. Sprigs were also worn by prostitutes to attract business.

Today people use lavender to protect their clothes from moth infestation. What is it that you need to take out of storage and safeguard before it is destroyed?

Cleansing of some type. In Latin, the word for lavender means "to wash," and Greeks and Romans favored lavender in the bath houses.

Improved moods. In aromatherapy, the scent of lavender is applied to ease melancholy.

•LEAD

(see Metals)

•LEAVES

(see Field, Forest, Plants by type, Trees)

Raking: Cleaning away something that's old, but not necessarily without a use. Note that old leaves nourish the land, just as your past makes you who you are today.

Budding on a tree: A fresh beginning (see *Fruits, Flowers, Gardens*).

Rustling: An omen or portent from the Universe to which you should listen closely. The ancient Greeks used the sound of rustling leaves from the sacred *oak* tree in Dodona as an oracular method.

•LEMON

(see Fruit, Juice, Trees)

Eating a lemon or drinking lemonade may reflect the need for cleansing and purification of your body. Lemon has a natural purgative quality.

Adoration, commitment, fidelity, and romance. In the Middle Ages, lemons were a common component in love potions.

If a woman dreams of lemons, it portends good luck in *relationships*.

A sour attitude.

Clever uses of adversity (e.g., "when life hands you lemons, make lemonade").

• LEPRECHAUN
(see Fairy)

• LETTUCE
(see Eating, Garden, Vegetables)

The white juice of this vegetable is equated with mother's milk or semen, thereby symbolizing fertility or productivity.

Among the Greeks, lettuce was used to reflect the fragile nature of life, parts of which can be lost or taken away. On the dream plane, this may equate to losing your pep.

Astrologically, this is a lunar food, and as such may be an alternative *moon* emblem.

The *green* color of lettuce and its consistency give it some correlations with *money*. For example, if something is nibbling up all the lettuce in your dream, perhaps you feel that someone or something is likewise eating up your cash on the material plane.

If the lettuce is being eaten in the dream, this reveals a decrease in sexual appetite.

• LICENSE (PERMITS)

Rights and privileges; things that we can and cannot do legally or morally. So, the questions here pertain to what type of license is pictured, and what's happening with the license in the dream. Is it being granted, taken away, torn up?

If you have a driving test or have to attend driving school soon, this is likely a circumstantial dream that requires no further interpretation (see *Car*).

• LIGHT
(see Candle, Fire, Torch)

Consciousness. The active, aware mind.

Enlightenment of a mental or spiritual nature.

Hope (e.g., "light at the end of the tunnel").

A spiritual presence (see *Angel, Ghost, Icons*).

An extension of personal auric energy, viewed from the dream perspective.

•LIGHTHOUSE

If you're about to take a sea voyage, this may indicate some hesitation on your part, especially a fear of trouble at sea or a fear of drowning (see *Boat, Water*). Alternatively, this may portend a safe vacation.

If you have been in distress, this dream shows that hope is on the horizon, and recovery will come.

A guiding energy, akin to an *angel* (see *Light*).

If someone is standing at the top of a lighthouse, this can be an alternative *tower* or *balcony* dream that implies that you are the one sending out a message of hope or help.

•LIGHTNING

(see Clouds, Disasters, Fire, Rain, Storms)

A phallic symbol. In ancient legends, lightning fertilized the womb of the *abyss* to begin creation.

Destruction and ruin. The Tarot cards depict a *tower* being torn asunder by lightning. The interpretation of the Tower card is devastation.

The flash and energy of inspiration.

Divine or righteous wrath. In African traditions, a person who survives being struck by lightning is banished because it's considered a sign of serious divine judgment. Many European cultures depicted the gods' anger similarly with lightning.

•LILY

(see Flowers, Garden)

In Christianity, a symbol for Christ (see *Icons*).

Domestic happiness and duties. In China, this flower is used regularly to honor the Kitchen God.

Driving away your sadness by replacing it with beauty. In Japan, the Festival of the Cleansing Lily is performed to similarly drive away excess *rain*.

If the lily is growing in a garden, this symbolizes a desire to keep unwanted visitors out of your private space.

In France, this is an emblem of luck and serendipity.

Among the Mexicans, lilies portend reasons for celebration.

Chinese: An emblem that shows welcome and hospitality toward people or ideas.

• LINES

(see Art, Ink, Writing)

Boundaries you may have marked, or that other people created, delineating personal space and ground rules.

Figuratively, drawing the line on a situation that has gotten out of hand in your opinion, or holding the line with regard to a belief or ideal that you cherish.

Crossing a line: Going beyond a specific stricture, or breaking a taboo.

Consequences of actions or inactions, specifically those reaching into the future (e.g., something happening "down the line").

Erasing a line reflects a purging of boundaries or limitations that were once important.

• LION

(see Animals, Cat, Tiger)

Your own aggression or anger, especially if the lion is *hunting* for prey.

The roar and clamor of a bragging individual, who announces her/his presence to all who will listen.

Rulership or authority. The lion is known as the "king of the beasts" and is a potent solar symbol.

Hindu: The destroyer of demons, which can include bad memories, past experiences, and even addictions. A lion was the fourth incarnation of Vishnu.

Buddhist: Defending the law, but doing so with a soft paw of compassion.

Attentiveness. In folk beliefs it is said that the lion sleeps with its eyes always open.

•LIZARD

(see Animals, Dragon, Snake)

Because of its primitive origins, many psychologists view this as an emblem of the Collective Unconscious or wild nature within.

In Egypt and Greece, an omen of luck.

African: Transformation and the ability to adapt to your surroundings. Here the lizard is regarded as a shape-shifter.

Lizards are very sensitive to land vibrations, and have very good hearing and keen eyesight, making them symbolic of awareness, especially psychically.

Impartiality and the ability to break away from various situations. When a predator pounces on a lizard's tail, it is surprised to discover that the tail breaks off, leaving the lizard free and alive to grow a new one!

•LOCATIONS

(see Directions, Landmarks)

Seeing specific cities, states, or countries in your dream may have some bearing on the overall interpretation. For example, if the region has a symbolic name like Taylor, MI, this could indicate the need to "tailor" your activities or character to fit a specific situation. Areas that have *animal* names can be interpreted similarly, like Buffalo, NY, revealing a personality that tends to stampede over everyone standing in her/his way.

•LOCKS

(see Keys)

Safeguarding something that you consider valuable or precious.

Closing away negative portions of yourself, including bad memories, habits, and characteristics.

Blockage or an *obstacle*. Having your creativity, emotions, or ambitions "locked out."

•LODESTONE

(see Crystals, Gems, Stones)

Strength and tenacity. This stone has associations with Hercules, and Alexander the Great gave it to his armies to ensure their might.

Personal focus on being attractive or charismatic. As a natural magnet, lodestone was used by prostitutes to increase their business. It was also sometimes painted various colors as a component for magical "drawing" spells, such as green for encouraging prosperity or red to ensure passion or love.

Concerns over being a satisfying sexual partner. In India and Assyria, people rubbed this on the body to ensure potency.

•LOTUS

(see Flowers)

Among Hindus, a golden lotus represents the preexistent matter of the Universe. On the dream plane, this symbolizes untapped potential just waiting for your attention.

An alternative emblem for the *sun*. In Egypt, the Mother Goddess was called the lotus who gave birth to the sun.

In China, a golden lotus embodies a soul's mystical quest, which is very similar to the more Western idea of the quest for the holy grail.

In India, this flower is sacred to Lakshmi, the goddess of good fortune. As such, it foretells better luck on the horizon.

•LYCANTHROPY

(see Animal, Wolf)

Changing into any animal form reflects moving backward into more primal ways of thinking and behaving. The type of creature portrayed in the dream will help you to determine what aspect of your personality is returning to this wildness.

Communion with the astral realm. Shamans often transform into animals to travel in the spirit world.

Because folklore portrays this as a lunar phenomenon, this may be an alternative emblem of the *moon*.

Taking after your family in ways that are not necessarily complimentary. The ancients often believed that lycanthropy was hereditary.

• MACHINERY

An alternative type of *body* dream, in which the machine's state of repair represents your physical condition.

The general working mechanism of a relationship or situation, what makes it run smoothly (or not). For example, machinery where the parts stop moving due to lack of lubrication may symbolize the halting of a project because some necessary components or steps are lacking.

Squeaky: The need to oil a situation with fresh, innovative ideas.

Rusty: Talents or knowledge that have fallen into disuse. Alternatively, things that you regard as old, antiquated, or outmoded.

Figuratively going through life very mechanically, without real emotion or attachments.

• MAGIC

(see Circle, Divination, Incantation, Knots)

A power greater than yourself, but one that you seek to control.

The creative spark that unites the self to the ego, the masculine aspects to the feminine, etc.

Black magic: Using manipulation and exploitation to obtain your goals.

• MAGNET

(see Lodestone)

Something that draws or repels you. In magnetism, opposite polarities attract, while things too similar repel. So, if the magnet repels something, it can reveal a characteristic in yourself that you see in others and do not like.

• MAGNIFICATION

Items that *amplify* or magnify, like *eye* glasses, microscopes, and telescopes, instruct the dreamer to look closely at something. Scrutinize and analyze any information that comes your way right now. Alternatively, these may be a counsel to examine your way of life more closely, taking care that each element is in its right place.

Items that get magnified out of proportion in a dream are meant for stressing a specific point. Anything overly large is something you likewise perceive as big to the point of overwhelming. Small items are those you consider more trivial (see *Size*).

• MALACHITE

(see Crystals, Stones)

• MANDALA

An image or symbol usually featured within a *circle* or oval shape as a map of the cosmos used for meditation. In dreams, this is usually more personal, being an emblematic expression of your feelings or a growing awareness. Here, the *circle* represents a natural cycle or possibly fate's *web*, within which you're presently operating. The emblem contained therein becomes the prevalent dream key.

• MARATHON

(see Olympics, Running)

A physically trying situation that has gone on seemingly forever.

Finishing a marathon reflects your ability to endure physical stress as long as you prepare yourself properly.

Handing off to someone in a marathon symbolizes placing your goal or responsibilities in someone else's care or trust, hoping they can complete something which you could not.

• MARCHING

Marching to an odd beat represents assertion of independence (e.g., "walking to a different drummer").

Marching to a military beat reflects the desire to fight for a specific cause or possibly wishing to attain a public office.

Marching within a group reflects structure, or wishing to belong and fit in.

• MARRIAGE

(see Bride, Engagement, Groom, Relationships, Wedding)

• MARY

(see Icons)

• MASK

(see Clothes, Costumes)

Facades. Things not being what they seem. Or, the image you present to the world being only a partial truth.

Adapting to difficult circumstances: Ancient people wore masks to help them commune with specific energies. Today, we don figurative masks and temporary personas when faced with new, unfamiliar, or demanding situations. This results in stressing particular characteristics that help us cope in these new settings.

The element of surprise and mystery, like at a costumed *dance* where you wonder what's behind the mask.

Emotions or ideas that abide in your subconscious may manifest through a dream mask's color, shape, or depiction. For example, a *red* mask that looks angry can reveal your own outrage that was either subdued or silenced.

Jungian: The dreamer's connection to the archetypes in the Collective Unconscious, mediating therein between two distinct factions, such as the mundane and the supernatural aspects of self.

• MAZE

(see Puzzles, Riddles)

• MEADOW

(see Garden, Field, Flowers, Grove, Trees)

Peace, growth, and nourishment, specifically if someone is lounging in, or eating, the *grass*.

Repose with danger. Just like a fawn being hunted, take care that you're not getting reckless at the wrong time.

A parched meadow reflects a wanting spirit. Consider what caused the dryness, and then water the grasses of your soul.

• MEASUREMENTS

Focus on outward appearances, specifically your *weight*, *size*, and proportions.

How does everything "measure up" in the dream, and what's being measured? Equate this to a prevalent situation in your life.

Check the numerical significance of whatever measurements you get for further interpretive value.

• MEAT

(see Cow, Eating)

Needing more hearty mental and spiritual sustenance in your life, instead of living on milky concepts alone.

An omen of improved finances, or an abundance of personal energy, especially if the meat is being consumed.

• MEDICINE

(see Healing, Physician)

Advice, ideas, rules, or taboos that you don't necessarily want to heed, but which are in your own best interest (e.g., "a hard pill to swallow").

Bas tasting: How are you doling out the recommendations and counsel you give others? Is it harsh, or do you remember to add a little sweetness to make it easier to accept?

Injections represent protection against those things that threaten our well-being. Alternatively, these can indicate a sudden increase in energy that comes at just the right time (e.g., a "shot in the arm").

• MELON

(see Fruit)

Metaphysically aligned with the *moon*, *water*, and positive energies for healing.

Among *Gypsies*, a fruit of love.

From contemporary jargon, an alternative symbol for a woman's breasts.

Moslem: Verdicts and decisions. In the Koran, this is one of the foods served on the day of *judgment*.

• MELTING

(see Ice, Snow)

Transformations that lead to liberation.

Warming affections, improved compassion and benevolence (e.g., the "melting of a hardened heart").

Flow, freedom, and forgiveness. What's melting here has great significance. For example, *metals* in a *forge* speak directly to a personal change that liberates you from old structures.

• MEN

Father figures.

Your conscious mind, especially in men's dreams.

The voice of logic, discipline, and rationality.

A protector, guide, or advocate (see *Angel*, *Icon*).

The masculine aspect of the self or Universe.

Boys, especially when dreamed of by a man, reflect youthful memories or the child within.

• MENU

(see Eating, Food by type, Prices)

• MERLIN

(see Icons)

• MERMAID

(see Fairies—Undines)

• METALS

(see Copper, Gold, Iron Ore, Silver)

Strength and resiliency.

How is the metal used in the dream? Are you building with it, and if so, what? For example, building a wall out of metal represents a very strong *obstacle* to intimacy.

As with *crystals* and *gems*, each specific metal has different symbolism:

- Aluminum: flexibility
- Copper: guidance and control
- Flint: durability and utility
- *Iron ore*: love, safety, and willpower
- Lead: foundations or delays
- Quicksilver: quick responses
- Steel: rigidity, hard-heartedness
- Tin: improved luck

• METEORITE

(see Iron Ore, Stones, Sky, Space, Gems)

Wishes (see *Stars*).

Messages from the Universe or your own subconscious. In ancient times, people often believed such occurrences were divine missives or omens.

• MICROPHONE

(see Amplification)

• MILK

A *beverage* symbolizing the maternal nature and love (see *Cow*).

If you are drinking the milk, this may represent the fulfillment of your inner child.

If poured on the skin, a dream that confronts self-images or prejudicial feelings. For hundreds of years in Europe, milky-white skin was considered the height of beauty and comeliness (see *Color*).

Spilled milk represents worrying over things which you cannot change (e.g., "crying over spilt milk").

In Hindu, Egyptian, Japanese, and Greek civilizations, this substance also represented the primordial cosmic matter of creation itself. In a personal setting, this may mean the development of a more intuitive, inventive spirit that can "tune in" and transmit the frequency of universal truths through a specific medium.

Sour milk symbolizes negativity toward your mother, or toward becoming a mother.

Warm milk is a positive omen, reflective of renewed peace and a sense of well-being.

• MINE

(see Excavation, Gems, Metals)

Something valuable within for which you should continue digging. This may be a characteristic, memory, ideal, talent, or a sense of the truth.

• MINT

(see Herbs)

Paying your dues in a situation, or making a gift to a worthy cause. The Pharisees paid their tithes in mint.

Effective communications. The ancient Greeks used mint to clear the voice.

Revitalization and/or hospitality. This was one of the favorite strewing herbs of the Middle Ages, believed to refresh those who smelled it.

A sense of peace and tranquillity. The folk names for this plant include heart mint and lamb's mint, because of its serene nature.

• MIRROR

Self-images, for boon or bane, as with the story of Snow White (see *Fun House*).

The mirror of truth that reflects genuine motivations, feelings, and fears. In ancient times, the mirror was thought to be able to reveal a soul within.

Metaphorical reflections and pondering, often of a personal nature about the essential questions of existence. There is an old *fable* about someone who sought the *book* of all knowledge and wisdom. When at last the book was uncovered, the person was amazed to discover it held but one page: a mirror.

The way you wish to be seen, or the way you portray yourself outwardly.

A broken or cracked mirror reveals total transformation in self-perceptions and distorted self-images. It also acts as an omen of ill fortune.

A cloudy mirror indicates unclear or uncertain outlooks, especially about yourself.

A *door* to other aspects of self or the Universe. People in both ancient Eastern and Western societies covered or turned mirrors after *death*, believing the *ghost* of a person could travel through the reflective surface and cause no end of trouble.

•MISCARRIAGE

(see Baby, Birth, Pregnancy)

Something that you hoped for suddenly being waylaid or totally called off.

Metaphorically feeling that there has been a miscarriage of justice or other honorable qualities in a specific situation or relationship.

For a pregnant woman, a reflection of fear that probably needs no further interpretation.

•MIST

(see Cloud, Fog, Rain)

•MISTLETOE

(see Herbs, Oak)

Invincibility. Teutonic warriors carried mistletoe into battle as protective amulets.

Setting aside bad feelings out of respect for a common belief or need. In Scandinavian regions, warring groups who met underneath this plant put away their *weapons* for the day.

Among Druids, a plant that heals all wounds and protects the bearer. What is it in your life that needs *healing*?

Romantic advances. A favored holiday tradition is to *kiss* anyone caught beneath the mistletoe.

A dream *key* to unlocking a specific door in your life. The German philosopher and theologian Albertus Magnus recommended this plant as a magical key that could open any locked door, including doors to the hidden realms of the *earth*.

•MONASTERY

(see Church, Holy Ground, Sanctuary, Temple)

Religious or spiritual confines and strictures that have distinct tenets and taboos.

The attempt or desire to maintain total religious autonomy through sequestration. The counsel here is caution, being certain that seclusion is the right answer to your questions or problems.

Reclusiveness that may or may not be in your best interest. Remember that by trying to avoid something, we often end up *running* right into it!

•MONEY

(see Bank/Banking, Coins, Gold, Poverty, Silver, Stock Market)

Financial worries, or the wish for prosperity.

Inaccessible funds: Something pent up within yourself, often an ability.

Corruption (e.g., "money is the root of all evil" or "dirty money").

Turning down, or turning away from, money: A change in personal priorities toward less material pursuits.

Clutching money tightly: A frugal nature, sometimes to the point of greed.

•MONKEY (APE)

(see Animals)

Anthropologically, a less evolved state. Slipping backward into more animalistic tendencies.

Darwinian: An ancestral dream in which the monkey, ape, or gorilla symbolizes your ancient roots.

Foolish behavior (acting like a "monkey's uncle").

The mischievous and playful aspects of self (e.g., "monkey shines").

Being deceived by flattery or amusing actions that hide other motivations.

Sagacious justice. Four apes attended the judgment hall of Osiris, and apes were also sacred to Thoth, the Egyptian god of wisdom.

Prudent speech, accurate vision, and good listening skills (the three monkeys who represent seeing, hearing, and saying no to evil).

Hindu: Bravery and swift action, being associated with the god of wind.

• MONSTER

(see Bed, Closet, Dreams, Dragon, Evil, Fables)

The feared or unexplored aspects of your own nature.

Slaying a monster: Becoming the hero for your own life; transforming fear into victory and creativity (see *Sword*).

Repressed drives and ambitions that need to be expressed.

• MOON

The lunar, feminine, *water* aspect of the Universe.

An influence that causes odd behavior, such as the full moon or a *blue* moon are purported to do.

If being covered by a *cloud*, a type of *eclipse* dream.

Each phase of the moon has slightly different associations. The waxing crescent symbolizes new beginnings and growth. A full moon indicates maturity, especially of a more maternal disposition, and a waning moon is the emblem of decline and old *age*. Note, however, that your ways of thinking can be metaphorically old without physical age.

Howling at the moon: A release of *animal* instincts and energies. Also possibly a sign of a superstitious person.

Something that is rare, and should be enjoyed while it lasts (e.g., "once in a blue moon").

• MOONSTONE

(see Crystals, Gems, Jewelry, Stones)

• MOOSE

(see Animals)

A solitary personality with tendencies toward being very territorial.

The ability to camouflage yourself and move quietly behind the scenes.

In metaphysical traditions, the moose is regarded as aligned with the feminine, watery, maternal nature. Allow this to develop in your life.

Alertness. Moose are born with their *eyes* wide open.

A portent that speaks of a long life lived fully.

•MOSES

(see Icons, Men)

•MOTHER

(see Women)

•MOTHER TERESA

(see Icons, Women)

•MOUNTAIN

(see Ascetic, Ascent, Balcony, Climbing, Ladder, Stairs)

Achievements. Overcoming the odds and getting a second chance. Many heroic figures await their rebirth in a mountainside tomb. Merlin is one such figure.

Doing something you've always wanted to do just for yourself (e.g., "*climbing* the mountain because it was there").

Transcending perceptions or taking a higher outlook, especially with regards to your own life (which then becomes the mountain).

Retreat. Getting some distance so that you don't have to be directly involved.

Finding problems where none exist (e.g., making "mountains out of molehills").

Freudian: An image of female breasts (this goes for hills too). Many earth religions describe their goddesses as possessing lush valleys, rounded hills, and tracts of land. Today there are still matriarchal mountain pilgrimage centers in Europe.

A path toward enlightenment and oneness with nature. In Burma (Myanmar), there is a set of stairs up the side of Mt. Popa called the Stairway to Heaven. Buddhists travel here to *ascend* to the shrine and honor terrestrial spirits that abide throughout the *earth*.

• MOUSE

(see Animals)

Frugality and resourcefulness. Saving and recycling even minute things effectively.

Someone overly soft in voice or who lacks backbone (e.g., being "mousy").

The size of this creature may reflect an underdeveloped sense of self-worth.

Aesop's Fables portray the mouse as an emblem that makes weaknesses into strengths.

A secret, well-hidden adversary of whom you should become aware. Note too that this enemy may be within.

Mousetraps have become an emblem of ingenuity and tackling a difficult problem with creative insight (e.g., "building a better mousetrap"). They may also be regarded as an alternative *cage* emblem, where you get caught by, or caught up in, technology.

• MOUTH

Matters of communication and self-expression. If you dream of being gagged, for example, this represents either swallowing your words, or having your speech repressed by societal or situational standards.

An overexaggerated mouth can reveal a propensity to gossip or to dominate a conversation with your own ideas.

Freudian: An alternative vaginal emblem.

With an extended tongue, the mouth becomes an emblem for gender unification, and therefore potent speech that affects all who listen. It is only in recent years that this symbolism transposed into an insult. Depending on the remainder of the dream, this might reflect the need to watch your words, being certain they carry the intended meaning for the most powerful impact on the listener.

A mouth with a forked tongue represents lies, and purposeful misrepresentations with an aim of personal gain or profit.

• MOVEMENT

(see Directions, Velocity)

• MOVIES

(see Costumes, Masks, Theater)

•MUD

(see Dirt, Earth)

•MURDER

(see Fighting, Weapons)

If the image is that of a young person, this represents having your goals or hopes figuratively "killed" before they could completely manifest.

Your own anger, hatred, fury, or prejudices revealing themselves through a heinous act.

This may be a circumstantial dream in which fears stemming from late night news manifest in the dream vision. Additionally, it may reflect your own abhorrence of such brutality.

•MUSEUM

(see Antiques, Art)

Your own past, or humankind's collective past.

The foundations of your thoughts, actions, and ideas, some of which can (and should) be dusted off so that understanding, integration, and growth can occur.

•MUSHROOMS

(see Vegetables)

Eating mushrooms among ancient Egyptians was a sign of rulership, as only the Pharaohs received this treat.

In Rome, an emblem of strength.

Metaphysics and/or the psychic nature coming to the forefront of your awareness. Shamans and medicine people have long known that some mushrooms produce visionary experiences. Additionally, they grow in dark, damp regions, equating with the fertile subconscious or Collective Unconscious.

The lunar aspects of the mushroom combine with fiery energy. Mushrooms are considered the child of lightning in folk tales. This provides a unique balance between conscious/logical thinking and the intuitive self. Consider if you have been heeding both voices equally of late.

•MUSIC

(see by specific instruments)

Inner harmony, or the song of your soul as it mingles with the Universe. Pythagoras believed that celestial objects sing as they move throughout the *sky*. When you learn that music, as well as your own keynote within the strain, it naturally engenders actualization and awareness.

The universal language that expresses your emotions to those who will listen. In this case, you are likely revealing hidden feelings to yourself.

Discordant: Being in an ill-advised *relationship* or situation that isn't healthy spiritually, physically, or mentally.

Note the selection of music, where it is played, the quality, and represented instruments. Each of these facets will add greater dimension to your dream's interpretation. For example, a mournful opera carries far different emotions from celebratory songs, or religious canticles. So if you dreamt of a *church* song being performed badly, this could reveal that your spiritual life has somehow gotten "out of tune" and needs your attention.

• NAIL

(see Hammer, Tools)

Someone who is being, or trying to be, impenetrable and rugged (e.g., "tough as nails").

The ability and wherewithal to hold things together. What objects get nailed together in this case is quite significant.

Being unjustly accused and sentenced (as Christ) by those around you, often a peer group. Alternatively, being caught in an untruth or illegal activity (e.g., "getting nailed").

Discovering an underlying, fundamental truth or reality (e.g., "nailing it down").

Correctly interpreting something that your Higher Self, others, or the Universe has been trying to communicate (e.g., "hitting the nail on the head").

Nails have a piercing quality that can be useful or harmful. Is there a relationship in your life right now that seems painfully binding?

Nails that are not flush with the woodwork represent those unseen snags in life. These can delay progress until you free yourself.

• NAKEDNESS

(see Barefoot, Body, Clothes)

Being, or feeling, overexposed.

Freedom; the loosening of conventional restrictions.

The real you, devoid of all exterior *masks*.

Total comfort with yourself to the point where you need no trappings for confidence. Also the ability to be totally open and honest.

The barest, most succinct facts (e.g., the "naked truth"). Look to see what appears naked in the dream for further insight.

• NAMES

(see Abbreviations)

Each name's meaning derives from its root *language*. Patricia, for example, means noble (which is the origin of the word patrician). Try looking in a baby's name book for more information along these lines.

Names can have symbols built into them. For example, someone in your dream named Mr. or Ms. Heart can symbolize your own emotions, or a person you know who is very loving.

Receiving a new name in a dream indicates drastic change and personal transformations to the point of a figurative rebirth. In European and Judaic folk traditions, healers often gave people new names to fool the spirit of sickness into leaving the body. Similarly, in many cultures a child is given a new name after undergoing a rite of passage into adulthood. This name marks the child's new role in that society.

A sense of individuality. Each person's name engenders images and feelings to those who hear it. People often chose nicknames that are more appropriate representations of their true natures.

The development of, or initiation into, an esoteric or metaphysical path. Many people practicing such faiths adopt a new name that reflects their spiritual vision and other positive qualities.

Control over aspects of the self or a specific situation. Many ancient peoples in Europe believed that if you knew a person's or entity's true name (like that of a *fairy*), you would have power over it. By naming something in a dream, you may be trying to exert or develop increased command, and make that item or characteristic more concrete.

• NEEDLE

(see Connecting Devices, Fabric, Sewing)

An alternative symbol of male sexuality, sometimes in a derogatory sense.

If attached to a thread, the emblem of repair, alteration, and reconnecting. Perhaps a relationship has been torn asunder and needs mending. Or, maybe there is an aspect of self that needs *healing* or other important adjustments.

Conducting fruitless searches or participating in unproductive worrying (e.g., looking for a "needle in a haystack").

Things, people, or situations that bother you to the point of distraction (e.g., "what's needling you").

Knitting needles can represent manipulating circumstances so that they come out a specific way. Alternatively, this may be a type of networking dream in which the fibers of a situation are carefully knit back together.

Embroidery indicates an intense attention to embellishing basic details and making sure everything has finishing touches that reflect your personality.

•NEST

(see Birds, Trees)

A dream manifestation of the nesting instinct common to pregnant women, or women who wish to conceive.

Building or finding a safe haven for yourself and your loved ones.

A bird sitting on *eggs* in a nest reflects the figurative hatching of ideas or plans, and knowing that all things come with time and patience.

•NET

(see Fish, Knots, Web)

•NINE

(see Numbers)

Changes that lead to completion, a sense of closure, and wholeness.

Matters of health and vitality. Folk medicine frequently mentions treatments being applied nine times, over nine days, and other similar applications for this number.

In Eastern beliefs, the number of self-mastery.

If the nine in your dream is seen as part of a set of 10, this reveals a situation that is just short of being finished. Take a second look and make sure all the loose ends are tied up.

•NOON

(see Light, Sun, Twelve)

•NORTH

(see Directions, Locations)

• NOSE

(see Body, Face)

Your investigative instincts (e.g., being able to "sniff" something out).

Truthfulness or lack thereof, like the story of Pinocchio.

Recognizing quality or the lack of it, like someone who has a "nose for wine."

If you dream of a stuffed nose, this indicates that something is stifling your ability to breathe freely and enjoy your leisure time. Alternatively, this may be a circumstantial dream caused by a cold or sinus condition.

A bleeding nose represents having your dignity somehow affronted.

• NOTARIZATION

(see Oaths, Writing)

Confirming to yourself or the Universe something's validity and sincerity.

Change in your life for which you feel witnesses or confirmations are required from an external source. Very often when making an effort to improve yourself, having someone note the transformation they see is a much needed motivator to keep pressing forward.

• NUMBERS

(see by individual number, Clock)

Duration of *time*: Hours, days, weeks, months, and years before something comes to fruition.

Personally significant numbers like birthdates or anniversaries that engender specific feelings and memories, or accent personal needs.

Counting: Pacing yourself, following a set routine without diverting. Alternatively, the number reached could indicate the number of people or situations you regularly "count on."

Fractions in dreams represent seeing only part of a greater picture. Before you make a decision here, make sure you get your facts straight and read the fine print.

Numbers appearing out of sequence portray chaotic undercurrents in life caused by procrastination or the lack of organization.

Upon what do the numbers appear? This object may help interpretation. For example, numbers on a house may equate to a real address that you know. Numbers on a *calendar* might be a special date in your life. Those appearing on an odometer might counsel you to slow down a bit so that you don't wear out your engine (see *Car*), and those on a *telephone* could be a nudge to call someone specific with whom you've been avoiding communication.

• NUMBNESS

(see Paralyzation)

A situational dream that comes from sleeping awkwardly on a body part.

Avoiding emotions by turning them off.

Experiencing so great a shock that the reality of a situation doesn't immediately sink in, leaving you feeling numb and out of touch.

• NUTS

(see Eating, Trees by type)

An emblem of male sexuality and virility, equated with the testes. Europeans used to eat nuts at the end of the meal to ensure continued fecundity (that's how we came by the expression "from soup to nuts").

If eaten by a woman, a symbol of fertility or *pregnancy*.

Cracking open: Seeing or revealing the core of the self.

As a play on words, this dream can relate to something that is literally driving you "nuts."

If eaten (or given) as part of a *wedding* or other gathering, the symbolism changes to providence and joy.

Among the Scots, nuts were favored for love divinations, and as such may speak of an increasing love in your current *relationship*, or a new partner. Much here will depend on the rest of the dream's contents.

•OAK

(see Forest, Leaves, Trees)

In northern Europe, this tree is strongly affiliated with god figures, including Jupiter, Thor, and Zeus, giving it a masculine overtone, with the *acorn* becoming an emblem of fertility.

Strength, firm foundations, and longevity. In folk beliefs, the oak's roots delve as far into the *earth* as its branches reach toward the sky.

An oak filled with *acorns* portends a promotion and financial increases.

Bravery and charity that benefits others. In Rome, any hero who saved the life of a citizen was crowned with a wreath of oak leaves and acorns.

•OASIS

(see Desert, Garden, Sand)

The ending of some type of deprivation or spiritual drought.

Fulfilling a thirst for knowledge or spiritual awareness after a long quest.

Mirage of: Your search has not yet ended, even though outwardly it may appear that it has. Look more closely at this situation or person, as there is something of which you remain unaware.

•OATHS

(see Notarization)

In dreams, these usually represent the promises and commitments made to yourself. Oaths may also reflect obligations for which you feel responsible.

•OBSTACLES

(see Abyss, Bridge, Cage, Cliff, Dam, Gate, Hole)

Traffic jams (see *Car*): Taking a direction perceived as free from trouble, only to find the way blocked for some unknown reason. Usually this pertains to external circumstances that you cannot control, but find frustrating.

Walls or barriers: If walls can talk, what are yours telling you? Is it too soon to move forward, or is the wall a kind of test to overcome? Also note that walls can symbolize limitations that are imposed by family, friends, *job*, or culture.

Fence: This reveals perceived class restrictions and prohibitions. Alternatively, if you're sitting on the fence, by all means make up your mind! Falling off a fence speaks of taking on a project that you are simply incapable of handling considering your other responsibilities right now. To avoid being the proverbial Humpty Dumpty, carefully balance your schedule and duties before taking on anything else.

Consider who or what is causing the barrier you see in your dream. What part of your nature provides the best tool to remove that obstruction (the rational, intuitive, or emotional self)?

Is the obstacle natural or human made? Natural obstacles represent something that would happen to anyone approaching this same situation. For example, a barrier reef standing between you and an *island* indicates everyday problems. Simply navigate around them so that you can rest in a safe haven. Conversely, human-made obstacles symbolize manufactured problems or delays. Such obstacles can be self-originated or caused by external forces.

•OCEAN

(see Abyss, Seashell, Water)

•OCTOPUS

(see Animals)

Being entangled by a very possessive personality.

Many *hands* make light work. Have you sought out assistance from those you know are capable of helping you right now?

An alternative figure for the number *eight*, a *wheel*, and a *circle*.

Inconsistency of words or actions, especially when you feel pressured. The octopus, like the *chameleon*, changes *color* under stress.

Deceiving others through appearance. Both Pliny and Aristotle hypothesized that the octopus changed its colors to fool its prey.

Creativity gone awry. In oceanic cultures, the octopus holds a place in creation myths, but often those that don't come out quite right.

• OFFERING

(see Altar, Sacrifice)

• OIL SPILL

(see Disaster)

• OLYMPICS

(see Acrobatics, Marathon, Running)

Because of the generally peaceful, positive atmosphere of the Olympics, this can represent your development or expansion of one-world thinking and actions.

Being a good sport and remembering the importance of fair play. Winning is not always the greatest prize if it comes undeservedly.

As the symbol of the Olympics is a lit *torch*, this dream may metaphorically relate to "carrying a torch" for a cause or person you idealize.

Undertaking projects or personal changes perceived as being Olympic in size.

• OM

(see Chanting, Languages)

• ONE

(see Numbers)

The creative, originating energy of the universe.

God (the first self-created power).

The self and the individual's relationship to, or awareness of, that essential nature.

Single-mindedness, focus, unity.

• ONION

(see Eating, Garden, Vegetables)

Onions have a power similar to *garlic* in overcoming *evil*, specifically our own *shadows*.

The shape and color of the onion makes it an alternative emblem for the *moon* or wholeness.

The layered skin of this vegetable represents having to probe to find the truth. Alternatively, it can represent layers of personal *armor* that you hide behind.

Strength. Alexander the Great fed his troops this vegetable along with *garlic* to ensure their vitality.

Peeling onions in a dream foretells of tears that come from your own actions.

• ONYX

(see Crystals, Gems, Jewelry, Stones)

• OPAL

(see Crystals, Gems, Jewelry, Stones)

• OPERATION

(see Healing, Medicine, Physician)

The radical need to change something that threatens your wholeness, happiness, or growth.

Destroying specific negative aspects of the self for renewal, like bad habits, bitterness, anger, etc.

Feeling fearful or helpless in connection with the health and welfare of someone close to you.

• OPPOSITES

Some dream researchers, especially at the turn of the century, theorized that the symbols in dreams were opposite to what they appeared. Good represented *evil*, joy represented sadness, a man represented a woman, and so on. This idea is worth considering if the other approaches to your dream have yielded little or no meaning.

To see two opposite items in a dream can reflect improved balance between different facets of the psyche. Alternatively, this can represent a dichotomy that causes inner turmoil over two equally important goals or ideals.

•ORANGE

(see Color)

An optimistic hue, denoting improved self-love, high energy, and a clear emotional state.

Bright, fiery oranges are the color of aggression. This hue needs gentle control so that angry outbursts don't occur.

Also the color of *autumn*, thereby denoting a harvest of characteristics that you have sown and tended with care.

•ORANGES

(see Eating, Fruit, Juice, Trees)

Because of its high vitamin content, this symbolizes good health or things that are good for you.

An emblem of the triune nature of humankind (body-mind-soul), because the tree bears *flowers*, *leaves*, and *fruit* simultaneously.

Buying oranges portends prosperity. In the Middle Ages, oranges were a highly valued and expensive commodity.

In the East, dreaming of oranges represents extending good wishes for joy and abundance to those you care about.

Controlling an unruly nature. Orange slices were originally put in drinks, believing they would prevent drunkenness. In this case, stopping the "inebriation" becomes a metaphor for self-regulation.

Russia: Faithfulness. Orange flowers were sometimes part of a *bride's* bouquet for this reason.

•ORGANIZING

(see Filing Cabinet)

Integrating or ordering recent experiences.

A fastidious personality expressing itself through your dream.

Exactly what's being put in order in the dream may hold tremendous import. For example, if detailing a pantry, this might be a situational dream (being hungry) or it might reveal a latent fear of going hungry. On the other hand, organizing a closet speaks of different life roles and which ones are most important (see *Clothes*).

•ORGASM

(see Sexual Encounters)

Stimulation and overexcitement that may cause you to expend all your energy in one shot. If so, take care that you make this a well-considered and well-aimed effort.

A common side effect for dreams focusing on sexual fantasies. In this setting, this likely needs no further interpretation.

A physical need manifesting through what you consider a safe medium—the dream.

•ORPHANED

(see Adoption, Baby, Desertion)

For adoptees, likely a memory surfacing that may or may not need further examination. If you have unresolved issues pertaining to your adoption, look at this dream more closely.

A type of *desertion* dream.

Estrangement or separation from family or a close circle of friends that you did not choose.

A portion of yourself that you've left behind, especially the trusting inner child.

Awkwardness in your present situation (e.g., feeling out of place like a stranger in totally unfamiliar surroundings).

•OTTER

(see Animals)

Native American: The feminine power of *water*. Also gracefulness and playfulness.

Forgetfulness or lacking closure. Otters are known to take one or two bites from their food, then leave the rest behind when distracted by something else.

•OWL

(see Bird, Feathers, Flying, Wings)

Wisdom.

The ability to traverse the figurative *darkness* in your life.

As a companion and messenger to the Greek goddess Athena, an owl may presage new artistic abilities or the development of a warrior's spirit.

A type of *death* dream. In Greece, dreaming of an owl foretold of death, the Vedic god of the dead sometimes sent owls as messengers, and the Celts associated owls with the god of the underworld.

Native Americans call owls the "night *eagle*," and consider them a symbol of silent observation with potentially deceitful motivations.

In Hopi tradition, the gift of an owl feather bestows truthfulness on the receiver. By accepting such a token in a dream, you accept yourself.

The ability to see what others are trying to hide from you, as the owl's golden *yellow eyes* pierce the night.

Moving silently, or remaining silent in a situation. Owls are considered silent fliers.

Snow owls in particular are able hunters, representing the instinct to know where your sustenance lies, and how to effectively reach it.

•OYSTER

(see Seashell)

Because of the chance of finding a *pearl* here, a type of *treasure* dream.

The shell of this creature equates to *armor* or *obstacles* to intimacy.

Life's little irritations helping you to develop wisdom and patience. *Pearls* in an oyster are actually formed due to the irritation in the skin caused by a grain of *sand* or *dirt*.

• PANTOMIME

(see Acting, Costumes, Masks, Theater)

A sense that your voice isn't being heard, or that the message you're presenting isn't being received as intended.

Going through the motions without properly expressing yourself to those around you.

• PAPERCLIPS

(see Connecting Devices)

• PARABLE

(see Fables)

• PARADISE

(see Garden, Island, Oasis)

• PARALYZATION

(see Lameness, Numbness)

The inability to make a decision leaves you in a *corner* or leads to a *dead end*.

A part of yourself has remained unexpressed or underdeveloped, and therefore it is unable to integrate properly, causing arrested progress. Look to see what region of your *body* is paralyzed for more insight. For example, having your hand paralyzed might reflect an inability to give charitably or accept aid when it's offered.

Fear and other intense emotions that leave you unable or unwilling to act.

• PARENTS

(see Men, Relationships, Women)

A reflection of your relationship with your parents now, or a memory from past experiences with them.

Archetypally, the God or Goddess parent to all humankind who guides and inspires (see *Angel, Icon*).

Any *authority figure* whom you respect in the same manner as a parent.

A personification of your Higher Self.

• PARROT

(see Birds, Feathers, Wings)

Mirroring habits, characteristics, or ways that are not necessarily reflective of who you really are.

Repetition of cycles or patterns in your life, some of which may not be positive.

Among Pueblo Indians, an alternative emblem of the *sun*, which also embodies the power of *color* and *light*.

If the parrot is in the *air*, possibly a type of *flying* dream.

A "yes" person who accepts everything she/he is told to do or believe without real scrutiny.

Mockery or gossip.

In a *cage*, the parrot embodies the inability to integrate the lessons you see reflected through other people's words and actions.

• PASSAGE(S)

(see Door, Highway, Path, Windows)

• PATH

(see Alley, Corner, Dead End, Highway)

Spiritual directions and focus. Taoism, for example, translated from the Chinese, means "the way" or "path." Buddhism teaches the eightfold path to enlightenment. Christ spoke of the path of righteousness.

A guideline, edict, or idea that you are following now, or plan to follow in the future. Paths have defined borders that set them apart from the accompanying countryside, showing the way to go.

A sign of *fairy* mischief or presence. In European and rural American folklore, bright *green lines* of grass were called fairy paths, and believed to be created by the passage of these elemental beings.

Meandering: Varying from your destiny or taking temporary detours away from a previously specified goal.

Divergent: A decision must be made, but both options appear equal. See if your dream reveals something about this choice that you have not seen yet, such as one path exhibiting *weeds* that might entangle you.

Well-worn: Either being in a rut, or staying so constrained to one way of thinking and living that the same old routes get walked again and again.

Straight: Staying true to your ideals, lifestyle, and/or goals.

• PEACH

(see Fruit, Trees)

Generally an emblem of wisdom, except in the East where peaches are given the additional attributes of a happy *marriage* and long life.

In China, the *flowers* that bear peaches are used within the home to avert negativity. If tensions have been high with your family lately, now's the time to begin the *healing* process.

Among Taoists, a source that offers productive energy, especially in a sexual sense. This idea seemed to hold true in other cultures too, as the Greeks attributed this fruit to the rule of Venus, and Albertus Magnus recommended eating peaches as an aphrodisiac.

A sarcastic visual pun that indicates a situation or person you find less than "peachy."

• PEACOCK

(see Bird, Feathers, Wings)

Outward displays of vanity or conceit.

Expressing yourself in a manner that others see as boastful.

Pride, dignity, or self-respect (e.g., being "proud as a peacock").

In Babylonia and Persia, an emblem of regality. Similarly in the East, peacocks represent rank and having obtained the favor of powerful people.

Buddhist: Compassion and fidelity. It was believed that Kwan Yin, the protectress of children and mothers, took this form, and that peacocks would die of loneliness if their mate passed away.

A warning that bragging will eventually bring sadness. This bird foretells rainfall by its *dancing*.

• PEARL
(see Gems, Oyster, Seashell)

Something that, once found, is worth all your sacrifice (e.g., the "pearl of great price").

Sagacity and the creative aspects of self (e.g., "pearls of wisdom").

An alternative symbol for *moon* and *water*.

Freshwater pearls: Strung together, they represent progressive learning, or serious thought that leads to a perspicacious decision, action, or conclusion.

Black pearls, while rare, are actually considered a negative portent due to their color (white represents purity). Something in your line of reasoning or current situation is likely flawed, and could lead to trouble.

• PEAS
(see Eating, Garden, Vegetables, Vines)

An alternative emblem of the male testicles, especially when dreamt of in pairs.

Black-eyed peas appearing in dreams portend improved good luck.

Comfortable companionship, relationships, or partnerships (e.g., "like two peas in a pod").

• PEGASUS
(see Fables, Horse)

• PELICAN
(see Birds, Feathers, Wings)

Rising above circumstances, or staying afloat when a sea of emotion threatens to overcome you. Despite their large, awkward size, pelicans are actually very buoyant.

Wise frugality, even during periods of apparent abundance. Pelicans do not immediately eat their catch, but save it in their bills.

Folkloric: Self-sacrifice for something you love, or a greater good. The *red* streak on the pelican's chest supposedly occurred when it opened itself to feed its starving young.

•PENGUIN

(see Birds, Feathers, Wings)

If *swimming* in *water*, this represents free movement through your dreams. Anticipate more frequent dreams, as well as those with increased detail.

A penguin has wings, but does not fly. These actually help them steer through the water. So, if you've been trying to "fly" in a specific situation that seems to be going nowhere, consider an alternative tact, using your given talents and insight as a guide.

•PENTAGRAM/PENTACLE

(see Five, Star)

This *pictograph* was used widely in the ancient world as a protective amulet, specifically to ward off the *evil eye* and malicious *magic*. On the dream plane, this may indicate that you sense some type of psychic or mundane threat to your well-being for which you should take proper precautions.

An emblem of the esoteric mysteries, and possibly the development of specific occult or magical abilities within. Note that the pentacle was often also called a wizard's star or witch's cross in the Middle Ages.

Among *Gypsies* and some earth-centered *religions*, the pentacle was an emblem of health and long life. This probably developed due to the natural pentacle formed by *seeds* when an apple is sliced in half.

•PERFUME (AROMAS)

(see Incense, Flowers, Smells)

In European and Victorian American folk beliefs, certain aromas indicate the presence of a spirit (see *Ghost*), especially favored colognes and perfumes of deceased family members.

Bitter aromas indicate anger, jealousy, and harsh attitudes. This scent can also indicate an attempt to cover up something foul.

Sickly sweet scents reveal insincerity, dishonesty, and hypocrisy.

Light, pleasant aromas are usually associated with positive emotions. For example, a gentle *rose* fragrance may symbolize tender love, and the aroma of honeysuckle may indicate accomplishment (e.g., the "sweet smell of success").

Memories: Some people respond very strongly to aromas, and can relive experiences through scents appearing in their dreams.

• PHOENIX

(see Fire, Fables)

Reincarnation, rebirth, and new beginnings. Known by the Egyptians as the *bennu*, this fire *bird* renews itself by making a *nest* in a raging conflagration from which it is born anew.

Longevity. Several ancient texts, including the Talmud, intimate this creature can live as long as one thousand years.

• PHOTOCOPIER

The loss of individuality and personal vision to that of your peer group, society, or culture.

Cloned ideas or lacking originality in your approaches.

The loss of value or appeal because of having been overexposed to one person, object, or situation repeatedly. Just as a child with candy, there can be too much of a good thing.

• PHOTOGRAPHS

Contemplation about your past. Look to see if any theme develops in the pictures envisioned, or if they have a central object or character. This item or theme will help your interpretation.

Memories that may have gotten pushed aside, but need to surface now to help you better understand or cope with a specific situation or individual.

If the photograph itself isn't familiar, look to see what it contains and review those emblems herein. In this case, it may be a snapshot from the subconscious or Higher Self of something that you need to know and remember in the days ahead.

• PHYSICIAN

(see Authority Figures, Healing, Medicine, Operation)

If you have a tendency to always help others while neglecting your own needs, the physician in your dreams is the Super Ego counseling that to be a healer, you must first heal yourself.

A gentle nudge to seek medical evaluation or treatments for something you have either ignored or overlooked up until now.

The patient in this dream can represent a person or group with whom you need to patch things up. It may also be situational.

• PICTOGRAPHS

By definition, pictographs are picture-like symbols used to communicate specific concepts. On the dream plane, these can be very potent keys for unlocking deeper meanings. A comprehensive listing of pictographs is a subject worthy of a complete book, but for the purpose of illustration, here are a few examples:

Pictograph	Name	Meaning(s)
=	Equal sign	The need for symmetry and equity.
○	Circle	An alternative lunar or solar emblem. Completeness and cycles. Enclosure and protection.
□	Square	The four elements in balance. A pictorial pun for someone who is socially awkward. Truthfulness (e.g., a "square deal").

Pictograph	Name	Meaning(s)
♭	Flat	Feeling as if life has lost its flavor. A project that fizzled out. Something that has gotten slightly off-key and needs tuning for harmonious interaction.
♂	Male	An emphasis on the masculine nature and associated characteristics.
↑	Tyr	The rune of the warrior showing strong convictions and the willingness to fight for a just cause.
△	Triangle	The triune nature, balance, and an alternative *fire* emblem.
⊕	Circle/wheel	The *winds*, the *four directions*, and a type of cross emblem.
∞	Infinity	Something that has longevity, or that goes on seemingly forever.
♥	Heart	Matters of love or emotions.
✓	Check mark	Correctness or incorrectness, *red* check marks denoting the latter.

• PIE

(see Eating, Fruit or Nuts by type)

An alternative *circle* emblem.

A sliced pie reflects your ability to judge things fairly and equitably. How even are the slices? Is someone getting the lion's share?

Dreaming of mince pies foretells the fulfillment of wishes and improved luck.

Birds or other unexpected items coming out of a pie symbolize the need to look at a person or situation more closely. Something here is not what it seems, and will surprise you.

• PIG

(see Animals, Farm)

Figuratively, someone who is always "hamming it up."

Among the Celts, an emblem of success and overcoming the odds. Pig was the favored food for Celtic victory feasts (see *Eating, Meat*).

Norse: Rebirth, honor, and new beginnings. In Valhalla, Valkyries feast on a reborn sow.

• PIGEON

(see Birds, Feathers, Wings)

The ability to maintain your roots and find your way back home, even when circumstances try to steer you off course. Pigeons are excellent navigators.

Fertility or productivity. Pigeons are close to *rabbits* in their ability to breed rapidly.

A pictorial play on words representing someone who seems gullible (e.g., having a "pigeon" on the line).

• PILLARS

(see Archway, Buildings, Concrete, Stones)

While these are sometimes considered phallic due to their shape, in ancient Greece pillars were regularly carved in the shape of a woman whose visage was modeled after a *priestess* of the Moon Goddess. In this form, pillars can emphasize the need to balance gender-specific outlooks, or to accept the traits you exhibit from the opposite gender as a building block to your whole personality.

What do these pillars uphold? If, for example, they support a *temple* roof, this implies having strong foundations and evidence for your beliefs. However, cracking and decayed pillars reflect a belief system that you have outgrown, but not left behind.

Ancient Egyptian: A hieroglyph called the Pillars of Horus was placed on the walls of homes to keep negativity away from the residents. Such symbols inscribed on your dream's buildings may represent feelings of oppression or danger from which you wish to protect yourself and your kin.

A person's best attributes that are worthy of recognition or honor (e.g., being a "pillar of truth" or "pillar of the community").

• PINE

(see Forest, Trees)

The scent of pine in a dream reflects either a need for cleansing and purification of some type, or refreshment for one's energy. The scent of pine was regularly used in sick rooms for both purposes.

Long lasting results from your labors. Pine trees stay *green* through the winter, implying immortality.

Sticky situations, clingy emotions, or barbed conversations: Pine needles are quite sharp and often bear tacky sap that seems to get on everything with which they come in contact. Are you being likewise prickly or sticky in the way you deal with people or a particular circumstance?

• PINK

(see Color)

Gnostic: The color of resurrection, notifying you that your old way of thinking, believing, or living is giving way to a brand-new adventure.

In the Victorian language of flowers, the color of friendship.

Health or well-being (e.g., being "in the pink").

• PIPE

(see Smoke)

• PIXIES

(see Fairy)

• PLAGUES
(see Healing, Medicine, Physician)

An alternative type of judgment dream. Many ancient cultures regarded widespread sickness as a sign of divine displeasure.

Blights perceived as being on your soul or spirit, like a curse.

Bitterness that rots away inside, creating all manner of dis-ease.

AIDS: In literal terms, AIDS is the plague of the 21st century, so this dream may express an honest fear playing itself out, or a homophobic reaction.

Leprosy: Feeling like your life is falling apart a little at a time, or that you are slowly losing yourself to someone or something. Alternatively, an experience or action that makes you feel "unclean" (see *Dirt*).

What or who does the plague affect? The answer to this question can reveal one's anger, moral conflict, or prejudice pertaining to a group, person, or situation.

• PLANETS
(see Space, Stars)

Someone (potentially yourself) who is constantly hovering around others for security, attention, or companionship.

Cycles that repeat themselves, but usually over very long periods of time. Think back over the years and see if what's happening right now doesn't have a twin in your past.

Astrologically, each planet has different attributes that it may represent in your dream. Here is a brief overview of the major planets noted in astrological writings:

♀ Mercury: Named after the Roman messenger of the gods, this planet governs communication and speedy action.

♀ Venus: Named after the Roman goddess of love, this planet governs relationships, matters of beauty/appearance, and passions.

♂ Mars: Named after the Roman god of war, this planet governs justice, anger, and the warrior spirit.

♃ Jupiter: Named after the chief Roman god, noted for protection, athletics, and excellence.

♄ Saturn: Named after the Roman god of agriculture, this planet governs manifestation, productivity, and abundance.

• PLOWING, PLANTING

(see Earth, Garden)

• POISON

Something or someone that is very bad for you, and needs to be purged from your figurative system.

• POLICE

(see Authority Figures, Cage, Judgment, Warrants)

A source of protection that stands between you and danger (see *Angel*).

Your conscience is policing your decisions or actions, based on your own sense of morality or lawfulness.

Being arrested by the police may reveal that your current course of action should be figuratively "arrested." Alternatively, the guilt generated by recent actions, or the fear of failure, causing halted progress.

Freudian: A manifestation of your Super Ego (see *Authority Figures*).

• POMEGRANATE

(see Fruit, Seeds)

Eating the seeds of a pomegranate, according to American lore, foretells the fulfillment of one wish.

In Babylonia and Asia, this was a positive omen for *marriages* or any matters of commitment.

Because of the *red* juice of these seeds, they were an accepted substitute *blood* symbol in both ancient Greece and Judaic tradition.

Seeing a heap of pomegranates (or a lot of seeds) in your dream reflects upcoming prosperity. In Egypt, pomegranates were so valuable that they were sometimes used as a form of currency.

• PORCUPINE

(see Animals)

Defense mechanisms working overtime.

Metaphorically bristling at any new ideas, possibilities, or relationships for fear of failure or being hurt.

You may be threatening others in order to get your own way, whether or not you actually intend to follow through on the warning given.

• POTATO

(see Garden, Farm, Vegetables)

An alternative *earth* emblem.

Because of its broad ranging use in folk remedies, a symbol for the return to health, usually in a physical sense.

Provision and the staples of life. Potatoes were an essential crop to many communities.

In a more negative sense, sitting on the side lines of life, getting sucked in by non-active pastimes (e.g., "being a couch potato").

• POVERTY

(see Money, Slum)

A beggar: Expecting to experience a loss, and anxiety that comes from this expectation. Alternatively, bad management and the need for improved frugality.

Starvation: An aspect of your personality or talents that is inadequately developed, or needs some type of infusion (see *Hunger*).

Things in your life that you have blatantly neglected. For example, seeing rags covering your head might coincide with needing to study more tenaciously so that your mind is not "poor."

Negative self-images. Feeling as if you deserve no better than rags.

An illustrative lesson in charity. If we turn to the pages of Dickens's *A Christmas Carol*, we can see how dream images of poverty can help improve a miserly disposition.

• PREGNANCY

(see Adoption, Baby, Birth, Miscarriage)

For a woman (or her partner) who is pregnant, or wishing to be so, a situational dream that needs no further interpretation.

Being figuratively fertile with ideas, energy, and creative insight.

A very good seed has been planted for a project near and dear to your heart, but now patience is required. It will take time for this effort to manifest, and it cannot be rushed without endangering your groundwork.

• PRICES

(see Bank/Banking, Menu, Money, Numbers, Shopping)

The prices on objects in our dreams reflect their value to us. For example, seeing someone buy an expensive designer outfit instead of an identical brand-name one illustrates a superficial personality, someone interested only in impressing others and looking more important. Or, paying an exorbitant price on a heart-shaped pillow could represent having given too much of yourself to a relationship, or valuing love as precious.

• PRIEST/PRIESTESS

(See Authority Figures, Church, Temple, Monastery)

An emblem of religious law, prohibitions, or taboos. In this case, the priest's or priestess's attitude in the dream will be very revealing (see *Religions*).

The Higher Self or a spiritual guide who may convey a message of a moral nature, or act as the voice of your conscience (see *Angel, Icons*).

What ritual or service is the priest or priestess performing? This might prove even more important to the dream's meaning. For example, if this person is setting up the altar, you may likewise be starting to settle on specific spiritual precepts. If the priest or priestess is performing a baptism, this might reflect a new beginning for you, in which your slate is wiped clean for a fresh start.

• PRISON

(see Cage)

• PROFESSIONS

(see by type, Jobs, Workers)

Each profession illustrated in dreams carries specific meaning, commonly the attribute that first comes to mind when you think of that profession. For example, an *astronaut* is adventurous and highly trained, bartenders are thought to be good listeners, and secretaries exhibit strong organizational skills. So, dreaming of all three of these individuals together might indicate the need to hone your personal listening skills for greater effectiveness.

Note that if you cannot find the specific profession dreamt of in the main listings, review that profession's central goal, location, and/or tools for possible meaning. For example, look up nurse under *healing* or *women*, and construction workers under *hammer*, *nails*, or *tools*.

• PROFESSOR

(see Authority Figures, Blackboard, School)

The conscious, logical mind and matters of learning. What subject is the professor teaching, and how does this affect or reflect upon your current situation?

Someone in your life whose knowledge you admire, especially in one specific field.

Your own faculty for self-learning, specifically from life's lessons.

• PROMISES

(see Oath, Notarization)

• PROPHYLACTICS

(see Orgasm, Sexual Encounters)

Concerns or thoughts centering around "safe sex."

Metaphorical protection, probably concerning vulnerability in relationships.

• PROSTITUTE

(see Men, Orgasm, Sexual Encounters, Women)

Feeling as if you've highly undervalued yourself, your work, or your art.

A sexual desire or drive that may not be healthy.

Illicit, immoral, or underhanded activities going on behind your back (although not necessarily pertaining to physicality).

Selling a service or idea to others that is not socially, religiously, legally, or culturally accepted.

• PUMPKIN

(see Eating, Garden)

A carved pumpkin often represents the specific emotions in the depicted face, so consider if it is happy, sad, angry, frightened, or whatever.

Traditionally an emblem of protection because of its use on Halloween to scare away mischievous spirits.

Made into *bread* or *pie*, this represents a positive transformation in either your finances or ability to act justly, respectively.

• PUNCTUATION

Quotation marks especially are the subconscious's way of drawing your attention to a specific key phrase in your dream. Make sure to remember this and ponder it. Each word, or the entire phrase, may have significant importance for your present situation or in the days ahead.

Each type of punctuation stresses something slightly different, even as it does in written form. The period denotes finality and completion, a question mark is uncertainty or inquiry, three dots (ellipses) reflect something that is unfinished or in progress, and an exclamation point indicates surprise or shock.

• PURPLE

(see Colors)

Dark: Mental *storms* and disorientation.

Royal purple: Personal rulership, self-control, and mastery.

Amethyst: Wisdom, especially of a spiritual nature (see *Crystals, Gems*).

Pale pastel purple: A spring color, often equated with Easter and rebirth.

• PUZZLES

(see Riddles)

The solution to problems in your life slowly piecing itself together. Look to see what's appearing in the pattern for more interpretive value.

Self-created confusion that comes from complicating simple matters. Go back to the basics and reevaluate this situation.

Brainteasers represent matters that you find confusing or overwhelmingly complex.

Word jumbles symbolize problems with communication, or difficulty in ordering your thoughts (see *Writing*).

A labyrinth is a type of three-dimensional puzzle that represents complex paths or situations that require patience and wisdom to traverse without losing your way.

Maze: Similar to a labyrinth, a maze reflects a situation through which it is difficult to navigate due to trickery or confusion that stems from external sources.

• PYRAMIDS

(see Landmarks, Locations)

Esoteric wisdom shared from the Collective Unconscious.

A good omen that portends achievement and financial gains.

Precision is needed in your evaluations to assure success. Scientists have shown the tremendous accuracy used in designing and building these great edifices; no less care should be taken with things you value.

In India, an alternative *fire* emblem. Similarly, in ancient Greece *the pictograph* of a pyramid could represent an idea or spirit that had fiery characteristics.

Mesopotamian: The meeting place between the gods and mortals. Edifices similar to pyramids were seen in Babylon at the core of the city around 3500 B.C.E. These buildings were called the *Gate* of the Gods. In your dream, such structures may represent a personally designed astral *temple*, where you can commune with your subconscious, your Higher Self, or the Divine.

• PYRITE

(see Gold)

• QUAIL

(see Birds, Feathers, Flying, Wings)

In the Middle Ages, quails were characterized as having amorous personalities, and were given the symbolism of erotic energy.

Courage and victory in battle. In Rome, these were *fighting* birds.

In a *cage*, the quail came to represent the embodied soul that seeks freedom.

Transmuting any poisons that threaten your physical, mental, or spiritual health. Aristotle believed that quails could safely eat toxins like hemlock that normally killed humans.

Unexpected blessing. The ancient Hebrews received quails as a miraculous feast (Ex. 16:11–12).

Among Hindus, the quail symbolizes spring and the returning *sun*. Similarly in Russia, this was an emblem of the dawn, a time of hope and new beginnings (see *Time*).

• QUARANTINE

(see Cage, Plagues)

Wishing to be removed from, or being forcefully removed from, a situation.

Avoiding some perceived health risk, sometimes by drastic means.

• QUARRY

(see Gems, Metals, Mine, Stones)

Tapping into the "mother lode" of knowledge or insight after concerted effort.

Fortunate discoveries that lead to literal or figurative prosperity.

Needing to dig a little deeper to uncover the truth or the *treasures* inherent in a specific situation.

• QUARTZ

(see Crystals)

A cold, distant person who never seems to let the walls down. In Greece, people believed that quartz was actually petrified *ice* that never thawed.

Pure, flowing inspiration and energy, especially in a religious context. The priestess of Vesta gathered *fire* from heaven using a quartz crystal for the sacred flames of the *altar*.

The ability to gain energy or power from your present situation. Note that quartz crystal holds a natural "charge," which is why it's used in watches.

•QUEENS
(see Authority Figures, Fables, Icons, Women)

•QUICKSILVER
(see Metals)

•QUOTATION MARKS
(see Books, Punctuation, Writing)

• RABBIT (HARE)

(see Animals)

The lunar, feminine aspect of self or the Universe.

Fertility, abundance, and sexuality (e.g., "breeding like rabbits").

Metaphorically: Prolific energy, as when a writer, musician, or artist overcomes creative blockage and creates a masterpiece.

Potentially sexual obsession that needs to be controlled or examined closely before it becomes destructive.

An overly large *white* rabbit in American theater represents the fine line between "imaginary" things and reality.

Rabbit's *foot*: The ability to move quickly and cleverly, or an omen of improved luck.

• RACCOON

(see Animals)

Getting into things that you're not supposed to. Raccoons are notorious and rather adept thieves.

A curious demeanor, eager for exploration. These are common traits of the raccoon.

The raccoon's *mask* represents privacy, ambiguity, or secrecy of some type. What's being hidden and from whom?

• RACING

(see Marathon, Running)

• RADIO

(see Amplification, Announcements, Music)

Matters of communication. How well are you "tuning into" the messages from others, yourself, and the Universe?

Static on a radio reflects similarly muddled discourse. Readjust your manner of conversation so that it can be understood clearly.

A terribly loud radio indicates someone with a strong personality who may try to dominate conversations through boisterous behavior. Frequently this is actually a manifestation of insecurity that needs attention. Alternatively, such amplification can indicate a message from the subconscious or Higher Self that has been trying to get through for some time.

• RAIN

(see Clouds, Fog, Snow, Sun, Water)

Fruitfulness. Spring showers nourish the *earth*, bringing forth *flowers* and *fruits*. What positive attributes have you been watering lately?

Possibly symbolic of sadness and grief where you are personified in the clouds.

Mist: Being melancholy or gloomy (e.g., "misty eyed").

Rain or *storm* clouds gathering: Increasing troubles, concerns, or despondency that seem to overwhelm all the bright moments.

• RAINBOW

(see Colors)

Biblical: A promise kept, as well as hope and forgiveness.

Birth, fertility, and creativity. In Africa, the rainbow *snake* made the world.

The *veil* between realities: In pre-Vedic traditions, and among the Norse people, the rainbow represents the *bridge* between this life and the next.

A rainbow appearing over any gathering of people represents divine blessings, unparalleled joy, success, and/or love.

• RAVEN

(see Birds, Feathers, Wings)

Scandinavian: A spiritual messenger. Heed well this bird's call, and look to the rest of the dream for more meaning.

During the Middle Ages, hearing the call of a raven during battle portended defeat or death. Are you fighting a lost cause?

Your ability to vocalize ideas and opinions. Note Edgar Allan Poe's use of the raven's call, highlighting this trait.

Creativity, especially in regards to using what's available to you. A raven will pick up and employ anything it can as a *tool* for nest building.

• RED

(see Blood, Colors)

Vital life, energy and passion, especially bright reds.

Brownish-red: Death, bitterness, or smoldering anger.

Danger! Stop whatever you're doing and look more closely, just as you would at a traffic light.

Red cape: Used in *bull* fighting, this is symbolic of controlling the masculine nature.

Red caps: Often worn by mischievous *fairies* or wizards in *fables*, this might indicate your own yearning for a little playfulness and knavery.

Bright scarlet: Anger or fury (e.g., "seeing red").

Red tape: Delays to the point of nearly being halted, often caused by bureaucratic approaches, people, or requirements.

• REFUGE

(see Sanctuary)

• RELATIONSHIPS

(see Bride, Engagement, Groom, Marriage, Parents)

These dreams frequently relate to real-life scenarios in which the relationships in the dream mirror those from waking hours. If, however, the relationship takes on different dimensions in the dream, this may reflect your hopes or fears for that association.

Building a relationship with strangers in your dream can indicate building similar *bridges* between your ego and psyche for self-actualization. It can also reveal a more social attitude developing in which you're not so shy about extending yourself to others.

Antagonistic relationships in dreams usually divulge your own hostility and conflicts with the persons seen. Alternatively, this may be self-hatred. In either case, the source of the anger needs to be detected and reconciled.

• RELIGIONS

(see Altar, Church, Monastery, Sanctuary, Sacrifice, Temple)

If the religion depicted is the one you currently practice, this dream reveals your feelings toward that faith, its tenets, and your activities within that organization.

The subconscious or Higher Self expressing a need to reconnect with sacred powers and spiritual ideals.

Different religions appearing in dreams may stem from your exposure to recent articles or documentaries on the subject. If this is the case, consider this part of the dream situational.

Each faith has a slightly different focus, which may reflect heavily on your current situation. For example, Buddhism is highly introspective and philosophical, which might reflect too much brooding on your part, or perhaps not enough, depending on the other dream images.

• RENTING

(see Apartment)

Transitory conditions in your life that exact a price, but produce no permanent results.

What's being rented here will improve your dream's interpretive value. For example, renting a *car* indicates that you may have a tendency to shuffle responsibility or run with other people's ideas instead of developing your own.

Wanting creature comforts without having to exert a lot of physical, mental, or emotional effort to keep them.

• REPAIRS

(see Hammer, Nails, Tools)

Look to see exactly what gets repaired in your dream. This can symbolize your *body*, mind, or spirit, or alternatively, a situation or relationship that needs mending. Usually repairs on a house equate to the self, whereas repairs to objects may be less personal in meaning.

The quality of the repairs performed here is also important. If, for example, a *castle* wall is patched with faulty materials and begins immediately to fall apart, this can reveal a halfhearted truce on the home front, or a makeshift cure for a malady that only covers symptoms.

• REVOLT

(see Fighting, Uprising)

• RHYME

(see Conversations, Riddles, Writing)

Something that seems, on the surface, nonsensical or baffling (e.g., "not having any rhyme or reason").

A mnemonic device that the subconscious or Higher Self uses to help you retain a dream key upon awakening. In this case, consider either the whole rhyme or each phrase for more meaning. For example, the children's rhyme of "thirty days has September, April, June, and November" might have numerical significance, or may equate to the symbolism of the months mentioned.

In poetry, rhyme helps establish a meter to the words, and carries ideas from one line into the next. So, consider how well you have paced yourself lately, or if your line of reasoning has been flowing in the right direction.

• RICE

(see Eating)

In Eastern lands, the emblem of providence and prosperity. Alternatively, this indicates the development of patience, as experienced when trying to pick up a single grain of rice with chopsticks.

If tossed at newlyweds in a dream, the symbolism is abundant joy and fertility (see *Wedding*).

• RIDDLES

(see Puzzles, Rhyme)

Some type of complexity that requires sound, creative thinking to solve. Unless time is of the essence, don't rush this answer.

Lacking clarity in the way you present something, or purposefully hiding your true motivations and feelings in a matter (e.g., "talking in riddles").

A lesson in disguise. In many *fables*, riddles are used to teach the main characters something specific about themselves or life. Similarly in ancient Japan, priests used riddles as a way of teaching seekers spiritual truths.

Something or someone who tries your patience by presenting everything in seemingly incongruous or incomprehensible terms.

• RINGS

(see Crystals, Gems, Gold, Jewelry, Metals, Silver, Stones)

An alternative *circle* emblem denoting eternity, repeated cycles, or longevity.

Binding *relationships*. In written history, *wedding* rings were exchanged as early as ancient Rome, and probably before. If depicted as a *nose* ring, this relationship may be very manipulative.

A symbol of authority or belonging. For example, high school rings indicate your place among that group, whereas a bishop's ring denotes a position of leadership.

A brass ring speaks of goals and hopes (e.g., "reaching for the brass ring"). Consider where this ring appears in your dream to see how close you are to obtaining those desires.

An *acrobat* on a set of rings reveals someone who has an excellent grip on a difficult situation in which they're in the spotlight.

A ring appearing around the collar of a shirt either indicates that you are paying too much attention to superficials, or that you need to clean up your act (probably the way you talk considering where a collar lies).

• RIVER

(see Water)

Free-flowing thoughts and actions.

Time's passage. The beginning of the river is the past, and where it goes represents the future. This is especially true if you dream of yourself *traveling* on the river.

If you see yourself in the water, being conveyed by an overwhelming current, this reflects either relinquishing yourself to your instinctive, emotional nature or having your individuality washed away by circumstances.

Traversing a river in a small water craft is an alternative type of *path* dream in which the current reflects your direction of personal growth.

Healing. Rivers figure heavily into folk medicine in which healers used the water's movement to convey sickness visually away from a patient. If this is the case, what is the water taking away? This item will give more meaning to the dream.

•ROBIN

(see Birds, Feathers, Wings)

As a harbinger of spring, the robin nearly universally represents renewed hope, fresh beginnings, reversals in negative attitudes, and a dawning *light* being shed on difficult situations.

In England, an emblem of fertility, especially if one comes pecking at a window.

•RODS

(see Divination, Sticks, Trees, Wand)

Traditionally an emblem of discipline, being applied to the backsides of ill-behaved children. If you have been acting childish lately, or found yourself lacking real restraint, this dream comes to make you more aware of how these things appear to, and affect, others.

Biblically: A divine tool that offers serenity (e.g., "thy rod and thy staff, they comfort me").

A fishing rod represents an augmented ability to use what's at your disposal to begin reaching a goal.

Authority (e.g., "the rod of rulership").

•ROLLER COASTER

Testing yourself by facing fear head-on.

Emotional ups and downs.

The thrill from dangerous adventures or liaisons. The question here is whether or not the danger is worth the excitement.

Anxiety over *sexual encounters*, or tension created by nonsexual relationships that constantly vacillate between love and hate, passion and passivity.

•ROPE

(see Knot, Ties, Web)

A surprising escape (e.g., the "rope trick").

Climbing a rope can be a type of *ascent* dream, whereas descending a rope reflects movement into the lower self—matters of a more physical or primal nature.

Walking a tightrope reflects finding yourself on a very fine edge between what's expected of you, and what you feel you can accomplish effectively. Alternatively, this can represent balancing fact and faith, or the beliefs of others against your own conscience.

A *jumping* rope may symbolize the voice of your inner child. Alternatively, it can reflect a restless spirit who finds that wanderlust often leads nowhere.

Being tied up by a rope may be a type of *obstacle* or *cage* dream.

• ROSE

(see Flowers, Gardens)

The loveliness of nature, or life itself.

A nearly timeless symbol of love, passion, and the spirit of beauty in all its many forms, having been originally associated with the goddess Venus. The *color* of the rose here provides more meaning. For example, *purple* roses are exotic emotions, *red* is for passionate love, and *yellow* is for friendship.

Thorny roses speak of the difficulties in all relationships. Native American shamans believe that nature hides its greatest *treasures* beneath such painful traps so that we have to work to receive the prize.

A rose with its bud just opening represents the blossoming of your highest conscious awareness.

Alchemically, the rose symbolizes wisdom; *blue* roses represent impossible tasks, and *gold* ones are an emblem for achievement.

Jung believed that in dreams a rose became a *mandala* representing an integrated person and wholeness.

In Babylonia and ancient Arabia, the rose became an alternative emblem for Paradise with strong sexual connotations of this also equating to a woman's vulva. Consequently, this can be a dream figure for *women*, and your feelings toward women.

• RUG

(see Carpet)

• RUINS

(see Archway, Buildings, Landmarks, Locations, Pillars)

The crumbling of a situation, relationship, or system of belief.

A reminder of transience. Even the greatest civilizations succumb to the hand of time. Therefore, live life to its fullest while you have the opportunity.

Falling from a place of glory, achievement, and respect, if only in your own *eyes*.

• RUNES

(see Languages, Pictographs)

• RUNNING

(see Acrobatics, Marathon, Olympics)

Something that's gotten out of control circumstantially or personally.

What's chasing you, or from what are you trying to escape? Perhaps the past or an unpleasant experience?

Hurrying, without necessarily having a defined goal.

• RUST

Disappointment in something or someone that, at first, appeared shiny and perfect.

Disuse of skills, knowledge, or talents. Check the meanings behind the item upon which the rust appears.

• SACRIFICE

(see Altar, Carcass)

Are you the one being sacrificed in the dream? If so, consider if you play the eternal martyr by denying your own needs and wants. Alternatively, for what exactly do you feel you should be punished?

Renouncing or forsaking something so that it can finally die away, especially an outmoded, harsh, or unrealistic self-image.

Feeling that your energy is abused, or efforts unappreciated, by others.

In the ancient world, sacrifices were made in order to gain divine favor. What is it that you must relinquish to achieve something better?

• SALAMANDER

(see Fairy)

• SALT

(see Eating, Herbs)

Worthiness (e.g., "a man worth his salt"). This saying actually dates back to ancient Rome where soldiers were paid in salt because it was so valuable.

Zest, or spicing things up.

Longevity and endurance. Salt is a natural preservative.

Cleansing. In the Middle Ages, priests commonly consecrated *altars* with salt, and salt can be used as an effective cleanser because of its gritty nature.

Painful reminders (e.g., "throwing salt in an open wound").

Being true to self and others, in word and deed (e.g., people who are the "salt of the earth").

Tossing salt over your shoulder in a dream is a protective gesture, so look to see on what or whom the salt lands.

Arabic: Promises made and kept. In ancient times, travelers in Arabia would take an *oath* of salt upon entering a home, as a way of saying they wouldn't harm anyone therein, or overstay their welcome.

• SALVE

(see Healing, Medicine, Physician)

A wound that is slowly being healed, within yourself or with others.

If an *insect* appears in cream, this reveals a temporary holdup in obtaining the restoration you desire (e.g., "a fly in the ointment").

A means of smoothing out a rough situation, sometimes unusual, that perhaps you haven't considered before. During the Middle Ages, one type of sympathetic cure was putting salve on the implement of harm (like a *knife*) instead of on the wound itself. Symbolically, this forgave the *weapon* for the pain inflicted, thereby aiding the cure. So, salve applied on the dream plane may also help bring peace to this matter.

• SANCTUARY (REFUGE)

(see Church, Holy Ground, Monastery, Temple)

A place or situation that offers you complete acceptance.

Protection and safety from someone or something perceived as wishing you harm.

Needing to take a retreat from everything to get some perspective (see *Desert, Island*).

• SAND

(see Desert, Oasis)

Spiritual or emotional dryness.

A self-imposed hermetic retreat for the purpose of delving further into your Higher Self or communing with God.

Being buried in sand, or engulfed in quicksand, equates to a kind of *death* or *burial* dream in which you feel completely engulfed by people or circumstances that drain your resources, but never give anything back.

Denial and refusing to see the truth for what it is (e.g., "having one's head in the sand").

Sand paintings among Native Americans represent *healing* and knowledge, especially of a spiritual nature. Observe this dream closely to see if any *pictographs* appear in the sand for further interpretive value.

• SAPPHIRE

(see Blue, Crystals, Gems, Jewelry, Stones)

•SATELLITE DISH

(see Radio, Telephone, TV)

Communication. The way you receive other people's signals. How effectively does the satellite dish work? Is it properly aligned?

Representative of the media's growing influence on contemporary life.

Tuning into a specific "wavelength" in a situation to improve your understanding.

An alternative *circle* symbol.

Remaining open and receptive to external ideas and input.

•SATYR

(see Animals, Fables)

Depicted as having the head of a man and the lower body of a goat, this creature represents the untamed nature within, especially procreative instincts.

Animalistic impulses and humankind's greater connection to the animal kingdom.

Biblically: An emblem of destruction and barrenness (Is 13:21), probably due to the connection between this image and various frolicsome pagan deities, including Faunus and Pan.

•SCALES

(see Balance)

•SCENT

(see Incense, Perfume, Smells)

•SCHEMATICS

Seeing any type of plans or *blueprints* in your dream often reveals symbolic or literal representations of your future hopes, what you are currently working toward, cycles that have repeated themselves in your life, or the patterns of fate currently at work in your reality.

The need to develop a solid outline for your life, including obtainable goals, so that growth can begin or continue.

• SCHOOL

(see Blackboard, Professor)

The classroom of life itself. What are you learning in this dream, and how can you apply it to your present situation?

Matters of education and training. What level of schooling is shown in the dream? Elementary school reflects the need to get back to basics, whereas college symbolizes preparation and learning as a key to success in our endeavors.

An unvoiced desire to return to school and achieve a specific personal goal, manifesting through the dream. If this is the case, check with your local institutions and see if you can't make this dream a reality!

• SCISSORS

(see Knife, Sword)

• SEAHORSE

(see Horse)

• SÉANCE

(see Death, Divination, Ghost)

Missing someone who has passed over, and wishing that person was nearby to provide advice or companionship.

Getting in touch with your own feelings regarding death and the afterlife.

Potential missives from beyond. The subconscious may choose this type of dream to convey ghostly messages because it is a familiar, less frightening apparition.

Matters of communication between yourself and the realms of spirit, including the Divine. How well does the séance progress? Does there seem to be an *obstacle* to effective mediumship? If so, consider what that obstacle is within your own life that likewise hinders your ability to accept or commune with the sacred.

• SEARCHING

For what exactly are you looking in the dream? This symbol will help you interpret the internal search that's going on. For example, seeking a missing *coin* might represent a longing to recapture financial security after a loss, and looking for a person can represent the desire for a mate.

How does the search feel? Is it futile or hopeful? If the former, perhaps your present focus is in the wrong place. What we think we need and what's best for us are not always in sync.

•SEASHELL

(see Oyster, Pearl, Water)

An alternative symbol for, and more ancient type of, a *cup*.

The voice of the *water*, the emotional, intuitive nature, reaching out to us from the swell of busy thoughts.

For some sea creatures, a type of *armor* that also becomes a home when necessary. Are you becoming too reclusive, or too picky about your personal space?

•SEASONS

Seasons in flux: Transformation of some sort, often *age* or activity related.

Autumn: The realization of maturity, and harvest from hard labors. Potentially also the need to conserve despite bounty; putting things in order before inclement "weather" (literally or figuratively) puts everything on hold.

Winter: A time of rest, or a cooling-off period when things can be reevaluated (see *Ice, Snow*).

Spring: A new beginning, refreshed hope, and the first signs of progress or growth with regard to a specific circumstance. Also, fertility (see *Rain*).

Summer: Warm feelings, potentially becoming "hot" (like a tiff turning to an all-out argument, or simple flirtation becoming passion). Alternatively, profuseness of energy and increased social activity (see *Fire*).

•SEDUCTION

(see Prostitute, Sexual Encounters)

Straightforward desires and passions.

A revealing dream that may indicate unhealthy relationships, like the siren who lures the sailor to doom and destruction.

Sensing that you've succumbed to a faulty bill of goods, sold by sweet words and pretty pictures that won't hold up under close examination.

• SEEDS

(see Flowers, Garden, Vegetables)

Seeds represent untapped potential, being the semen that fertilizes in earth's womb. Each type of seed holds a wealth of promise, if properly sown, watered, and cared for. What attributes are you trying to develop, and how conscientiously are you tending those seeds?

• SEPARATION

(see Divorce)

An alternative type of *desertion* dream.

Seeing something that is whole divide into two parts equates to either a situational separation (such as in *relationships*), or purposefully separating your conscious self from a portion of subconscious awareness/feelings.

Separation into several sections may reveal your own multifaceted nature and parts of yourself that you are unwilling or unable to recognize consciously. This can also be an indicator of multiple personality disorder; however, any such serious malady should be professionally determined, not assumed or hypothesized.

Separating yourself from a person or situation in a dream is often a signal from your subconscious that you are actually ready to break those ties and venture out alone.

• SERVANTS/SERVITUDE

(see Jobs, Professions, Workers)

Giving of yourself freely, but perhaps in excess.

Being in a situation or relationship in which one person is dominated by another's rules, ideas, expectations, and/or requirements.

Discovering that those around you are taking advantage of your good-hearted nature by having you wait on them hand and foot. Remember to say "no" once in a while!

• SEVEN

(see Numbers)

The unfolding of mystical relationships and the understanding of universal truths. Alternatively, a renewed focus on spiritual matters as they pertain to you personally.

Marvels. There are seven wonders in the world, seven colors in the *rainbow*, etc.

Inventive energy that comes to fruition. Biblical creation took seven days, including God's day of rest.

• SEWING

(see Fabric, Needle)

The need to repair a relationship, a system of belief, or any other situation that has somehow been allowed to disintegrate, or torn apart by negativity.

Sewing machines represent having all the *tools* you need to fix a situation. Don't be afraid to rely on your wisdom, talents, and insight.

Thread symbolizes the lines of fate and destiny that we all work within and weave. To break a thread is a negative omen of bad fortune or mishaps on the horizon.

• SEXUAL ENCOUNTERS

Aspects of physical relationships that you may be unwilling to recognize, or those about which you feel timid. For example, some people are uncomfortable talking about what really makes them feel good, or about what types of things they fantasize.

Fears and uncertainties about your physical performance in bed.

Unexpressed desires toward specific individuals. Sometimes these people are unobtainable and uninterested. In this case, the dream allows you to live out the fantasy in a socially acceptable manner.

• SHADOW

(see Black, Darkness)

Dark forces that threaten to undermine your spiritual quest. Note that these forces can also come from within.

Your own shadow or alternate persona. For the goodness to mean something quantifiable we must all overcome this darker side of the soul.

Shadow boxing represents an internal argument you're having with your sense of morality.

Not having a shadow equates to someone with a soulless character, without depth or passion. In earlier times, anyone who did not bear a shadow was considered cursed, like *vampires*.

• SHEEP

(see Animals, Wool)

A symbolic representation for a passive, shy, or docile person.

A sign that you, or someone you know, are too easily led astray by strong or charismatic people.

Black sheep represent the shadow, or feelings of isolation and rejection. Alternatively, this may reveal you are unafraid to pursue your own way, despite others' opinions.

Among Christians, an emblem of those saved by grace.

Hebraic: Wealth, purity, and innocence. This was the only creature acceptable for the Passover observance.

• SHEPHERD

Being able to guide and control yourself or others. If the shepherd is seen with a flock, the flock represents those people whom you guide, or the characteristics within yourself over which you are exerting management.

Gentle love and concern that always maintains a respectful distance.

• SHIP

(see Boat, Water)

• SHOES

(see Barefoot, Clothes, Foot)

Old, torn shoes symbolize snares along the path, or long, hard roads traveled to obtain your heart's desire. These can also reveal a tendency to always fall back on what's comfortable and known to you, instead of taking risks.

Boots are protective, so this dream may portend some rough footing ahead for which you should prepare.

Wearing unusual shoes in a dream may indicate a need to see things differently. Try looking at this situation from another perspective (e.g., "walking a mile in someone else's shoes").

The kind of shoes seen in the dream can reveal how you walk through life. For example, seeing *baby* shoes means that you're very unsure of things, and compensate by moving slowly. Ballet shoes can disclose a person who either tiptoes through difficult situations, or someone who has unique grace and mobility.

Trying on shoes represents testing various options until you find the perfect one (e.g., "if the shoe fits, wear it").

Wearing new shoes symbolizes change and transitions with which you may not be totally comfortable yet.

In Egypt and Greece, shoes were part of fertility rights, which is how they became part of *marriage* rituals today. So, the throwing of a shoe or seeing numerous shoes following behind you in a dream represents productivity or abundance.

Small shoes symbolize virginity, or being naive about worldly matters, as in the story of Cinderella.

•SHOPPING

(see by item, Money, Prices)

•SIGNAGE

(see Billboard, Pictograph)

Read any sign that appears in your dream, be it a *highway* marker, a street sign, an advertisement, or whatever. The messages thereon will often provide clues to the deeper meaning of your dream, if not unlock its meaning for you completely.

Traffic signs: On the dream plane, each traffic sign has some synonymous meaning to what it signifies to a *car's* driver. For example, stop signs mean just that—stop whatever you're doing and look all around for signs of danger or trouble. A yield sign indicates that you're probably being too rigid and need to learn the value of flexibility. Signs for roadwork usually reveal that the path ahead may be a little bumpy or slower moving than you might like, so prepare to be patient. One that reads "no shoulder" shows that you overexposed yourself in some situation, and need to back off a bit for your own good.

Exit sign: We look for exits when we want to find the way out of a *building*. From what or whom are you trying to withdraw?

Street signs: If these signs are those that you pass regularly in your travels, consider this a circumstantial dream that needs no further explanation. On the other hand, street names can have very symbolic meanings. For example, one called "Normal Avenue" might reveal thoughts about your own sense of normalcy, and how you fit in with your peer group.

Written advertisements can show up in numerous places in your dream, from being part of a newspaper to appearing on a supermarket wall. The meaning for each is interpreted similarly to street signs, using the product name or use as the key. For example, a vitamin ad might be construed as an admonition to take better care with your health, whereas an ad for a cruise ship might reveal a personal desire to take a vacation, or get more in tune with the *water* element.

• SILVER

(see Colors, Metals, Moon)

Depending on what is seen as silver, this may be an alternative type of *coin* or *money* dream.

An emblem of the feminine, lunar, intuitive nature.

Something within yourself that you treasure. See what shape the silver takes for more interpretive value. For example, seeing a silver heart may reveal that you consider a loving nature very valuable, and an essential part of your being.

Tarnished silver shows disuse or poor upkeep. What is it that's being neglected?

• SINKING

(see Directions)

Not realizing that you're retreating from the real world, or a situation, only to be in worse trouble.

In quicksand: Losing your identity to a group, corporation, or set of circumstances. Alternatively, having your mobility or normal escape mechanisms impeded by a person or situation.

Feeling hopelessly swallowed up by problems, emotions, or a relationship.

If this is not a frightening or uncomfortable sensation, it may be that you are traveling into your own subconscious, the animal nature, or Super Ego, and integrating the content.

If a *boat* is sinking, this can symbolize the end of a relationship, partnership, or other joint efforts, particularly profitable ones.

• SIX

(see Numbers)

In mainstream religions, six is often associated with *evil*, such as the number of the Beast (666) in the Book of Revelation.

Protection. The six-pointed Star of David, the emblem of Judaism, was frequently used as a protective talisman, bearing specific potency against evil.

An alternative type of *crystal* symbol, as many natural crystals have a hexagonal form.

May also be considered a number of completeness, as creation took six days, with God resting on the seventh (see *Seven*).

Among some Native American tribes, this is the number of mental or emotional strength.

• SIZE

(see Magnification)

How large or how small things look in a dream is a very revealing factor. For example, seeing yourself as minute might indicate that your self-esteem needs work. Conversely, seeing someone in giant form reveals idolization, sometimes to a dangerous point that a person cannot possibly live up to in reality. Over- or underemphasized objects can be interpreted similarly, like a large heart equating to an immense capacity to give and receive love, or a tiny wall indicating something you see as only a very small obstacle to your goals.

Narrow or wide: Narrow might reveal narrow-mindedness, while wide angles show more openness and receptivity.

• SKUNK

(see Animal, Smells)

Self-assertion and confidence. The skunk's scent is a protective odor, but it is uniquely its own.

Getting the respect one is due. Skunks do not like confrontation, and usually withhold their spray until no other option is left. Have you been holding back in some area where recognition of your abilities is long overdue?

Irritating people or situations. Being sprayed by a skunk causes all kinds of distress, most of which stems from frustration about being in the wrong place at the wrong time!

• SKY

(see Blue, Clouds, Space)

Frequently a masculine symbol. Both Hindus and Native Americans speak of "father sky" (see *Men*).

An alternative, higher level of awareness. Possibly a type of *flying* or *ascent* dream.

The transcendent, limitless self. An image that reconnects the dreamer to her/his heritage as a universal being (see *Star*).

• SLUM

(see Garbage, Poverty)

Disorderly, chaotic, or corrupt thoughts.

Financial or personal difficulties that create impoverished sensations, or lower self-esteem.

A subconscious editorial on urban conditions. How do you see this area? Is it improving or getting worse, and what role do you play in making things different?

An indicator of personal health. If the *buildings* are badly run-down, and litter lies everywhere, you're probably not eating right or getting enough rest.

• SMELLS

(see Incense, Perfume)

On the dream plane, smells frequently engender memories of past experiences and our reactions to those experiences. Like other senses, the way we feel about each aroma is very personal, and should be interpreted accordingly.

• SMOKE

(see Fire, Fog, Incense)

Not being completely truthful with yourself or others (e.g., "putting up a smoke screen") in order to avoid an issue.

If you see yourself or someone else smoking a cigarette, this may be an oral fixation, or a symbolic substitution for other desires.

What feelings are you allowing to fester inside? Where there's smoke, there's fire, and something is definitely burning!

A type of message or oracle. The Native Americans sent smoke signals to communicate with one another, and many ancient civilizations used the smoke from sacrificial fires for *divination*. In this case, see if images appear in the smoke, and watch its *direction* of movement for more interpretive material.

Smoking a pipe is indicative of peace, and the sealing of a bond, especially if the pipe is offered to someone else, or shared around a group.

• SNAKE

(see Animals, Dragon, Lizard)

In the Old Testament, the emblem of temptation and *evil*.

Greco-Roman: A symbol of renewed health and well-being. Note that the caduceus, a symbol of physicians, appears as two snakes entwined on a staff.

Transformation and development. The snake sheds its old skin to make room to grow.

Being bitten by a snake is not a bad omen, as it might seem initially. Instead, because of the snake's regenerative power, it represents a new awareness developing within.

A phallic symbol that sometimes comes to women upon conception, or when the dreamer is figuratively pregnant with creative ideas and psychic impressions.

• SNOW

(See Clouds, Ice, Rain, Sun, Water)

Cold or distant demeanors that cover up one's true feelings.

Feeling momentarily halted, frozen, or paralyzed by external forces that will eventually give way.

A temporary barrenness or time of rest that leads to personal growth and refreshment.

Individuality, and asserting that sense of self without remorse or uncertainty. Note that no two snowflakes are ever alike.

Snowperson: Indifference or frigidity toward men or women, depending on the gender indicated in the sculpture. Alternatively, trying to mold others into an image that you find pleasing, but one with which they may not be comfortable.

A snow *storm* represents confusion or the inability to see things clearly due to external hindrances.

• SODA POP

(see Beverages)

The bubbles in this drink reflect an upbeat, happy attitude that can lift the spirits of those around you.

Health: In the Victorian era, soda was only available by prescription, and used to help overcome sickness.

Refreshed energy, zest, or outlooks.

• SOUTH

(see Directions)

• SPACE

(see Astronaut, Meteorite, Planets, Sky, Stars, UFO)

An *abyss* that seems vast and untouchable, but one that the wonders of human technology are slowly making accessible. What new parts of yourself lie just beyond your reach that might likewise soon open up?

A more universal mind-set that ponders many potentialities and dimensions to any situation before making a decision or drawing a conclusion.

If you are moving toward, or *flying* in, space, likely a type of *ascension* dream.

Metaphorically representative of the immense potential of the mind.

•SPACESHIP

(see Airplane/Airport, Alien, Flying, UFO)

As a symbol of the future, this ship may take you forward in time to see where your current course of action leads.

Because of its otherworldly nature, this may represent the Universal Mind, and missives from same.

If approached expectantly, this dream expresses a strong desire for *travel* and adventure, especially to exotic places.

Like other vehicles, an emblem denoting movement, transition, and change (see *Airplane, Bus, Car, Horse*).

If the vision makes you apprehensive, this reveals some anxiety over experiencing new things, unfamiliar circumstances or places, and rapid change.

•SPEEDS

(see Velocity)

•SPIDER

(see Insects, Web)

In men, this is frequently a maternal image (see *Woman*).

Ancient Grecian and Egyptian, and Native American: Fate and our ties to all times and all peoples. In Greece, Arachne spun the thread of people's lives. Egyptians had Neith, who wove the world, and the Pueblo Indians have Spider Woman, who created the world from two strands of thread (see *Web*).

Feeling trapped in someone's well-executed snare.

Creating connections that help you to finish a goal. Note that the line of networking here may not be direct, even as the spider's *web* may take unexpected turns.

• SPINNING (WEAVING)

(see Fabric, Needle, Sewing, Web)

The passage of time.

A creative process that sometimes seems as long and arduous as spinning *gold* into straw.

• SPIRALS

(see Pictographs)

The swirling powers of creation.

The essence of individuality (note the shape of DNA molecules).

Depending on its direction of movement, this can indicate a type of *ascension* into higher thought patterns, or a descent into self and introspection (see *Sinking*). Downward spirals can indicate a strong focus on the less evolved animal nature within.

Stationary spirals can be an alternative type of *stair* or *circle* dream.

Matters of love and caring. Sacred geometricians depict the heart chakra as a spiral flame.

The cycle of *death* and rebirth, in a literal or figurative sense. This is why many ancient sacred dances (see *Dancing*) had circular patterns.

Divinatory ability: The ancient Roman augurs carried a staff called a *littus* which was often capped with a spiral pattern, likely acting as a focus for the seer (see *Rods, Sticks, Wand*).

• SPORTS

(see Acrobatics, Jumping, Marathon, Olympics, Running)

Each sport depicted in a dream reveals different dynamic emotions or actions on your part. For example, seeing an acrobat is far different from dreaming of a football player. The first likely symbolizes a recognized need for flexibility in your current situation, whereas the second might reveal aggressive action needed to achieve your goals. Consider each vision separately, as well as how the athlete(s) performs, for more insight.

Team sports speak of the ability to act in concert with others. How well does the team play together? Does one person seem to dominate the field, or is it a cooperative effort?

Extreme sports like windsurfing and skateboarding reflect the need to push yourself to the limits of excellence, but sometimes with tremendous risks involved. Start considering the *price* you may pay for trying to obtain that proverbial *brass ring*.

• SQUARE

(see Four, Pictograph)

Metaphorically, the inability to fit in due to social awkwardness (e.g., being "square").

Trying to adapt to an impossible situation, like putting a square peg in a round *hole*.

Boundaries. Like the outlines in a coloring book, the *lines* of a square may contain something, or keep something out. Look to the rest of the dream for more information to see if this fits. For example, if a house sits amid a high square fence, this probably shows that you're very private and keep a strong wall between yourself and others.

If a square *frame*, highlighting a perspective.

• STAPLES

(see Connecting Devices)

• STAR

(see Darkness, Sky, Space)

Your unrealized wishes. The tradition of wishing on stars is very ancient, going back to Northern peoples who wished on the first star (Venus) as a type of supplication to that goddess. This custom also tied into astrology and the belief that the heavens influence life on earth (see *Zodiac Signs*).

What constellation or portrait do the stars form? Draw the pattern that you saw in the dream, then play connect the dots and see what appears. Use this image to help interpret the dream further.

Being overly romantic or idealistic (e.g., "starry eyed").

Dreams, hopes, and goals (e.g., "reaching for the stars").

Deliverance or help in a time of great need. A star heralded Christ's birth, and the Good *Fairy* of *fables* carries a powerful *magic wand* topped with a star.

Falling stars and comets are usually some type of warning or announcement (see *Meteorite*). Historically people believed they presaged important events or disasters.

The direction the star is moving, if or where it lands, and other scenery in this dream may qualify it more for you.

Star *fish* dramatically reflect the New Age precept of "as above, so below." Nothing exists in the heavens that is not likewise on the *Earth* or within you. They are also an alternative *pentacle* emblem.

Your soul, or matters of spirit. In ancient times, people often believed that their soul was tied to a specific star, and when that star was low in the sky it represented peril to their life.

•STATES

(see Locations)

•STATIC

(see Radio, TV)

Tension or friction that develops between people, or in situations, due to different outlooks and approaches.

Not communicating ideas and concepts clearly, or having your communications interrupted by external sources.

The inability to "tune into" other people or circumstances effectively so that tolerance and understanding can ensue.

•STEALING

(see Bank/Banking, Money)

Having something or someone you don't feel you deserve, whether or not this feeling has any foundation.

Someone taking credit for an idea or accomplishment, instead of sharing the recognition with those who deserve it.

Look to see what is taken in the dream, as this can provide more meaning. For example, seeing someone rob a house symbolizes a person or situation threatening your personal space or possessions.

•STEEL

(see Metals)

• STICK

(see Trees, Rods, Wand)

Depending on its size and shape, this can be an emblem of leadership (e.g., "speak softy and carry a big stick").

Freudian: An alternative phallic symbol.

A metaphorical message to perk up and stop being a "stick-in-the-mud."

The type of wood, its shape, and how it is used or seen in the dream will further delineate this image for you. For example, a piece of hazel wood with a forked end may symbolize improved divinatory talents or the ability to empathically "douse" out a situation (see *Divination*), as this wood was traditionally used for *water* witching.

• STIFFNESS

(see Lameness, Numbness, Paralyzation)

A circumstantial dream that comes from sleeping in an uncomfortable position.

Arrogant, strict, and uncompromising attitudes exhibited by yourself or others.

Because stiffness impedes your ability to move, this can be an alternative type of *obstacle* dream.

• STOCK MARKET

(see Bank/Banking, Money)

Things in which you place your trust, but which may not be very secure.

Closely reviewing your assets and resources (e.g., "taking stock").

If the stock market crashes, this represents having the rug pulled out from under your hopes and dreams to the point of despondency.

If specific stocks appear in your dream, consider their *names* or *abbreviations* for alternative symbolic value. For example, a company with a name like Environmental Design may equate to needing to make changes in your surroundings, specifically those that will be more healthful.

•STONES

(see Crystals, Excavation, Gems, Jewelry, Mine, Minerals)

The central self; the core of your being.

Being hard-hearted or having a stony disposition.

A place of origin; beginnings with foundation. Ancient beliefs contended that humankind was born of stone, which is one of the reasons why uniquely shaped stones or those with unusual markings were worshipped as goddesses.

A rolling stone: By gathering no moss, the stone (representative of self) keeps progressing along its *path*. The caution here is not moving so fast that valuable lessons get left by the wayside.

Standing stones: Indicative of nature worship and *earth religions*. This may reveal an interest in same, or an urge to get closer to the land. This can also be an alternative *circle*, *cross*, or *wheel* emblem, depending on the stones' configuration.

Holed stones formed from *water* are considered harbingers of improved luck. Similarly, small stones called *saivo* in Finland were carried as talismans, being gathered from the same region as the standing stones.

Throwing stones: Casting aspersions that may or may not be accurate. Placing the blame on others without seeing your own faults.

Birth stones: Dreaming of your own birth stone is very serendipitous.

Boulders: An alternative type of *obstacle* dream, where going around this issue is not the answer. You must find a way to clear this *path*, or go over the boulder instead of avoiding the issues. Alternatively, the boulder may block your path for a good reason, such as one balanced at the edge of an *abyss*.

Geodes: A hidden *treasure*. Don't always judge a *book* by its cover alone—look a little further than the superficials in this situation. The effort will yield life's intangible riches, all of which are well worth your time.

Fossils: Evolutionary states in ourselves, others, or situations. Alternatively, a historical connection with the greater chronicles of *earth* and humankind.

Patience. In the East, wise people will often instruct their students to learn diligence by watching rocks grow.

Skipping stones: A kind of childhood release that allows the mind to wander. Count the *number* of times the stone skips and consider its numerological value. Or, take this as a simple treat from your inner child, that gently reminds us that leisure does not have to equate to being lazy.

•STORK

(see Birds, Feathers, Wings)

The dance of a stork represents the ability to make the right moves to ensure your success.

Due to children's stories, this is an emblem of fertility, especially physical.

Maternal instincts toward people or special projects and goals. Storks are fiercely dedicated to their young.

•STORM

(see Disasters, Lightning, Rain, Snow, Wind)

Internal or external conflict.

Emotional buildup that threatens to rage freely if you don't find a constructive outlet for that energy.

An emotional release that leads to liberation (like a good cry), just as *rain* is figuratively "released" from *clouds* to nourish the land.

•STORYTELLERS

(see Books, Fables)

The preservation of history, culture, religion, or central truths. Among many civilizations, this person equated to the medieval bard, or Hebrew cantor, who by their talents kept an oral legacy for a specific group alive. In interpreting such a dream, consider what story is told, by and to whom, and how it is received for more meaning. For example, the rejection of a Bible story from your youth in a dream might likewise symbolize your personal rejection of that idea or belief system.

Morals or lessons from the subconscious or Higher Self, neatly disguised in a more enjoyable construct. Storytelling has always been an effective teaching tool because it draws our attention away from the chore to something we perceive as fun.

Potentially, a personal creation that should find its way into a tape or book, if only for your own enjoyment. Inventive energies are much more fluid when we sleep, and many excellent artists have received inspiration for a story, song, or painting this way.

Religious stories denote a change in perspectives from mundane to more devout matters, whereas hearing things like fables reveals a romantic nature prone to daydreaming.

• STRANGERS

(see Crowd, Men, Women)

Freudian: Unsatisfied or unrecognized libido; repressed emotions.

Situational: Think back to see if you met someone recently who made a stronger impression than initially realized.

A part of yourself with which you have remained unfamiliar.

Does the stranger say anything? This may be an important observation, insight, or question to ponder. Strangers are sometimes easier to talk to because they have no personal involvement in our situations, so your subconscious may personify itself through such images.

• SUFFOCATION

The inability to express yourself as freely or honestly as you might wish (see *Choking*).

Being unsatisfied and unfulfilled by your present situation to the point where this slowly "kills" creativity or individuality.

Being overwhelmed by restrictions imposed upon you by others, your culture, society, or religion.

If you see yourself suffocating someone else, this either expresses aggression toward that person, or something so morally or ethically offensive that you want to stifle it.

• SUN

(see Candle, Gold, Fire, Hearth, Red, Torch)

The masculine nature. Many ancient gods were affiliated with, or represented as, the sun, including Apollo in Greece and Ra in Egypt (see *Icons, Men*).

Noontime: A fullness of conscious awareness or rationality. You can trust that your current course of reasoning is "right on" (see *Time*).

Sunrise or sunset: Beginnings or endings, respectively. Each stage of the sun equates to phases in our own life, situations, or relationships, sunrise being *birth*, and sunset representing *death*.

Increasing physical energy or mental activity.

An omen of good fortune. Many cultures regarded the sun's presence at special occasions as a sign of divine favor and blessings.

The egoic, conscious, intelligent aspect of your mind, versus the intuitive, feeling portion, which is lunar (see *Moon*).

Sunburn: Getting figuratively "burned" by a man, or feeling resentment toward men in general. Alternatively, too much use of the logical mind causes neglect of the instinct, leading to fiery times.

• SWALLOW

(see Birds, Feathers, Wings)

The arrival of this bird in spring makes it an envoy of hope and new opportunities.

In heraldry, the swallow represents conscientious attention to duty.

China: A symbol for daring and fearlessness. Also a stern protector of marital fidelity.

Biblical (Old Testament): Communications, sometimes those with little meaning. In this setting, the swallow is called a chatterer.

• SWAMP

(see Sinking, Water)

The current situation you're encountering has a weak foundation that simply won't endure over time. Rethink your approach here, and rebuild on sturdier ground.

The situation around you is murky and confusing, and there seems to be little if any insight on which to draw. In this instance, taking yourself away to fresher water is recommended.

Memories that are either being dredged up, or those you would prefer to bury. Look to see what else is in and around the swamp for more interpretive insight here.

• SWAN

(see Birds, Feathers, Wings)

A recognition of finality and ending (e.g., "singing one's swan song").

Among Hindus, this bird is interchangeable with the *goose*, representing creative origination and the breath of life.

The Celts regarded the swan as a solar bird that was beneficent and a shape-shifter. In a dream, this can relate to your ability to adapt to a new situation gracefully.

Native American: An emblem of trust and forgiveness.

Swans are also representative of love interests, being sacred to Aphrodite, Venus, and Zeus, the latter of whom changed himself into a swan to pursue the affection of Leda.

Dreaming of two swans together portends very devoted *relationships*. Swans mate for life.

Because of the story of the Ugly Duckling, swans also represent positive transformations in self-image. It can also reflect spending time with the wrong groups of people who engender lower self-esteem.

• SWELLING

Having an overinflated ego on a specific matter. The exact location of the swelling will delineate this dream further.

Self-originated *obstacles* that slow down any progress you hope to make.

Any matter that gets out of control, especially those things caused by emotional poisons like anger, bitterness, and jealousy.

Something or someone that has infected you physically, mentally, or spiritually, from which you are beginning to see the negative effects and consequences.

• SWIMMING

(see Sports, Water)

Water represents the intuitive nature and the subconscious. The movement through this liquid indicates either a willingness to traverse hidden portions of the self, or focusing on a defined aspect of subconsciousness as the goal of your swim.

Success in a situation in which you were asked effectively to "sink or swim."

Regulation of the feminine aspects of self so that instincts or emotions do not overcome rationality.

A balance between the spiritual and mundane, leaning slightly more toward spiritual matters depending on the amount of the body shown as immersed.

• SWORD

(see Knife, Weapons)

Jung felt that this represented the conscious ego seeking freedom and singularity, separate from one's place of origin or core group.

A *tool* that can help or harm. Just as the sword Excalibur could inflict wounds or keep a nation strong, swords represent all the things we have at our disposal—talents, knowledge, resources—that we have the responsibility to use wisely.

Truthfulness. Edged weapons cut through deceit in our dreams to the heart of any situation, even those things in which we deceive ourselves.

Feudal Japan: The emblem of a warrior's soul. The Katana is a long sword that represents a samurai's soul and will, while the Wagasahi was shorter and the implement of honor and defense.

Honorably fighting for a just cause, often taking an integral leadership role in that fight (e.g., "taking up a sword"). Note that kings used a sword to bestow knighthood, and knights in turn regularly swore oaths upon swords.

A masculine emblem and alternative phallus. In pagan Europe, swords were owned by men, and often buried with them, whereas women held the house and land.

Breaking or misplacing a sword reflects the loss of authority or heroic mettle, or falling from an honored position in the eyes of those you respect.

An ancient emblem of the Sacred King, which may equate to your own masculine nature or the God aspect of the universe (see *Men*).

In the Tarot, an emblem of trouble and conflict.

• SYLPH

(see Fairy)

• TAPE

(see Connecting Devices, Music, Red)

• TATTOOS

(see Body, Ink, Pictographs)

Taking pride in something specific. For example, many people put the name of a wife or husband on a tattoo, or the *flag* of their nation to honor that affiliation. What does the one in your dream depict?

Allegorically, the marks that life leaves upon us. People in some tribal cultures tattoo their personal history on their bodies for the world to read. What types of markings has your life's experiences left behind?

• TAXES

(see Bank/Banking, Money)

Feeling financially burdened by someone or something over whom or which you have little control.

Paying exorbitant taxes can reflect oppression from a specific source (the payee in the dream).

A situational dream caused by aggravation over recent tax increases or issues.

• TEA

(see Beverages, Herbs)

In the East, this beverage is sacred to Buddha, making it one of tranquillity and meditation. This symbol expresses that actions and words are in accord.

An ability to see beyond the surface of a situation and discern hidden truths. Tea leaf reading is still a popular form of *divination*.

Universal ideals and community. In Japan, the tea ceremony becomes a group meditation on the higher truths common to all humankind.

Two people pouring out of the same teapot in your dream portends arguments.

•TEETH

(see Body, Mouth)

Hostility or an attack, such as when dream figures deliver "biting words" or "bare their teeth."

Losing teeth in a dream may reflect words said in haste, or losing the ability to speak candidly.

Because this bony part of the body endures long after death, it has some associations with the cycle of *birth*, *death*, and rebirth. In this context, losing teeth might equate to losing the will to live or having your personal power taken away.

Rotten teeth equate either to the fear of old age, or someone whose words are filled with so much insincere sweetness that decay in that *relationship* is inevitable.

Having teeth pulled out represents an end to suffering that is aided by an external force.

•TELEPHONE

(see Answering Machine, Conversations)

Matters of communication and effective speech.

News or messages from your Higher Self, others, or the Universe.

Endlessly ringing: Overlooking or misconstruing the signals you're receiving.

Out of order: Closing yourself off from communication or socialization with a large group of people. This situation may have been by personal choice, or something that was caused circumstantially.

A telephone left off its hook indicates not wishing to listen, often to a specific person. The question here is whether or not turning a deaf *ear* is the right solution to your problem.

Dialing a phone in your dream and always getting a busy signal implies that other people always seem too busy to listen to your ideas or problems.

Being put on hold represents people or situations inhibiting free discourse in some way, including the constraints caused by propriety and societal expectations.

• TEMPERATURE
(see Fire, Hearth, Ice, Snow, Sun)

Blisteringly hot: A similarly heated situation exists in the waking hours, from which you need to protect yourself or you will get hurt.

Frigid: Emotional apathy or distance. Whether this pertains to you or someone else will become more clear by examining the rest of the dream.

Warmth: Kindness, compassion, friendship, and other warm feelings that are not forced or coerced.

Lukewarm: Indifference or nonchalance with regard to a specific person, situation, activity, or goal.

• TEMPLE
(see Church, Holy Ground, Monastery, Sanctuary)

Temples have connections with ancient ideas, history, sacred beliefs, and rituals. While similar in meaning to a church, the theme indicated by a temple is not one linked to Christian ideals. What type of temple appears in your dream? A Japanese shrine, for example, has strong ties with Buddhist teachings regarding proper speech and action. A Grecian temple, on the other hand, might relate to the development of oracular senses.

According to both Edgar Cayce and Carl Jung, this *building*, like other structures, may be an emblem for your *body*. Take special notice of the condition of each portion of the building for more interpretive information on your physical condition.

Esoterically, this edifice represents a personal astral temple, a place of safety, and learning on a higher plane. The Templars, older Masonic mysteries, and other similar teachings tell of developing or finding such a place through meditation.

• TEN
(see Numbers)

Manifestation; an alternative type of *one* numerologically.

Cabalistic: Alterations in your spiritual goals or *path*.

Divine or mundane law. In the Old Testament, Moses received 10 commandments that were to be obeyed by the Israelites (see *Stones*).

The muse: David, the great bard of the Old Testament, had a harp with 10 strings (see *Music*).

•TENT

Transitions and movement, or an actual shift in residence. Tents are temporary shelters, easily relocated.

Inviting someone into a tent is akin to welcoming them into your family and/or sharing your house with them. Please note, however, that these people can represent principles and beliefs that you accept into yourself.

•THEATER

(see Acting, Costumes, Masks)

Unrealistic fantasies; the desire to escape to a personal imaginary realm instead of facing reality.

Glamorizing or romanticizing aspects of yourself or a situation.

The stage of life itself. Shakespeare once said that all the world's a stage. So, the movie or show that is playing at this theater is very important to the interpretive value of the dream. For example, seeing a production of *Arsenic and Old Lace* might indicate some treachery afoot, whereas seeing *Die Hard* reveals the development of tenacity and courage.

•THREAD

(see Fabric, Needle, Sewing, Spinning)

•THREE

(see Numbers, Trident)

The triune nature of humankind as body-mind-soul; and the triune nature of many divine figures (Father-Son-Holy Spirit; Maiden-Mother-Crone).

Stability. Three legs gives the tripod or *cauldron* greater strength.

In ancient Greece, the number representing fate. External, powerful forces are at work here, whose source is wholly or partially unknown to you.

If the number appears on a die in the dream, this portends excellent luck (e.g., "three is a charm").

Oracular experts claim any dream that repeats itself three times will come true.

Jung felt this number represented some type of incompleteness, like a table that's missing one leg.

• THRESHOLD
(see Archway, Door)

Breakthroughs or setbacks, depending on the *direction* of movement.

Changing your basic values, or status as is shown by the *groom* carrying the *bride* over a threshold.

Birth and *death*, depending again on the direction of movement. Generally, coming into a threshold marks a beginning, while leaving one indicates an ending.

• THUNDER
(see Storms)

Reverberations or waves of emotion, especially ire, that goes much further than expected or intended.

Vocalized wrath.

Some type of omen. In the 14th century, an entire manual detailing the interpretation of thunder portents was written.

Inner altercations with yourself, or heated disagreements with other people, like the thunder caused in Greek legend by Zeus and Hera's arguments.

Similar to *lightning* in indicating divine displeasure. Here, however, the chastisement may be coming from your own conscience.

• TICKETS

Traffic tickets are a message from the subconscious that something you're doing is going to get you into trouble. If the ticket in your dream is for speeding, for example, definitely slow down and become more observant (see *Velocity*).

Theater tickets represent a brief respite from your normal focus. If you've been thinking about taking a break, do so! It's exactly what you need.

Lottery tickets may reflect a wish for prosperity or improved good fortune. This is perfectly normal and healthy, as long as you're willing to back up that wish with practical actions for manifestation. While some people try to dream of their lucky lottery numbers, getting those numbers is very rare. Don't count on your dreams to bring about your future realities—begin manifesting them yourself today!

Dry cleaning tickets indicate that you recently trusted someone to clean up a problem. Now it's time to check and see if the work got done.

• TIES/TYING

(see Connecting Devices, Knots, Rope, Web)

Our connection to other portions of the self.

Ties to other people or situations that may or may not be desirable.

The network of life that goes beyond *time*, *space*, and dimensions. This type of dream helps you to recognize your place in the greater scheme of things, and the importance of each individual.

Too much attachment, the need to loosen binding ties.

A necktie represents business matters, protocol, and attention to the social graces. It is worn when we wish to present a specific image of ourselves to others, or as a recognition of a societal expectation (see *Clothes*).

Bow ties speak of old-fashioned formality. Possibly you are trying to be too conventional or reserved with regard to a project, person, or situation.

• TIGER

(see Animals, Cat, Lion)

In India, an emblem of divine wrath being unleashed.

China: The Lord of Animals, who embodies the attributes of authority, courage, passion, adventure, and prowess. Similar symbolism exists in Japan where the tiger represents heroic energy and self-regulation.

Riding a tiger: Confronting dangerous elemental powers that might get quickly out of control without constant monitoring.

Learning patience and the value of silence in achieving your goals. Tigers are slow, meticulous, and silent hunters.

• TIME

(see Clock, Hourglass)

An awareness that life sometimes passes you by unnoticed, or far more quickly than you might wish (e.g., "seeing time fly").

Recognizing your mortality (e.g., "time waits for no man").

Seeing a clock that is not moving represents a wish that time would momentarily stand still so that you can enjoy it more fully, or catch up on things that you feel you've missed.

Transformations that take a while to achieve (e.g., "time for a change").

Knowing when to act, when to wait, when to speak, and when to remain silent for success (e.g., "timing is everything").

Seeing a stop watch in a dream represents effective time management, and making every second count. Alternatively, feeling under time constraints.

• TIN

(see Metals)

• TOMB

(see Cemetery, Death)

An emblem of rebirth, especially if empty. Besides the Christian stories of Christ's victory over death, the ancient Celts buried people in tombs to await their next existence.

Is something inside the tomb? If so, consider what it represents of yourself that you may have buried or recently uncovered.

Tombs can also represent the collective past of humankind and our link with archetypal ancestors. Have you honored this connection in some manner recently? If not, this dream may be calling you to a figurative graveyard visit where you can explore your past as a member of humanity.

The portions of the self, the subconscious, or the Collective Unconscious that have been ignored so long as to be figuratively dead and buried.

An alternative womb emblem if rounded in shape.

• TONGUE

(see Face, Mouth, Teeth)

• TOOLS

(see Axe, Hammer, Nails)

Something that you are building or destroying. This can refer to personal characteristics, a relationship, a project, and so forth.

Abilities and knowledge that abide within, and can be effectively applied to your present circumstances.

Wisdom, discretion, and education. Having a tool and knowing how to use it correctly are two different things. Likewise, recognizing the right tool for the right job takes training and good judgment. So, what tool are you trying to apply to your life right now? Have you properly developed your skill with it?

• TORCH

(see Candle, Fire, Light)

Metaphorically "carrying a torch" for someone or a situation.

Improved light with which to navigate whatever *darkness* surrounds you.

Does the torch ignite a fire? If so, this can mark any type of momentous beginning, like the opening of the *Olympic* Games continues to be heralded.

• TORNADO

(see Disasters)

• TORTOISE, TURTLE

(see Animal)

A tortoise that withdraws into its shell is protecting itself (see *Armor*). From what do you feel the need to hide?

In Chinese and Hindu mythology, the tortoise carries the world on its back, and personifies endurance. What burdens are you carrying for which you need support?

In Taoism, this is the symbol of cosmic and prophetic power. As such, a tortoise appearing in your dream may presage some positive spiritual developments.

From the story of the Hare and the Tortoise, this creature may become an emblem of persistence in your dreams (see *Rabbit*).

Japanese: A messenger from the gods of the sea, which equates to a bulletin from your subconscious, intuitive self. Watch and listen closely!

• TOWER

(see Ascension, Balcony, Climbing, Ladder, Stairs)

Freudian: A phallic symbol.

Being rescued from a tower: Getting long-awaited relief from a constraining or *cage*-like situation. Frequently this assistance is from someone you regard as noble, or who has your best interest at heart.

Where are you? If at the top of the tower, take care that it is not made of ivory, lest your ideals fall short of the reality.

In the Tarot, the Tower card marks ruin and destruction, often self-initiated.

• TOYS

(see Games)

Toys may be a reflection of the inner child who wishes to come out and play.

These can be memorable toys from your own youth, or those for which you longed as a child.

Each toy envisioned will likely carry different connotations. For example, seeing a rag doll could indicate that, in this situation, you feel as if you've lacked backbone or firmness. A fire truck may act as counsel to put out a figurative *fire* that's been raging. Building blocks reflect self-construction and foundation work, and an ABC's coloring *book* might symbolize the need to return to the "basics" again, instead of focusing so much on frills.

• TRAIN

Freedom, especially in regard to instinctive drives.

Freudian: An emblem of the male penis, primarily when combined with *tunnel* imagery.

Similar to other vehicles in terms of movement and transitions (see *Bus, Car, Horse*).

Each car of the train may represent aspects of yourself, including hidden talents, knowledge, fears, hopes, and memories. So, exploring the train symbolizes introspection and integration of some of these portions. For example, searching the caboose may symbolize routing out your feelings about *death* or endings.

• TRANSFUSION

(see Blood)

• TRAPPED

(see Cage, Escape)

• TRAVEL

(see by mode of Transportation, Journey)

Desiring a change of scenery and refreshed perspective. Sometimes in order to truly grow, you have to leave someplace comfortable.

Freedom, liberation, and self-discovery. Getting away allows you to be free of other people's images and expectations so that you can build your own foundations for living.

The beginning of a personal quest that requires some type of mental or physical "travel" into the unseen portions of self or to new places, respectively.

Possibly an OBE (Out-of-Body Experience) (see *Dreaming, Flying*).

• TREASURE

(see Antiques, Excavation, Gold, Mine, Silver)

Gifts, talents, and abilities within you that are just waiting for discovery.

Friends, loved ones, and other precious things in life.

Unexpected prosperity that comes through a windfall.

Digging deep to reconnect with the subconscious, Higher Self, or Collective Unconscious.

Consider each piece of treasure for additional symbolism. For example, unearthing a jeweled *crown* can represent taking up your rightful role as the ruler of your destiny, and finding a string of *pearls* can symbolize following the voice of wisdom for successful outcomes.

• TREE

(see by type, Forest, Fruit, Rods, Stick, Wand)

Familial lines (e.g., "the family tree").

Free will and the ability to choose (note the Garden of Eden).

Life, knowledge, and wisdom. Many cultures have a mythological Tree of Life, including that of the ancient Hebrews, Assyrians, Babylonians, and the Norse.

The tree of self. How do your roots and fruits fare?

A personal branching out, or improving your foundations by putting down firm roots.

• TRIDENT

(see Three, Water, Weapons)

Ancient: The union of the God aspect with that of the triune Goddess. Out of this union, tremendous creative power is born.

Alchemical: An alternative emblem for water. Note that the Greek and Roman gods Poseidon and Neptune are frequently pictured holding a trident representing their dominion over the waters and all that dwells within. Therefore, this dream may symbolize a new sense of control over your emotions.

• TROLL

(see Bridge, Fairy)

• TUNNEL

If a light appears at the end of the tunnel, this symbolizes hope.

A voyage toward self-discovery

Freudian: A sexual dream, especially if a *train* is traveling through the tunnel.

Because tunnels often appear inside a *mountain* or the *earth*, they may be an alternative womb emblem, in which the birth process equates to personal transformation.

• TURQUOISE

(see Blue, Crystals, Gems, Jewelry, Stones)

Maintaining your balance and an emotionally even keel during a difficult situation. In the Middle Ages, turquoise was favored as a talisman to keep riders from falling off *horses*.

Overcoming negativity from outside sources. Buddha used a turquoise to defeat a terrible monster in Eastern mythology.

Among Turkish people, a lucky omen.

Arabic: A warning of impending danger. This stone supposedly alerts the owner to peril by changing color.

• TV

(see Satellite Dish, Radio, Telephone)

A reflection of your personal views about this media and its representations of reality.

Tuning into a specific "frequency" of ideas, morals, spiritual views, and the like. Look to see what images appear on the TV for more insight.

Perhaps you've spent too much time lately being a "couch *potato*." Try reading a good *book* instead.

If the TV screen appears blank, this indicates some sort of problem with connections or receptivity. Are you listening to sound advice from others? Are you figuratively "turned off" by something or someone, and have consequently severed that connection? Are you remaining open to the messages from the Universe?

• TWELVE

(see Numbers)

The culmination of forces, processes, and cycles. Many initiations into esoteric mysteries take place a year and a day (or 12 months) after beginning study.

The ever moving *wheel* of time (note that there are 12 hours marked on a *clock* face and 12 months in a year).

The number of enlightenment. This can also equate to the mental "ah ha!" that occurs when something elusive is finally understood.

• TWO

(see Numbers)

Division or unity that results in improved strength or accented weakness.

Duality, adversity, ambivalence, or insincerity (e.g., being "two faced").

Partnership; two forces joining to improve each and create a stronger oneness (as in *marriage* or business).

•UFO

(see Astronaut, Space Spaceship, Stars)

An unexplored, unrecognized, or unexpected aspect of yourself, brought out by a specific situation or *relationship*.

Possibly an alternative *flying* dream, especially if the ground is seen from the UFO's perspective, or if you are inside the UFO.

A potential abduction memory. Many people claim to have been taken aboard UFOs for examination and experimentation, and often remember these experiences through dreams. Tremendous caution is issued here—the amount of public attention given to this topic can create false impressions that leak into the conscious mind during sleep.

A message from the Universal Mind, often pertaining to brotherhood and oneness among all Earth's people. Look to the rest of the dream for more insight.

•ULCER

(see Body, Medicine, Physician)

Something that gnaws away at you, often causing distraction and irritability.

An indicator that there is an excessive amount of stress in your life that could eventually cause this malady. Take a break!

An open sore that seems difficult to heal because of inaccessibility or complications.

•UMBILICAL CORD

(see Baby, Ties/Tying)

For someone who has been gravely ill, this represents holding on to life tightly and tenaciously.

Your connection to, and relationship with, your mother. Is this cord still tied to her? (see *Women*)

What *color* is the cord? If *silver*, this may be part of an OBE in which you see the silver cord that connects the *body* and spirit together.

A familial source of metaphorical nourishment. If you have needed support lately, and haven't turned to your own family (especially your mother), consider this option.

Being broken: Having the connection between yourself and your family (specifically your mother) cut off in some manner.

• UMBRELLA

Safety and protection from one's emotional nature represented by *rain*.

An alternative type of *armor* that shields the bearer from elements of a situation to which she or he prefers not to be exposed.

If the umbrella won't open, or collapses in the *wind*, this represents being beset by annoyances and little troubles that increase stress levels.

A leaky umbrella symbolizes having attention distracted from little but important details that can make the difference between success and failure.

Because of its shape, this can be another type of *circle* or *wheel* dream. See if any patterns appear on the umbrella, for more interpretive value.

• UNDERGROUND

(see Dirt, Cave)

An alternative type of *death* dream, in which being underground equates to *burial*.

What exactly appears underground? This can be symbolic of something that you've covered up so completely as to hide it even from yourself.

Digging underground may symbolize your own quest to uncover subconscious signals, spiritual gifts, or positive characteristics (see *Excavation, Mine, Treasure*).

The womb of *Earth*; a place of introspection.

• UNDINES

(see Fairy)

• UNEMPLOYMENT

(see Jobs, Professions)

• UNICORN

(see Animals, Fables)

Traditionally an emblem of purity. In fairy tales, the unicorn becomes a mount to only chaste maidens, and befriends only those who are pure in spirit.

The *horn* of this creature is an alternative phallic emblem. It is also considered the most potently magical part of the animal—the "magic" in this sense being the *seed* of life (sperm).

If the horn of the creature is dipped into *water*, this represents the purging of some type of *poison*, be it emotional, physical, or spiritual.

In Greece, an alternative emblem for the *moon* goddess, and as such reflects a predominance of the intuitive nature in your decisions and interactions.

In China, this is a most beneficent dream. Here, the unicorn symbolizes the perfect balance between Yin and Yang, and all five elements in harmony (earth-air-fire-water-ether/void). Seeing one indicates goodwill and kindness toward you from others, as well as the presence of gentle, wise companions.

•UNIFORMS

(see Apron, Clothes, Hat, Professions, Workers)

Wishing to conform to, or fit in with, a specific group or situation. The message of this dream, however, is that a uniform is only an external expression. The person inside does not change. So, the question you have to tackle is whether the changes necessary for this group or situation are conducive to personal growth and wholeness.

•URINE

A figuratively "pissy" attitude that dampens everyone and everything it touches.

Ridding oneself of toxins of a literal or figurative nature, such as addictions.

Anger that is not expressed positively (e.g., getting "pissed").

A way of marking your territory. *Animals* do this regularly.

•UTOPIA

(see Garden, Island)

Hopes and wishes depicted in the most idealized, quixotic form. Be aware, however, that such perfection is rarely achieved in waking hours. So, ask yourself if you're expecting too much too soon from a situation or other people.

• VAMPIRE

Ancient meaning: Eternal life and the vital power of *blood*. Vampires used blood as their source of rejuvenation and, in a sense, reincarnation. Among ancient Greeks, the underworld was filled with souls who craved life's blood in the hopes of finding this renewal. On the dream plane, such symbolism can equate to finding ways to make the results of your efforts more durable and abiding.

Someone or something figuratively sucking the life away from you a little at a time. This person or situation may be very appealing on the surface, but definitely has an agenda that isn't in your best interests.

• VASE

(see Bottle)

• VEGETABLES

(see by type, Eating, Garden)

If this is a play on words, your subconscious is saying that for some reason you have begun to feel as productive as an inanimate, uprooted vegetable. Get up and become an active participant in life again!

Each vegetable in a dream has a different interpretive value. For example, a carrot is a masculine emblem that also represents vision and luck. Additionally, as an omen, carrots symbolize forthcoming wealth, health, and happy marriages. Dreaming of eating celery is an omen of love and affection. Cauliflower growing in a garden foretells increased business prospects, *corn* might depict a "corny" personality or the promise of improved finances, and *beans* carry a magical overtone thanks to the story of "Jack and the Beanstalk."

Root vegetables denote grounding, a connection to your family, and the staples of both spiritual and mundane life.

Jungian: Because vegetables get nourished by all the elements, they represent the depths of the subconscious, the deepest roots, and the fundamental self.

Societal, cultural, or religious limitations. Many vegetables have been shunned because of one of these contexts, such as tomatoes being thought poisonous, or potatoes not being eaten by Puritans because they are not in the Bible.

Eating vegetables in a dream is a portent of odd luck and coincidence on the horizon.

•VEIL

(see Curtain, Dancing, Fabric, Wedding)

Separations between people, situations, or dimensions. The Hebrew veils of the temple marked the line between the outer and inner sanctuary, the latter of which was YHWH's abode.

Societal transitions, just as marriage veils mark the transition from single woman to wife.

Insecurity. The need to hide behind something so that your true feelings cannot be seen.

Dreaming of bridal veils, especially for a woman, portends successful changes.

Putting aside a veil reflects a willingness to accept a change in status or role in a situation.

Celtic: The movement of fate, which can never be totally seen or known within mortal limits. It was believed that a peek behind fate's veil presaged *death*.

Seven veils, such as those possessed by Salome and Isis, represent the planetary spheres (see *Planets*, *Zodiac Signs*). On the dream plane, this may open new insight into the weavings of fate or destiny as they interact with your free will.

Veils may also reflect endings, as they were often worn by widows during mourning.

•VELOCITY

(see Bus, Car, Travel)

Moving slowly in a dream may reflect taking your time and considering each step necessary for success. Alternatively, it can indicate procrastination or delays that may or may not be of your own doing.

Rapid movement represents hasty actions which may not have been thoroughly thought out. This can also reflect that you are moving through life so quickly and busily that you never stop to smell the roses.

Dream sequences that go in very slow motion are usually replays of something that's happened so that you can examine the details more closely and from an alternative perspective.

• VINE

(see Grapes, Ivy, Leaves)

A clingy, uncertain personality type, but also likely very faithful.

Pretty appearances that threaten to entangle you in something in which you may not wish to participate.

In a *jungle*, vines offer a way of *escaping* danger by *climbing* or swinging upward to safety. If you're being offered a way out of a situation right now, seriously consider taking it.

• VINEGAR

(see Eating)

Making the best of a bad situation. Vinegar is actually wine or cider that has turned, but still gets effectively applied. What situation seems negative right now, and how can you mix things up so that they turn in your favor?

Placing objects into vinegar: Safeguarding or saving things for when they are most needed. Vinegar has a natural preservative quality that allows it to last for up to a year along with any herbs placed therein.

Drinking vinegar: Being a sourpuss, as if you've just swallowed vinegar along with your words (e.g., someone who is full of "piss and vinegar").

• VIOLET

(see Flowers, Gardens, Purple)

Passion: This flower is astrologically ruled by Venus.

In the Victorian language of flowers, this represents enchantment or being charmed, for boon or bane.

The *color* of this flower directly relates to the spiritual condition. So, how does the flower appear? Is it healthy, wilted, uprooted, surrounded by *weeds*?

Among the ancient Greeks, violets represented undisturbed rest and safety from *ghosts*.

• VOLCANO

(see Disaster)

• VOTING

(see Elections)

The right to choose the ideas and beliefs that govern your life.

Deciding upon the best person to lead a group, or help you with a specific situation by taking the leadership role.

Having to make a single selection from a large group of options regarding something that affects your future. Make sure this decision is an educated one.

Singling out aspects of yourself to develop more publicly. In this case, note the *name* of the winning candidate for possible symbolism. For example, if Ms. Lovage Charity appears, you may be trying to develop a stronger charitable image in your community.

• VULTURE

(see Animals, Birds, Feathers, Wings)

Targeting a vulnerable situation or person.

Ill feelings aimed toward you from a exploitative or predatory person.

The desire to focus on a particularly susceptible opportunity for personal gain.

Ancient meaning: An archetype for the goddess of *death* and reincarnation among the Egyptians especially. Here, vultures were believed to nurse the spirit of dead Pharaohs, maintaining them in the afterlife.

• WAGON

If the wagon is *red*, this might reflect a childhood wish or *toy* that was special to you. Alternatively, red wagons can reflect anger toward a person (e.g., "fixing her/his red wagon").

Falling off of a wagon symbolizes a failure to stick to a promise made to yourself, or moving away from an ideal that you hoped to keep.

Putting yourself or something onto a wagon may represent some type of *travel*, or the beginning of a new commitment to better living.

• WALLS

(see Obstacles)

• WAND

(see Divination, Rods, Stick)

An emblem of rulership over yourself, or being put in a place of respected leadership for a group, as shown by a king's scepter.

A blossoming wand represents figurative or literal fertility and productivity.

A phallic symbol that combines with an orb or *star* at the top, thereby illustrating the union of male/female, or Yin/Yang energies, for potent personal transformations. Note that a *fairy's* wand is topped in a star to show that a magical creature possesses it.

• WANDERING

(see Foot, Highway, Journey, Path, Travel)

Aimless thought patterns that cause problems with maintaining your focus on a current project or goal.

Lacking direction in life, not knowing exactly which *path* to take, or what choice to make in order to succeed in your objectives.

Introspection and exploration of the various alternatives currently available. Take care, however, that you don't wander so far off as to lose sight of the primary purpose.

•WARRANTS

(see Police, Writing)

Warrants allow access into normally "forbidden" or "private" realms. Through what *doors* does this paper give you the freedom to glimpse? Take care, however, as the discoveries in such a search can be both wonderful and disconcerting.

•WATER

(see Flood, Fountain, Ice, River, Rain, Snow)

Changing tides: Among the Teutonic people, each tide carried different meanings that may apply to your dream. The tide occurring just before sunup is one of introspection, while the one at dawn bears fertile waves. Noon tides speak of tenacity, dusk tides bring transformation, the night tide edifies, and the one occurring at midnight heals.

An ocean: The earth's womb and beginnings of all humankind. Also representative of the vast subconscious, superconscious, or Jungian Collective Unconscious (see *Abyss*).

Among Native Americans, water appearing in dreams indicates your spiritual state. For example, if the water is flowing smoothly, your spirit is calm and moving in a natural direction.

Moving water: The seen and unseen ebb and flow of all energies.

Baptism: New life, forgiveness toward yourself, and renewed purity of thought and actions (see *Baby*).

Bathing: Getting rid of your figurative "*dirt*," like old habits, guilt, anger, and even sexual repression (e.g., feeling "dirty").

Hot water: Trouble's afoot, so look for the wellhead (see *Temperature*).

Drowning in water: Overwhelming circumstances, problems, or emotions that threaten to defeat your efforts or sense of individuality. Esoterically, this may also reflect a memory from a past life experience (see *Choking, Suffocation*).

Floating upon: Dependence on your feminine nature or a mother figure. Alternatively, skimming the surface of spiritual potentialities without ever really diving in and experiencing that aspect of self.

Stagnant water: Something, often a situation, that is unhealthy for you to the point where it causes a standstill in personal growth and in your quest for wholeness.

Shallow water represents a similarly frivolous personality that avoids delving into any aspect of life too deeply. Alternatively, this can represent a fear of confronting the depths of your own subconscious.

Tidal waves: Powerful emotions or instincts that you have let build up to a critical mass. This dream reveals the need to express those things before they come crashing over the floodgates.

Surfing on water: Taking control of, and accepting the power in, the feminine aspects of self and the Universe. Also maintaining a rather haphazard balance between the intuitive nature (the water) and the conscious self (the surfer).

A geyser: A sudden, unanticipated outpouring of creativity, goodness, inspiration, spiritual gifts, or whatever.

Wearing a life preserver in the water represents getting a second chance at something. Grab it before it gets away!

Ripples appearing on the water's surface indicate the waves of energy we send out without even knowing it, similar to a *web*. This will eventually touch everything and everyone because you are part of the network of life.

Lakes: As the abode of several magical creatures, including the Lady of the Lake and water nymphs, dream lakes reflect the search for the wonders that lie just beyond the surface of reality. What does the surface of the lake cover? Are you fishing here, thereby trying to catch a little magic?

•WEAPONS

(see Ammunition, Armor, Axe, Knife, Fighting, Sword, Whip)

Taking up a weapon reveals hostility or fear that you may be repressing during waking hours. Turn to look upon the object of your actions. Sometimes just facing your true feelings is enough to begin the *healing* process.

Guns are violent, but impersonal. These reveal a source of anger or anxiety that you would prefer to keep at arm's length. How healthy this distance is for you, however, is questionable, or your dreams would not reveal it.

A catapult indicates the ability to circumnavigate an *obstacle* by ingenious thought and assertive action.

Cannons can fire over a large distance, meaning the perceived threat is not nearby. Additionally, they may symbolize things that you value very little (e.g., something best used as "cannon fodder"). As an omen, cannons portend a struggle that engages powerful forces.

Maces represent blunt realities that are so cold and firm as to nearly knock you off your feet with their realization.

Nuclear devices represent tremendous buildup of frustration to the point that it leaks into your life as a futile attitude that poisons everything.

•WEB (NET)

(See Knots, Rope, Spider, Spinning)

In the immortal words of Shakespeare, "Oh, what a tangled web we weave." This dream may represent the web of deception or some other trap of which you need to be aware.

The web of life that interconnects all things, from the smallest grain of *sand* to the *stars*. In this case, your subconscious is trying to remind you of your importance in this scheme, and how your life touches everything directly or indirectly.

Attachments and associations. Nets participated in ancient Russian *wedding* ceremonies to indicate the unity of the couple and ensure fertility ("a teeming catch").

Being caught in a net can be an alternative type of *cage* dream, with slightly looser constraints indicated (rope is easier to get out of than steel). Alternatively, in China this is a symbol of protection. Pregnant women were sometimes surrounded by fishing nets to safeguard the *baby* from any *evil* influences.

•WEDDING

(see Bride, Engagement, Groom, Relationships)

Wishful musing for a long-term commitment from one desired.

Marrying yourself figuratively to an ideal, situation, or group. The caution here is to remember that such commitments, if healthy, do not require the loss of individuality.

Reconciliation and resolution among warring factions within or without. In earlier history marriages were often arranged to bring peace between two tribes or two families.

The harmonious union of opposing energy for a mutually beneficial outcome.

Being the bridesmaid or groomsman at a wedding represents standing on the sidelines of a situation with which you would like to be more intimately involved.

•WEEDS

(see Garden, Path)

Negative aspects of your own behavior, or unhealthy ideas, that need to be cleared away before real growth can occur.

Problems growing into a *relationship* or situation that must be rooted out for any type of positive results.

Overgrown: Something in your life that's gotten out of control, and now obscures the natural beauty within.

Positive outcomes from annoying situations. Not all weeds are useless. Dandelions, for example, may be made into coffee, salads, and wine. The difference is in how they are viewed and applied. Try looking at your current circumstances differently for a moment, and see if you can't make the most of them.

•WEIGHT

Situational: Have you been focused on your own weight loss or gain lately?

Burdens that you are carrying.

Anything you perceive as hindering your movement or growth. What exactly is weighing you down?

•WELL

Tossing a *coin* into: Your wishes and hopes

A font of creativity, wisdom, ideas, or knowledge that lies within just waiting to be tapped.

Because of the *water* element here, this can represent your emotions, or possibly the subconscious, into which your dream effectively lowers the bucket.

A source of healing. Sacred wells dotted the land in Old Europe. Sick people would travel to them and bathe in the water hoping the well's nature spirits would grant rejuvenation.

Falling into a well reflects a sudden force or situation that propels you into deep introspection. Take care, however, in such a journey that you don't forget where the rope lies so that you can return with your discoveries safe and sound.

•WEREWOLF

(see Lycanthropy, Monsters, Wolf)

•WEST

(see Directions, Locations)

•WHALE

(see Animals, Fish, Water)

A difficult journey to transformation and enlightenment as in the story of Jonah and the whale. Similar whale myths appear in other cultures too, all of which equate this creature's belly to a *cauldron* of change and rebirth, or an initiation.

A whale *swimming* in deep waters often represents your own search for deeper awareness about yourself or the Universe.

A whale spout is a type of *air* or *wind* dream, in which you seek out the breath of life, and perhaps a break from being emotionally or empathically immersed. Alternatively, this may represent the liberation of positive ideas and energy.

A symbol reflective of the regenerative power of water to refresh your ideas, bring peace and *healing*, and smooth out the rough spots in life.

Among the Norse, whales have magical power all their own, and would sometimes carry witches to their destination. So, a whale surfacing from the ocean depths may indicate a surfacing interest in, or ability with, the occult arts.

Whales have sonar like that of *dolphins*, making them an emblem of "sounding things out" and knowing your *direction* in life.

The humpback whale, specifically, reflects finding your own song; a harmony that mirrors your soul, especially with regard to the way you interact in relationships. The song of the humpback changes every breeding season, reflecting the environmental changes that surround it (see *Music*).

•WHEEL

(see Car, Circle, Seasons)

Time's cyclical movement, especially the seasons. In India, Kali ruled the Time Wheel that fixed life and *death* for all things. In ancient Greece, the *12* zodiacal houses are fixed around a wheel.

Native American: The *medicine* wheel that symbolizes everything's equality. If one part of the wheel is ignored or broken, the entire thing doesn't function right.

A *mandala* that equates to the cosmic model or pattern that maintains congruity of life-death-rebirth, beginning-middle-end-return on both intimate and universal levels. It is thereby a vital representation of the rede "as within, so without."

The power of fate and destiny. The Etruscans and Romans both had goddesses whose domain was the wheel of time and fate. In the Tarot, there is also the Wheel of Fortune that marks the succession of human and universal affairs.

A source of control and regulation (see *Car*).

A cycle that the psyche sets into motion, resulting in internal change, or external events.

•WHIP

(see Weapons)

If being used to tame an *animal*, this dream speaks of bringing your less evolved, more instinctual, characteristics under control.

Quick adjustments that gain approval or help move something ahead (e.g., "whipping it into shape").

Possibly reflective of a dominatrix fantasy, depending on the other dream components.

Subordination, punishment, or abuse. Is this directed toward you from others, or vice versa? Are you directing such negativity toward yourself?

Generative force. In some ancient cultures, people whipped *trees* to ensure abundant harvests.

•WHISTLE
(see Air, Music, Wind)

A signal from within that asks for attention to specifics, just as you might whistle up a taxi, or whistle to stop someone with whom you wish to speak.

Accusing or condemning someone whose responsibility in a situation has not yet been implied (e.g., "blowing the whistle on them").

A way of lifting burdens, or a reflection of joy (e.g., "whistle a happy tune").

A release or augmentation of power, specifically *spiritual*. In ancient times, it was believed that witches could whistle up the *wind*.

•WHITE
(see Colors)

In Eastern cultures, the color of *death* and mourning.

Purity, as with the cleansing white *light* of New Age beliefs, and the blinding light of God in the Bible.

Covering up a mistake or blemish, as is accomplished with white-out and whitewash.

Alchemical: Following white light in a dream is a step that takes the dreamer on the path of *ascent* toward purity.

•WILLOW
(see Forest, Rods, Stick, Trees, Wand)

Symbolic of flexibility and tolerance because of its supple branches.

Wishes and *magic*. An ancient willow wand, topped in a *star*, and carried by the Greek goddess Helice was a cosmic emblem connected strongly with the *moon*, *divination*, and the Mystery traditions.

Pain's abate. Herbally, willow bark is a substitute for aspirin.

The weeping willow represents personal mourning or sadness. Remember the lesson of the willow, however, that also shows us how to bend without breaking. Do not let grief break your spirit.

• WIND

(see Air, Fan, Whistle)

Strong winds or *storm* winds reveal powerful forces at work in your life, some of which may cause confusion about your *direction* and *path*.

Change and movement, which often meets with some turbulence before positive transformations occur.

A sign of latent psychic abilities developing.

In Christian theology, the presence of the Holy Spirit.

Angry winds are often considered a sign of *evil* or negativity. Note that Lucifer is called the Prince of the Power of the Air, and in the Koran, demons control stormy winds (see *Monsters*).

Howling winds: In folklore, this portends either trouble on the horizon, or an unsettled spirit (see *Ghost*).

Anciently an emblem of the masculine nature, with the four directions becoming a natural *wheel* or *cross* that later became the weather vane.

Weather vanes that show which way the wind blows are an alternative emblem for both a *wheel* and a *cross*, indicating the originating source of energy or problems.

• WINDOWS

(see Apartment, Buildings, Castle, Curtains)

Do the windows in your dream appear open, closed, or shuttered? How accessible this opening is indicates how open-minded you are as an individual.

In earlier history, windows were open to let fresh luck in with spring breezes, and bad fortune out. Do you need a change of pace, or some fresh outlooks?

• WINE

(see Beverages, Fruit by type)

Drinking fully of life's nectar; living each moment to its fullest.

Celebration, and reasons for same. Also, hospitality being offered and accepted.

In ancient Greece, wine and the god Bacchus were one and the same. Bacchus was somewhat of a mischievous and randy figure, who may represent unrepressed sexuality, liberation, and the power of nature.

Red wine is an alternative *blood* emblem, as seen in Christian communion rites.

The spirit of truth, or as the Romans said, "*in vino veritas.*" It is interesting to note that in Mesopotamia the goddess Saki personified the *vine* and epitomized the revelation of truths.

Among the Norse, an emblem of taking care of things that you value. The deceased had to drink all the wine they had spilled before being allowed to enter Valhalla, their version of paradise.

•WINGS

(see Birds by type, Butterfly, Feathers, Flying, Insects by type)

Freedom and liberation.

The ability to lift your vision above circumstances and see a broader picture.

Flexibility and spontaneity (e.g., "winging it").

A source of protection and safety, as when an *angel* covers you with its wings, or when a *bird* is able to escape a predator through flight.

•WIZARD

(see Authority Figures, Icons)

•WOLF

(see Animals, Lycanthropy)

Things that you fear about yourself, a situation, or others, and have been unwilling to face directly.

Some type of obscured threat (e.g., the "wolf in sheep's clothing"). In Freudian analysis, this threat is construed as sexual intimacy.

The loss of innocence and naive outlooks.

In *fables*, the emblem of *evil* craftiness that threatens to devour all goodness.

Alchemically, a symbol of duality; the light and dark aspects of all things.

Howling at the *moon*: Discovering and announcing a secret alliance or treacherous plan. Alternatively, acknowledging the lunar/feminine aspect of self.

• WOMEN

Three appearing together: During the 1100s and before, writings from Norway, Sweden, and Iceland tell of the Vanir Cult. This was a group of Germanic people who followed fertility goddesses. From writings entitled *Flateyjarbok*, it seems the manifestation for these goddesses often came through dreams. Specifically, the women would appear as protectors, luck-bringers, and counselors. They were also associated with the ancestors and the Three Fates of Greek mythology.

Mother figures: The maternal aspect, and attachments to same. Feeling toward the feminine side of self. Alternatively, the spirit of *earth* (earth as our mother).

Wife: The literal wish for a wife, or someone in your life who would act as a companion and helpmate (see *Bride*).

The archetypal Goddess who is maiden, mother, and crone combined (see *Icons*).

An old woman: An emblem of folksy, time-honored wisdom, especially in matters of love and health (this may also be true of an old *man*). Alternatively, an emblem of the ancestors who act as guides in important life decisions.

Maids represent neatness and an attention to appearances either for yourself, in a situation, or in your home.

Nuns reflect religious dedication and lifelong devotion to an ideal. For those who attended Catholic school, a nun may also be an *authority figure* stressing the need for discipline.

Waitresses symbolize service to others (see *Servant*). Do you feel as if people appreciate your time and efforts (for example, does the waitress in the dream receive an acceptable tip)? Are you giving too much of yourself?

• WOODPECKER

(see Birds, Feathers, Trees, Wings)

An alternative emblem of the *drum* because of its rhythmic pecking.

Among the English, Babylonians, and ancient Greeks, this bird was a weather prophet. What's gathering on the horizon for you?

Among Native Americans, the woodpecker represents the sacred rhythms of the *earth*, to which you are learning to listen.

Discrimination in what one accepts as truth. The woodpecker uses its sharp bill to carefully reach the specific foods it wants and needs.

•WOOL

(see Fabric, Sheep)

Daydreaming or engaging in too much random thinking (e.g., "wool gathering").

Being naive about someone or something (e.g., "having the wool pulled over your eyes").

Soiled wool represents a lack of principle or derailed convictions.

Biblically, *white* wool reflects spiritual purity.

•WORK

(see Jobs, Professions by type)

•WORKERS

What are these individuals doing? Their actions may reveal the answer to a perplexing question or problem. For example, if they are building a *bridge*, this indicates that you are preparing to become more social and traverse the gaps that lie between yourself and others.

•WORM

(see Animals, Dirt)

An alternative emblem for *dragons* and *serpents*, but on a smaller scale.

Because the worm has no *eyes*, an alternative type of *blindness* dream in which you navigate the depths of self or *earth* with little to guide your way.

A visual pun for someone who cannot be trusted, or whose actions are routinely crass.

Something that appears worm-ridden represents ideas, plans, or beliefs that have bugs which need to be worked out before proceeding further.

•WOUNDS

(see Blood, Healing, Physician, Salve, Surgery)

Unresolved issues or an open emotional trauma that has not had time to heal.

Infected wounds represent the festering of resentment and bitterness. Remember that these negative emotions produce nothing positive, and only hurt you. Find a constructive outlet for your feelings instead.

•WRAPPING PAPER
(see Box)

What is the paper covering? This may represent portions of yourself that you have hidden, suppressed, or concealed for whatever reasons. If the paper is being removed in your dream, then you are likewise opening up those aspects for closer examination and eventual integration.

•WRESTLING

Your own struggle to survive in life's never-ending *ring*.

Conflicts that exist within your own psychological makeup that need to be resolved (e.g., "wrestling with your conscience").

Playful wrestling may symbolize *sexual encounters*.

•WRITING
(see Books, Billboard, Blackboard, Ink, Punctuation)

Consider what the writing says, and to whom it's addressed first. Very often the words are a message from your own subconscious or ego that need your attention.

The creative process. Many writers tell me that they dream of writing things before they actually put pen to pad.

Writing with footnotes is a subconscious message to be certain you're carefully checking your sources of information with regard to a specific person or situation. Don't believe everything you read and hear without some other confirmation.

If writing appears in a journal, this represents the need to record events carefully. This information will prove useful later.

Writing with a quill pen symbolizes the power and responsibility for your words. Great documents like the Declaration of Independence were scribed with this implement, with due diligence. What declarations are you writing into your life?

Writing a manuscript that never gets finished, or finishing one that gets rejected, portends similar disappointments on the horizon.

• X-RAY

Examine this situation closely to be sure you're seeing everything that's important.

A useful tool or technique that can also be dangerous if misapplied. Take care with your abilities so that no one gets accidentally hurt.

• YELLING

(see Amplification, Conversation, Fighting)

A dream expression of anger or frustration that you could not exhibit during waking hours.

A way for the subconscious or Higher Self to get your attention. What message is being shouted?

Yelling that has no discernible words represents making such a fuss over a situation that people just don't want to hear about it anymore. Alternatively, this can reflect pointless arguments that cannot be won.

Echoes symbolize those thoughts, actions, or words that inevitably return in some manner: anger breeding anger, love rendering love. What types of echoes are you hearing, and what types of energy can you expect to return from them?

• YELLOW

(see Colors, Gold, Sun)

A color strongly associated with the element of *air*, this represents the mind and your ideals.

Bright: An extroverted personality who gains much energy from being around people and is very upbeat.

Depending on the shade observed, this may also symbolize cowardice.

Jaundiced yellow reflects the need to get some sun, metaphorically stressing a reconnection with one's masculine, logical nature.

• YEW

(see Forest, Trees)

Norse mythology portrays the yew as *Yggdrasil*, or the World Tree. As such, this is a great symbol of security and firm roots.

Folkloric: Protection, specifically against *magic* meant to charm or beguile.

For someone who has been sick, this is a good omen. It foretells long life.

Celtic: A hunt or search. This was a favored wood for bows because of its flexible strength. What is it that you're *hunting*?

Among the Druids, yew wood was used to foretell the future. If you accept this interpretation, look at the rest of the images in the dream as potentially prophetic in content.

•YGGDRASIL (THE WORLD TREE, OR TREE OF LIFE)

(see Trees)

Creation and subsequent nourishment or support of what was created. In many myths, including Mayan, Norse, Indian, and Saxon, a special tree was part of humankind's origins and the world's beginning, its roots reaching out and feeding the *earth*.

The ability to communicate effectively. This is especially true if the tree's *leaves* are rustling. In India specifically, the gift of *language* was provided to humankind through the World Tree's leaves, each of which had a mantra written upon it.

Renewed life, health, wisdom, and knowledge. In Eden, the central tree bore the *fruit* of knowledge. In Celtic tradition, the Goddess's trees in Avalon bore *apples* that granted longevity. Finally, in Asia, the Tree of Life has mantras that must be gathered by the souls of the dead to assure their reincarnation.

•YOUTH

(see Age, Baby)

Having optimistic, utopian outlooks that may or may not have any practical applications.

Abundant energy welling from within.

A playful spirit, renewed health, and innocent happiness.

•ZERO

(see Circle, Numbers)

The beginning of something, as occurs with a countdown. It is worthy to note here that the Fool card in the Tarot, representing the beginning of the spiritual adventure, is numbered zero.

Feeling worthless, or realizing that your ambitions lack merit in terms of personal growth and maturity.

•ZIP CODES

(see Numbers)

A way to locate someone or something for which you have been searching. Make special note of these numbers, and see if you can't find a waking representation of them.

Effectiveness of communications. Having the wrong zip code on a letter will keep its message from being delivered promptly. Are you directing your words in the right way, to the right people?

A numerological code equating to basic personality traits that either need to be developed or honed to improve your relationships. Add all the numbers together (for example, 14127 = 15 = 1+5 = 6), and look that number up herein for more ideas.

•ZODIAC SIGNS

(see Divination, Space, Stars)

The signs of the zodiac carry different meanings based on their depiction. Frequently they represent aspects of your personality that are not wholly known or acknowledged, and therefore need developing. For example, dreaming of Virgo may represent your need to reconnect with feminine attributes or clean up your act physically (Virgo is the virgin). Here are some other sample correspondences which may be expanded by reading any good astrology text:

Aquarius: Erratic creative energy; feelings of unrest.

Aries: Quick decisions that may not be wise; courage and zeal for things to which you commit yourself.

Cancer: Paradoxical actions that others find confusing.

Capricorn: A cool, patient temperament that hides deeper passions.

Gemini: A restless, artistic nature; often impedes meeting goals due to getting bored or distracted.

Leo: Strong leadership skills always need to be tempered with wisdom so that you don't become boastful or pompous.

Libra: The need for balance, especially with the emotions.

Pisces: A strong spiritual nature is starting to develop along with a new sense of responsibility.

Sagittarius: The mark of an overachiever. Make sure your goals are reasonable.

Scorpio: A bold, determined nature that sometimes "stings" to achieve its goals or communicate a vision.

Taurus: Watch your temper and tendency to want "things" to fill up your life.

• ZONE

(see Blueprints, Directions, Locations)

A space with limited access over which someone or something has control. Consider the type of zone portrayed. For example, a radioactive region might imply a situation that's way too hot to approach right now. Conversely, approaching an end zone in your dream reflects the successful undertaking of a task, or a completion on the horizon.

• ZOO

An alternative *cage* dream, in which parts of your personality are displayed to others. What *faces* are you showing the world? For example, are you growling at everyone like a *bear*, or perhaps being overly playful like a *monkey*?

Parts of yourself that you keep firmly under lock and key, especially the animalistic urges and instincts. Look to the *animal* symbols given sein for more insight.

A zookeeper reflects aggression. Something restrains you from truly being yourself. Alternatively, if you are the zookeeper, consider what or whom you're trying to control unfairly.

BIBLIOGRAPHY

Andrews, Ted. *Animal Speak*. St. Paul, MN: Llewellyn Publications, 1993.

Artemidorus. *The Interpretation of Dreams*. Translated by Robert White. NJ: Noyes Press, 1975.

Budge, Sir E. A. Wallis. *Amulets & Talismans*. NY: University Books, 1968.

Cayce, Hugh Lynn. *Dreams, the Language of the Unconscious*. VA: ARE Press, 1962.

Cavendish, Richard. *History of Magic*. NY: Taplinger Publishing Co., 1977.

Cirlot, J. E. *A Dictionary of Symbols*. NY: Philosophical Library, 1962.

Complete Book of Fortune. NY: Bracken Books, 1936.

Cooper, J. C. *Symbolic & Mythological Animals*. England: Aquarian Press, 1992.

Coughran, Jane N. and Daniels, Pat, Assoc. eds. *Psychic Voyages*. VA: Time Life Books: Mysteries of the Unknown Series, 1987.

Cunningham, Scott. *Crystal, Gem and Metal Magic*. St. Paul, MN: Llewellyn Publications, 1995.

_____. *Encyclopedia of Magical Herbs*. St. Paul, MN: Llewellyn Publications, 1988.

_____. *Magic in Food*. St. Paul MN: Llewellyn Publications, 1991.

deLys, Claudia. *The Giant Book of Superstitions*. NY: Citadel Press, 1979.

Douglas, Mary. *Natural Symbols*. NY: Pantheon Books, 1970.

Feinstein, David and Stanley Krippner. *Personal Mythology*. Los Angeles: Tarcher, 1988.

Freud, Sigmund. *The Interpretation of Dreams*. NY: Avon Books, 1965.

Gackenbach, Jane and Jane Bosveld. *Control Your Dreams*. NY: Harper & Row Publishing, Inc., 1989.

Garfield, Patricia, Ph.D. *The Healing Power of Dreams*. NY: Fireside Books, 1991.

Gordon, Leslie. *Green Magic*. NY: Viking Press, 1977.

Guirand, Fellips, ed. *New Larousse Encyclopedia of Mythology*. NY: Prometheus Press, 1973.

Gustavus, Miller. *10,000 Dreams Interpreted*. NY: Rand McNally & Co., 1995.

Hales, Dianne. *The Complete Book of Sleep*. CA: Addison-Wesley, 1981.

Hall, Calvin. *The Meaning of Dreams*. NY: Harper and Brothers, 1953.

Jung, Carl G. *Man & His Symbols*. NY: Doubleday, 1964.

Kaplan-Williams, Strephon. *Elements of Dreamwork*. Shaftesbury: Element Books, 1990.

Kowalchick, Claire and Hylton, William, eds. *Rodale's Illustrated Encyclopedia of Herbs*. Emmaus, PA: Rodale Press, 1987

Kunz, G. F. *Curious Lore of Precious Stones*. PA: Lippincott Co., 1913.

LaBerge, Stephen. *Lucid Dreaming*. Los Angeles: Tarcher, 1985.

Loewe, Michael and Blacker, Carmen, eds. *Oracles and Divination*. CO: Shambhala Publications, 1981.

MacKenzie, Norman. *Dreams and Dreaming*. NY: Vanguard Press, 1965.

Perls, Frederick S. *Gestalt Therapy Verbatim*. CA: Real People Press, 1969.

Roberts, Jane. *Dreams, Evolution and Value Fulfillment*. NY: Prentice Hall Press, 1986.

Sechrist, Elsie. *Dreams, Your Magic Mirror*. NY: Warner Books, 1974.

SummerRain, Mary. *Earthway*. NY: Pocket Books, 1990.

Telesco, Patricia. *The Budget Herbal: Pantry Spices*. Johnson City, TN: Geneva's Greetings, 1996.

_____. *Folkways*. St. Paul, MN: Llewellyn Publications, 1995.

_____. *Kitchen Witch's Cookbook*. St. Paul, MN: Llewellyn Publications, 1994.

_____. *Victorian Flower Oracle*. St. Paul, MN: Llewellyn Publications, 1994.

_____. *Witch's Brew*. St. Paul, MN: Llewellyn Publications, 1995.

Ullman, Montague, MD & Zimmerman, Nan. *Working with Dreams*. NY: Dell Publishing Co., 1979.

Walker, Barbara G. *The Women's Dictionary of Symbols and Sacred Objects*. NY: Harper & Row, 1988.

Whittick, Arnold. *Symbols: Signs & Their Meaning and Uses in Design*. MA: Branford Press, 1971.

Wortman, Camille and Loftus, Elizabeth. *Psychology*. NY: Alfred A. Knopf Company, 1981.